Greenland's Icy Fury

TEXAS A&M UNIVERSITY
MILITARY HISTORY SERIES

32

Greenland's
Icy Fury
Wallace Hansen

TEXAS A&M UNIVERSITY PRESS · COLLEGE STATION

Library of Congress Cataloging-in-Publication Data

Hansen, Wallace R., 1920–
    Greenland's icy fury / Wallace Hansen.
        p.   cm. – (Texas A&M University military history series ; 32)
    Includes bibliographical references and index.
    ISBN 0-89096-579-X (alk. paper)
        1. Hansen, Wallace R., 1920–. 2. World War, 1939–1945–Greenland.   3. Military
    meteorology–Greenland–History–20th century.   4. World War, 1939–1945–Search
    and rescue operations–Greenland.   5. United States. Army–Search and rescue
    operations–History–20th century.   6. World War, 1939–1945–Personal
    narratives, American.   7. Geologists–United States–Biography.   8.
    Meteorologists–United States–Biography.   I. Title.   II. Series.
    D810.M42H36   1994
    940.53'982–dc20   93–36823
                                                                                          CIP

Photo credits
Sgt. Mark J. Johnson: pages 33, 35, 48, 58, 66, 71, 74, 91, 96, 102, 129, 131, 136, 147, 155, 170, 172, 173, 174, 185, 198, 202, 206, 209, and 214. Other photos by the author.

To Ellen and
to those GIs
whose service in
the far backwaters
of the planet
has passed
unrecorded
in the annals
of World War II

Contents

Illustrations
and
maps

Illustrations   ix

Preface

Writing this book was largely an exercise in recall. No one's recollections are infallible, certainly not after half a century, but I had substantive help from several sources including, first and foremost the diary of my old World War II friend and fellow GI, Donald S. Galbreath. I admire people like Don who have the self-discipline to make regular entries into a journal. I learned from Don that a good journal has real practical value far beyond mere personal vanity. Don and I have remained in touch ever since the war, largely through annual Christmas messages, but occasionally through other notes and phone calls. Another wartime buddy, Robert R. Grahl, has also stayed in touch and just by doing so has helped me retain memories of that high and far-off time.

Most ex-GIs have vivid recollections of their wartime experiences. Dramatic or traumatic events such as those are more deeply ingrained than other happenings, and the memories of World War II tend to hold on more strongly than lesser incidents that have happened more recently. Obviously, no two veterans of the war recall things exactly the same way. Each person's experiences are unique, and if all nineteen men of the Greenland Base Ice Cap Detachment were to record their own stories, they would write nineteen different books. My outdoor experiences as a skier, weatherman, and dog driver were very different from those, for example, of a chairbound radio operator in the same outpost who spent virtually all his time in the smoky gloom of the radio shack. My recollections would also differ greatly from those of the outpost commander, the late Maj. F. A. "Hardrock Al" Wade, who of necessity looked mostly at the forest and made decisions, whereas I looked mostly at the trees and made ski tracks.

But I speak metaphorically, of course, there being neither forests nor trees in all of Arctic Greenland. My recollections must also differ somewhat from those of anyone else in camp, partly because I was a geologist and no one else could have seen the total environment quite as I saw it.

Not through the same eyes. Wade was a geologist, too, but as commanding officer he had little time to look at the rocks, glaciers, or icebergs
or contemplate the stunning vistas of the Ice Cap across Kjoge Bugt. I
traversed, gazed at, and peered closely at more of the local scene than
anyone else in camp.

I also was privileged to have had a marvelous set of official U.S. Army
photographs at my disposal, some of which are reproduced here, thanks
to our talented camp photographer and medic, Sgt. Mark J. "Doc" Johnson. Doc and I corresponded for several years after the war; we eventually lost contact, but Doc's photographs are still immeasurably helpful
as documentary memory jogs.

I had planned to write *Greenland's Icy Fury* ever since the end of
WWII–largely at the intermittent prodding of my dear wife Ellen. By
helping me keep that plan alive, Ellen reinforced my memories. But the
project came to fruition only when my retirement from a long career in
geologic research provided the needed motivation and leisure to get on
with the task. I was fortunate to have the great technical library of the
U.S. Geological Survey nearby to lean on for backup information. Even
places as remote and little known as southeast Greenland are well represented on the stacks of the Survey library, in literature going back–in
Greenland's case–more than a hundred years.

Most of the Greenlandic terms and place names mentioned here date
from the 1930s and 1940s. Many of them are archaic or obsolete in modern usage and have been supplanted by different spellings or whole new
words that have evolved through the spread of the East Greenland written language since the war. Many words of West Greenland origin on
old maps have been replaced on newer maps by East Greenland equiva-
lents. The old name Ikerssuak ("large bay"), for example, has been supplanted on maps by Ikertivaq (the same meaning). The American name
Comanche Bay, which appeared on maps issued by the Geodaetisk Insti-
tut of Copenhagen right after the war, has been preempted on more
recent maps by Igtip Kangertiva ("small bay buttressed by a cliff"). Probably these changes are for the best; the name Comanche Bay has little
meaning for today's young Greelander, but for my purposes I felt that
the old spellings and names preserve more appropriately and authenti-
cally the historic flavor of the early 1940s. These are the names and
spellings we used and identified with at that time, and for your convenience they are all listed in the glossary at the back of this book. With
the disappearance of the few American names from the official maps–
names such as Bluie West-1, Bluie East-2, Atterbury Dome, and Snowy
Slope–small bits of Greenland's history and heritage have been lost,

even though America's short wartime occupation of the great island surely altered the lives of its inhabitants as much as any other event in its long history. The term "Ice Cap," written as two words here and in the older literature, is now generally shown as one word.

After the manuscript was written it benefited greatly from a very helpful critical review by meteorologist Dr. Aylmer Thompson, professor emeritus at Texas A&M University. Finally, my discussions of the astonishing, if not incredible, southeast Greenland weather were greatly assisted by old archival maps from the files of the National Weather Service, maps kindly provided by John L. Tierney of the NWS, himself an old World War II weatherman. My thanks go to all those people who helped make this book possible. I hope *Greenland's Icy Fury* will help you as reader feel the spirit of southeast Greenland as I felt it so many years ago.

W. R. H.
Lakewood, Colorado

Greenland's Icy Fury

1

The Polar Connection

No area of military operations in World War II received less attention from the media or more neglect from the public than the diffuse network of Arctic outposts scattered across northern Alaska, northern Canada, and southern Greenland. There was even a disturbing tendency for the public to confuse Greenland with Iceland—a very different place, and a tendency that still exists. Yet these remote operations, unsung as they were, routinely provided ground support and weather information essential to the overall success of the Allied war effort, and not without hardships, personal sacrifice, and physical danger. In proportion to the number of men involved, casualties in the Arctic were especially high, through such nonhostile actions as aircraft accidents, frostbite, and psychological burnout. The Arctic wilds gave quarter grudgingly. Some poor souls unready for the tedium and stress of long isolation under severe climatic conditions took their own lives. One soldier in southern Greenland blew his brains out with a Colt .45. No Purple Hearts were awarded in this theater, but the victims were war casualties no less than any combatant killed or injured in the fire of battle. This was the original cold war, literally not figuratively, and it demanded its toll.

Most of the few books that have been written about the late cold war of the north were authored by ex–brass hats: highly motivated, highly qualified, and courageous polar experts—old hands who had put in time in the north long before their induction into the service but who had little empathy with or understanding for the men under their commands. They were chosen for their polar backgrounds and adaptability to harsh living conditions, but they led lives better and more comfortable by an order of magnitude than those of their dogface subordinates, and they enjoyed amenities unheard of by the men in the outposts. By outposts, I mean stations manned by a dozen or two dozen soldiers. To the foreign correspondents and the high brass in Washington, "outposts" included big installations like Bluie West-1 (BW-1) in southwestern Greenland and Bluie West-8 in central western Greenland, each with two or three thousand men. Our nineteen men of the Greenland Base Ice Cap Detachment (BICD) regarded Bluie East-2 (BE-2) at Ikateq in East Greenland, with its two or three hundred men, as a big-time air base. If the correspondents ever visited BE-2, they never mentioned it in their writings. None of them visited the Ice Cap Detachment.

In my limited experience, most of the officers in the arctic, even some of the old hands, viewed the GIs with subtle contempt and disdain. A visiting inspector general, just up from the States to check the outposts at the end of the long winter, when at last the ice was out and they could be reached by boat, described our Ice Cap Detachment as "lacking military discipline, men out of uniform, floors not scrubbed." Even some of the books refer to "Officer Smith or Jones and an enlisted man," as if the GI had no identity, or "Captain Doe and a corporal," and they mention "a dozen enlisted men from some southern part of the country," or "officer X and a miscellaneous staff who spent their time grousing about how lonesome and miserable it was to be stationed in the wilderness," or an "elaborate setup of malcontents." Yet the GIs were the heart, sinews, and soul of those forlorn outposts, and whatever success their operations enjoyed was due largely to the combined efforts of malcontented patriots from all walks of life, just as in all previous wars. The brass, of course, pushed most of the buttons and turned the knobs, but from their vantage points they just couldn't quite see or experience the humdrum details of Arctic outpost existence, and their published reports show it. They describe the grand strategies, as viewed from headquarters, and perhaps the goals and aspirations, but not the nuts and bolts of barracks life in the blizzard.

There were notable exceptions: Most small outposts were run by sergeants, but our gang of malcontents included two officers, Cpt. Franklin A. Wade and Lt. C. Barry Borden, who were proud of their affiliation with an expedition to one of the most hostile areas on Earth. All of us shared that feeling. Both officers mixed and fraternized gracefully with their enlisted subordinates; outpost living was too confining and restricting to think of doing otherwise. Basically inducted civilians—Wade was a college professor and Borden an army reservist—neither was what most personality profiles would portray as typical officer material, and in their capacity as bosses of the Ice Cap Detachment, they lacked the after-hours amenities of a base officers' club and an officers' mess. They competed as equals in chess, acey-deucy (a variation of backgammon), and snow shoveling. Weather officers were a breed apart also; they were mostly laid-back intellectuals who just wanted to get on with the war. They were engrossed in the weather, they thought more about airmasses and storm tracks than about discipline, posturing, or the Articles of War, and I never met one I didn't admire. In contrast, the autocratic commandant at BE-2 had his own private trout stream, and no subordinate—let alone a GI—dared approach it.

Weather stations in the Arctic were urgently needed in World War II—the first global war—for at least four reasons. On America's entry into the war, supply routes had to be established between the home front—what Franklin Delano Roosevelt called the "Arsenal of Democracy"—and the fighting fronts of Europe and Asia. The Arctic air routes required accurate weather information and forecasting for safe travel. The climatic influence of the huge Greenland Ice Cap reached into mainland North America and Europe. Under the leadership of the Ferrying Command, later the Air Transport Command (ATC), thousands of bombers and fighter airplanes were delivered to Britain, the Soviet Union, and our own forces at the fronts. A worldwide weather network, moreover, was needed for planning tactics and strategy at all levels of military and marine operations, such as D-Day itself, and the Arctic outposts were key ties in the network. In the vastness of the Arctic wilderness, these tiny points of miserable humanity were beacons and refuges for the in-transit aircraft.

Two main flyways, anchored in Great Falls, Montana, and Presque Isle, Maine, reached northwest and northeast respectively from the American heartland. Great Falls led northwest to Anchorage, Fairbanks, and Siberia. Presque Isle led to Gander, Newfoundland; Goose Bay, Labrador; Bluie West-1, Greenland; Keflavik, Iceland; and Prestwick, Scotland. Alternate routes, seldom used, had stops at Churchill, Manitoba; Ungava Bay, Quebec; Frobisher Bay, Baffin Island; and Sondre Stromfjord, West

Map 1–1.   The wartime Arctic air route to Europe. Alternate route is shown by dotted-dashed line.

Greenland. Bluie East-2 at Ikateq, East Greenland, was mainly a weather, rescue, and antisubmarine patrol base; big bomber aircraft would have been hard put to set down successfully on its short, icy runway, or to take off.

As the war progressed, antisubmarine warfare gradually swept the North Atlantic free of Nazi submarines, and shipping of airplanes via surface convoy became more practical than fer-

6

rying by air. Longer-range aircraft were developed, too, and wing tanks increased the flight ranges of existing fighter planes, but the outposts were still needed. Stations were needed high up on Greenland's Ice Cap to provide emergency rescue bases for downed aircraft, to transmit regularly scheduled weather reports for flight planning, and to fill holes in the four-times-daily synoptic weather map. Nowadays, deep lows and powerful highs in the North Atlantic region are readily tracked by satellite, but in World War II the only way to locate and follow them was with the densest possible weather-reporting network.

Ice Cap operations in Greenland entered the scene when Nazi U-boats still threatened the shipping lanes, a time when the Strait of Belle Isle, between Labrador and Newfoundland, was known as Torpedo Junction. There the "wolfpack" subs, in the words of FDR, lay in wait for the transports. At BW-1 I talked to a survivor of the S.S. *Dorchester* disaster. The *Dorchester* was a troop ship sunk off Labrador; the survivor described the mayhem and carnage. Men in the water tried to climb aboard overloaded lifeboats as other men in the boats tried to keep them out, even to the extent, he said, of slashing one another with knives. Most of the victims, though, died of hypothermia in the icy Atlantic Ocean. People in those waters had little time to be rescued.

Houlton Army Air Base in northern Maine was the recruitment, training, and staging area of our group, later known as the Base Ice Cap Detachment. When I received orders to report to Houlton for training for "rigorous duty in the Arctic," I was working in a four-man weather station at the Bell Aircraft Company in Niagara Falls, New York. In its factory there Bell was making a hot little fighter plan called the Airacuda. The assembly line was run mostly by women, all ravishingly beautiful sexpots in the eyes of the lonely, homesick soldier. The Airacuda was heavily armored, especially around the cockpit, and not very maneuverable, and hence was a poor match for a Japanese zero in a dogfight, but it had a cannon in its nose that was widely used for strafing missions and ground support, and it scared the scats out of the Germans in the North African campaign. It was also used for ground support by the Russians, under lend-lease, and the Kremlin had a glowering liaison officer right at the factory to handle the shipping arrangements. Our guys ferried the planes to Great Falls and Fairbanks, but Russian pilots took over from there—the reds didn't want Americans flying over their territory.

One pilot who came into the weather station at Bell Aircraft about once a week for a flight clearance used to sneak up behind me as I was plotting the synoptic weather map and wrestle me to the floor in a half nelson or hammerlock. As we scuffled about the room, the operations officer frowned disapprovingly but said nothing. The pilot outranked him. Air force pilots in those days were notably high ranked: a brigadier general from Santaquin, Utah, was only twenty-three years old, and a sign on the door of one officers' club, according to legend, said, "Lieutenant colonels and under admitted only with parents." Niagara Falls was known as a weatherman's gravy train in those days, partly because of the relaxed atmosphere, partly because of the male shortage at the factory, and partly because we were serving on "detached duty" in a nonmilitary area. But I had volunteered for rigorous Arctic service, following an announcement of openings for weathermen, and the army had picked up my option. I went down to historic Fort Niagara at the head of Lake Ontario for a physical. The weather was appropriately cold and blustery, as a chill wind blowing across the lake piled up the drifting snow around the buildings. An army garrison was there, I presumed, to secure the international boundary against any hostile Canadians. The doctor who checked me over said, "Good luck, son, I wish I were going with you," and I knew at the time that he meant it. Then I packed my duffel bags and headed for northern Maine, taking the New York Central to Albany and the Boston and Albany to Boston-the-Hub-of-the-Universe, and seeing for the first time the beautiful Berkshire Hills of western Massachusetts.

I changed trains in Boston, transferring by taxicab from the South Station to the North and getting my first view of the Hub's Old-Worldy cobblestone streets. In the days before one-way streets, we drove right down Washington Street past the Old South Meetinghouse, then by Faneuil Hall, Haymarket Square, Canal Street, and the Union Oyster House. I took the Boston and Maine to Northern Maine Junction in Bangor, then transferred to the Bangor and Aroostook—the famous square-wheeled potato line—to Houlton. Part way to Houlton, the train halted in the north woods while the engineer swilled a cup of coffee with a friend on the front porch of a log cabin beside the tracks. I didn't mind; we had a warm potbellied stove near the door of our car and a grand view of Mount Katahdin through the window.

At Houlton, now in early May, 1943, I checked in and was immediately assigned to "rigorous Arctic training"–skiing most of the day, hiking through the woods, fishing through the ice, and climbing mountains, just as I had done all my life. Mount Katahdin, over near Millinocket, still had six feet of snow on its flanks. Its hulking mass is the first place in the United States to catch the morning sun, and I climbed to its summit before daybreak with a couple of instructors, one of whom was a rugged mountaineer from Oregon. The temperature on the peak was fifteen degrees Fahrenheit and the wind was about thirty-five miles per hour out of the west. We had new square-toed ski-mountain boots, and the Oregonian had trouble walking; on the summit ridge line he discovered that he had his boots on the wrong feet.

Near the end of the month five of us returned to Boston to draw out Arctic gear and clothing. We were housed temporarily at the army dock in the Boston Port of Embarkation, right next door to the navy aircraft carrier *Lexington,* an enormous vessel that a disputatious GI in the local stevedor battalion insisted was just a "baby flattop"; it was about three blocks long. The army brought in a bunch of German POWs, captured in the Africa campaign. They were shipped to Boston, they claimed in broken English, because the army didn't want them to see the bombed-out ruins of New York. Had they arrived in the Bronx forty years later, their argument might have sounded more plausible.

Unexplained foul-ups in our orders delayed our mission. The captain who ran things at the army dock said, "We know why you're here, but your orders don't say so." We reclined on our sacks, looked at the ceiling a lot, and read old magazines while the machinery of war cranked on. The captain next feared we were getting "stale," so he ordered one of his sergeants to march the five of us up Summer Street twice daily to Winter Street and back, to fine tune our close-order drill–any soldier headed for rigorous duty in the Arctic had to know how to march. No two of us wore quite the same uniforms–we sported a mix of khakis, ODs (olive drabs), flight jackets, garrison hats, and overseas caps–and our picturesque if ragtag phalanx drew cheering crowds all along our daily route through downtown Boston. We drew only hoots and catcalls from the sailors in the navy barracks up the street. When we finally collected all our impediments, our travel orders were quickly cut, and the warrant officer in charge ordered us to "take off for Presque Isle like striped-ass apes." He was a charming, refined, personable Irishman.

Presque Isle seemed like the very gateway to the Arctic, and I thrilled with anticipation. On the broad plains of northern Maine, Presque Isle's evergreen forest stretched to the far horizon. Drizzly stratus clouds hung dark and low in the sky, and weedy little brooks meandered across the back lots of the air base; one was dubbed Cripple Creek, its name posted on a crudely lettered sign staked alongside by some homesick Coloradan. On clear nights at Presque Isle, you could see the northern lights.

Presque Isle also was a noisy, bustling war base, run by B. F. Giles, commanding general of the North Atlantic Wing of the Air Transport Command. Giles was a skilled commander, and morale at Presque Isle was high. Everyone worked together to keep the planes flying. Big long-range bombers, mostly B-24 Liberators, rolled regularly down the runway, some headed for Scotland and some for North Africa. Look on a globe and don't be surprised to see that Africa is a lot closer to Presque Isle than to Miami, Florida. Africa and Scotland are about equidistant from Presque Isle.

My buddies and I were housed in the transient barracks, where guys on orders waited to ship out and where a jukebox played a lot of Harry James and Judy Garland records. Though barely out of childhood roles in the movies, Judy had a voice that was rich, full, and mature, and her rendition of "That Old Black Magic" stirred men's souls. Nineteen-forty-three was the heyday of the big band, and there were many great vocalists such as Helen O'Connell and the Andrews sisters—more talented to my mind than today's counterparts—but the voice that really blew away all the flyboys was that of Wee Bonnie Baker in her interpretation of "You'd Be Surprised." Just a few years ago I heard her again on a radiocast of nostalgic old hits, and the impression had not changed.

At Presque Isle we had five days of intensive briefings on Arctic geography, weather, and living conditions, exciting and informative, given mostly by rough-hewn veterans of the Eighth Weather Squadron who had been north, experienced things firsthand, and looked it. This, I thought to myself, was the major league. The Eighth Weather Squadron was run by a meteorologist aptly named Colonel Merewether, whose domain covered all the northeastern Arctic, from Maine to Iceland. Thirty or forty weathermen were being briefed and processed for assignments to outposts scattered across northern Canada and Greenland. With our briefing completed, all our group but me were ordered back to Fort Devens, Massachusetts, and Camp Miles Standish for further overseas training and rifle marksmanship. I was given a week's furlough and when I asked, puzzled, if I'd been washed out of the expedition, they said, "No, just go home for a week." When I replied that I couldn't possibly get to Utah and back in a week, they arranged travel part way by military aircraft and told me to wire for a week's extension when I reached home. Asking no more questions, I followed orders. Then I went spring skiing at Alta, high in the Wasatch Mountains, and dated all the girls I knew who hadn't left town for defense jobs.

To this day I'm unsure what happened, but I suspect that my high-school ROTC paid off: as an ex–junior first lieutenant I didn't need combat training, in the eyes of the U.S. Army Air Corps. At any rate, I returned refreshed to Presque Isle, then took off for Greenland in a big new C-54 Skymaster (the military version of the four-engined Douglas DC-4). We crossed the Gulf of St. Lawrence at Anticosti Island, overflew the scrubby lake barrens of southern Labrador, and put down at Goose Bay to refuel and chow down. Goose was close to the true border of the Arctic in an open forest of stunted evergreens amidst a carpet of deep, gray reindeer moss, a tall lichen much favored by caribou in winter. But Goose was best known for its voracious mosquitoes, and we were happy that our visit was brief.

The southern border of the Arctic is the northern limit of trees–the Arctic tree line–where the mean temperature in July is fifty degrees Fahrenheit. This border also coincides with the average southernmost reach of Arctic airmasses over the continent in summertime. The Arctic Circle, on the other hand, at sixty-six degrees and thirty-three minutes north latitude, is merely an imaginary line that marks the point where the sun stays below the horizon on the winter solstice. Astronomically, it is very significant, having to do with the Earth's orbit and the plane of the elliptic, but it has little to do with the climatic boundary of the Arctic. In some places the tree line reaches well north of the circle–at the Mackenzie delta, for example, in Canada's Northwest Territories. In other places it is far to the south. An

Map 1–2. Ocean currents (shown by arrows), pack ice, and tree lines. The northern limit of trees, rather than the Arctic Circle, is the climatic boundary of the Arctic. Limits of discontinuous pack ice are averages for July; in southeast Greenland discontinuous pack ice approximately coincides with the area of the East Greenland Current. Note that in the north polar regions, except in Arctic Canada and the Beaufort Sea, land will be to your right if you drift with the ocean current. See also map 15–1.

Arctic climate, in fact, exists in all the mountains of the western United States high enough to maintain an upper tree limit, where the mean temperature for July is fifty degrees. Mount Washington, in New Hampshire, has such a climate. So has Mount Katahdin.

Out of Goose Bay, we were soon heading northeast across the Labrador Sea, beyond sight of land, and over an awesome expanse of ice slowly drifting south with the cold Labrador Current. Old charts show this area as Davis Strait, named for an ill-fated sixteenth-century English navigator, but modern maps generally place the strait far to the north opposite Baffin Island. At any rate, the ice cover was broken, not solid—a vast mosaic of interlocked ice pans, each of perhaps thirty to forty acres, or perhaps twice that size. With nothing for scale, their size was indeterminate, but countless thousands of large ice pans reached to the horizon in all directions, separated only by narrow leads of inky black water, and from the air they suggested the marble-chip terrazzo floor of an uptown bank lobby.

A stir of excitement gripped all passengers on board, but the sameness of the dazzling scene and the drone of the engines soon brought on contemplative silence, and my thoughts turned to the flood of personal events of the past few months. In Salt Lake City, where I had volunteered for induction a few months before, the local draft board had obligingly and quickly scheduled a physical examination at a former automobile agency made over into an army processing center, where scores of naked men stood silently in line on the concrete floor, waiting to be checked over, as tittering women giggled and watched from second-story office windows across the street. My prior visit to the draft board had been viewed with some suspicion by those present when I appeared at the door with a cane and rigidly stiff knee caused by a fractured femur and five months in a body cast, following a skiing collision with a pine tree at nearby Alta. But at the ex–automobile agency, noting my volunteer status, the examining physician said, "I'm sure we can find something for you in limited service, son," and with that and the oath of allegiance, I was sworn into the army.

I shipped out to historic Jefferson Barracks, high on the bluffs overlooking the beautiful Mississippi River south of St. Louis, for air force basic training and a battery of aptitude tests. Basic training, normally about a month long, ended four days later, when a sympathetic testing officer told me I was qualified for any job I wanted in the air force, from sheet-metal worker to flight crew to Officer Candidate School, though they favored shorter men for aerial gunners. Reminding him that I was in limited service, I asked, "How about aerial photography?" He grimaced. "You don't want to spend the war in a darkroom. What you want to be is a weatherman."

The Army Weather Service, I soon learned, contained many graduate geologists like myself, chiefly because of their technical background and facility with maps; the fact that my college transcript also showed a course in meteorology made me a shoo-in for admission to weather training. Besides, there was a shortage of qualified candidates.

As the plane droned on, my reverie was abruptly broken by shouts from the cabin. The inside starboard engine had suddenly begun to throw off buckets of oil and clouds of black smoke. Worse, it seemed about to catch fire. At the shouts of the passengers, the crew chief came aft, glanced quickly out of the window, fought off cardiac arrest, and dashed headlong back to the cockpit, where an alarmed but unruffled pilot coolly shut of the engine, feathered the propeller, and banked steeply back toward Goose Bay. Few places on earth could be worse for ditching a plane than the pack ice of the Labrador Sea, but at the time, in the folly of youth, I was more excited than scared. Like all good young soldiers, I was convinced of my own immortality. What an adventure, I thought. A red-faced major seated nearby—older and wiser—was less entranced, and cold sweat beaded his brow, but we landed at Goose on three engines without further incident. Then, on checking back in again at the transient barracks, I was assured by a gloating duty sergeant that I'd sit out the war there: "Once stuck in Goose, you'll never get loose," he smiled wryly, brushing aside a mosquito, but next morning, after bumping passengers off another C-54, we took off again and arrived a few hours later at Bluie West-1.

Approaching Greenland on a clear day, I got my first glimpse of the snowy crags of the southwest coast from the right-hand window of our C-54. On our left was a dazzling arm of the Ice Cap. We were already in a descending glide, skimming low over frothing skerries and rocky islets and racing past buildings and people below at the village of Julianehaab, heading up Eriksfjord at rim level, and closing rapidly on the air base. Suddenly we were on the steel-mat runway at Narsarssuak—"the big plain"— and taxiing to a stop in sight of a massive glacier just beyond the edge of the field. Greenland!

Meanwhile, all my buddies—Don Galbreath, Bob Grahl, Mark Johnson, Homer Loar, Max Morris, Larry Phillips, and others— had been drifting around in the North Atlantic on the troop ship *Yarmouth*, throwing up their breakfast each morning, and suffering three weeks of antisubmarine drills while the crew shot off depth charges. Just practice, they were told. I reached

BW-1 two weeks after they did. Air time from Presque Isle: about seven hours. Outwardly happy to see me again, my pals were both outraged and incredulous, but theirs was not to question why. Uncle Sam simply meant for them to travel by boat, and me to fly.

2

The 1940s in Perspective

To appreciate the constraints on life in the Arctic in World War II, one should review the enormous changes in our lives since then. Much that we take for granted simply didn't exist in the first half of the 1940s, least of all in the Arctic wilderness. Half the people who ever lived on Earth had not yet been born. Environmental changes wrought by humankind since the 1940s, and mostly in the name of progress, exceed those of all preceding human history. Technologically, we have perhaps advanced farther since the early forties than in all preceding history also— (culturally and morally, perhaps not).

In 1943 the top speed of the world's fastest airplanes—military fighter planes, called pursuit planes in those days—was about 450 miles per hour. Few bombers could reach 300, and passenger planes rarely exceeded 180. Jet aircraft were being developed in Germany, but they didn't exist in America and, anyway, the sonic barrier was supposed to place an insurmountable ceiling on the ultimate speed of travel—about 750 mph—if planes could even be made to reach it. Modern helicopters hadn't yet been designed, though builders were experimenting in the late 1930s with a curious forerunner called an autogyro, which had a powered propeller up front like an ordinary airplane and an unpowered, windmilling prop on top. When an autogyro flew over your house, everyone ran outside to look. The atomic bomb had yet to be detonated (first detonation was on July 16, 1945), and its development was a military secret. Matter, we were told, could neither be created nor destroyed, but if we could split the atom, unimagined benefits would accrue.

Most people in 1943 had never heard of penicillin, which was new and not widely available. All supplies went to the military. Sulfonamides, also quite new, were the big hope in the fight against infection. DDT was thought to hold the key to our salvation, being partial to insects, we thought, and harmless to all other creatures. Diphtheria, mumps, and measles were common, especially during the winter months. Polio victimized thousands of children yearly, and summer was thought to be the most infective time. Childhood deaths were common. Pneumonia took many lives annually, and tuberculosis was still rampant in some quarters. Meningitis was nearly always fatal; so was peritonitis– a ruptured appendix meant death. Effective insect repellents were just appearing. In the short Greenland summer, we made do with mosquito netting.

Plastics were brand new, were not yet in commercial production, and would have to await the postwar world. Most molded products were made of a substance called Bakelite. Television was rumored but unseen. I saw my first picture (black and white) in December, 1944, in a demonstration in Grand Central Station; a big screen at that time was seven inches on the diagonal. Most sets had four-inch screens with magnifying lenses. News and commercial breaks were new on radio. The singing commercial was "in" for catching the listener's ear. Most radio programs had single sponsors, such as Jell-O, Kraft cheese, Maxwell House coffee, or Ford or General Motors.

Few automobiles had hydraulic brakes. Almost none had power brakes or power steering. Manufacturers were experimenting with various kinds of automatic transmissions, with mixed results. Few people had air conditioning, either in their cars or their houses, and few cars had effective windshield defrosters. Radial tires didn't exist; most people bought recaps if they could get them when their tires wore out–tires were strictly rationed to certain eligible groups, such as medical doctors.

Most households had four or five electrical appliances: a refrigerator, a toaster, maybe an electric stove, and a curling iron. Some people had electric egg beaters (mixers), but no one had an electric razor. Before the late thirties most households had iceboxes rather than refrigerators. Most houses were heated with coal, though the better ones had semiautomatic stokers on their furnaces, but the clinkers had to be removed by hand tongs. Walls and ceilings had to be cleaned annually with a doughlike compound to remove the coal soot. Home dishwashers didn't exist, and the kitchen dishpan always ended up with a greasy ring for want of detergents that didn't yet exist either. Automatic washing machines weren't available and laundromats didn't exist; nor did clothes driers. Computers and calculators were years away: scientists and engineers used slide rules and adding machines, pencils and erasers.

Few people had charge accounts or checking accounts, let alone credit cards. Most people held off buying until they could pay cash, except for cars and appliances. Layaway deals were common. Most neighborhoods had a corner grocery store, but there were no supermarkets.

Modern snow vehicles hadn't been designed, let alone built— there was nothing like today's popular snowmobiles. Skis were made of wood, the best ones of laminated hickory. Ski bindings replaced leather harnesses in the late thirties. The new improved bindings were mostly steel-cable and spring arrangements that fitted around the heel of the leather boot, with metal toe irons and rat-trap tension releases. Safety bindings hadn't been invented. Aluminum ski poles had largely replaced bamboo in the late thirties, but aluminum was in short supply during the war, and the army switched back to laminated bamboo or to steel tubing, painted over with white enamel.

Dehydrated and fast-frozen foods were still developmental. Nobody had yet marketed prepackaged frozen dinners—these things evolved later along with TV. Grocery stores didn't have refrigerated food sections, anyway. Water-based latex paint didn't exist. There were no ball-point pens, and few dial telephones. People dreamed optimistically about the great postwar world, but nobody felt deprived. Everyone was confident of the rightness of our cause and of America's moral position in the world. Everyone knew that good would prevail.

3

Getting Under Way

Our marshalling point in Bluie West-1 was the headquarters of the base rescue officer, Cpt. Harry Strong. Captain Strong generously provided plenty of room in his storage yard to board our two teams of dogs and to stash our growing mountain of supplies destined for use at our base camp and on the Ice Cap itself. Our base camp was to be at Comanche Bay, about four hundred miles up the east coast of Greenland at the very edge of the Ice Cap. We would also maintain a weather station nearby on a mountain called Atterbury Dome. Captain Strong's rescue shack contained a fascinating assortment of Arctic gear of all sorts: guns, skis, snowshoes, harnesses, ropes, dogsleds, ice axes, tents, lumber in assorted sizes, and all manner of tools. In the summer of 1943 Captain Strong was a dashing figure who had already been involved in several rescue missions on the Ice Cap, including one near Comanche Bay. Deeply tanned and weathered, square-jawed, tall, and muscular, he had had previous experience in the north of Alaska, and he liked to tour the camp area in his jeep, towed by a team of huskies, while glancing sideward at the admiring footsloggers along the way. His dogs, he said, needed the exercise. He also owned a handsome black Newfoundland dog which he had fitted with saddlebags to carry his .38 automatic pistol and lunch during expeditions upcountry. Once when Captain Strong invited several of us greenhorns on a training hike to Narsarssuak Glacier (Kiagtut to the Greenlanders), northeast of the air base, the big black dog decided to swim a river draining off the ice, saddlebags and all. The pistol suffered only a minor wetting, but the captain's lunch—gourmet fare especially prepared at the officers' club—was irretrievably lost. Ironically, our lunches could have survived indefinitely long submergence, secure in our daypacks and hermetically sealed in waxed card-

Fig. 3-1. The pinnacles of Kangerdlugssuatsiaq, southeast Greenland near Tingmiarmiut. Based on a photograph by Gustav Holm, 1888.

board. We graciously offered the captain his choice of our selections, but he equally graciously declined. We carried K rations, and Captain Strong had eaten K rations before.

Narsarssuak Glacier was an immense picture of suspended animation. You could almost feel its potential energy. Its power was manifest in a groundswell of seracs and crevasses, blue ice, and wet, dripping walls. Bouldery moraines at its snout were cored with dirty gray ice. Just beyond the ice terminus and partly held in by moraines was a small, turbid lake, possibly twenty acres in area, and near its center a great fountain of muddy water erupted above the surface. The fountain was discharging from a subglacial stream flowing from the glacier under hydrostatic pressure. Here, I thought, was an esker in the making, before my very eyes. (An esker is the gravelly deposit of such a subglacial stream, left standing as a meandering gravel ridge after the ice melts. You can see them in Minnesota, Maine, Wisconsin, or Massachusetts, fifteen-thousand-year-old relics of the Great Ice Age.)

At the rescue shack Lieutenant Borden inventoried and arranged all incoming supplies. He meticulously painted different colored triangles on the corners of all the cartons, each color fitting into a prearranged scheme, so that each item could be properly loaded and stowed in its correct order aboard ship, then systematically unloaded and properly warehoused at our destination at Comanche Bay. When our ship, the *Nevada*, finally arrived in port, all expeditioners worked around the clock hauling supplies aboard, moving them first from Captain Strong's bailiwick, then down to the dock. The local stevedore battalion felt duty bound to offer minimal token assistance. We ourselves worked forty-six hours without interruption, which was quite feasible in the perpetual daylight of summertime Greenland, and we took time out to snack and catnap only as opportunities arose on the job. Though the result was utter bedlam, no one was decked by the ship's swinging cranes, no bones were broken, and no one fell into the fjord. But Lieutenant Borden's carefully planned inventory did go awry, as the mounting piles of cargo grew helter-skelter in the hold and spilled out onto the deck.

When we finally pulled away from the dock in the afternoon of August 22, 1943, everyone crashed below to their bunks in the bilges. Well, nearly everyone. I stayed on deck and fought to stay awake. All my life I had wanted to see the fjords of Greenland and I was not to be deterred by a little loss of sleep. We had a fifty-mile trip down Eriksfjord (Tunugdliarfik–"turnaround place"–to the Greenlanders) through a district of classic geology and scenery, and I didn't want to miss any of it. Just across Eriksfjord from the air base was Brattahlid, tenth-century headquarters of Erik the Red, harboring ruins of a Viking church and outbuildings. (Erik never abandoned the Norse gods, but his wife Tjodhild accepted the Christian faith when a Christian priest first arrived in Greenland.) Up and down the fjord other stone ruins could nearly be touched from the deck. There were ancient lava flows, strange rock formations called rhythmites, and deposits of rare minerals found at few other places on Earth. I longed to go ashore but soon succumbed to exhaustion, staggered below, and numbly hit the sack.

When I was awakened by the motion of the ship, we were rolling in the swells of the Labrador Sea. To our port side was the jagged coast of southwest Greenland, and I marveled at the array of icy granite peaks. One wag thought they looked like dogs' teeth, another like a row of broken whisky bottles. For the next four hundred miles, awesome coastal Greenland would be to our left, and my pulse quickened as we rounded Cape Farewell. Cape Farewell's Greenlandic name is Umanarssuak, and it literally means "big heart." The mountain shaped like a big heart–a nice simile. *Umanak*, "heart," is a common place name for mountain peaks in Greenland, or for villages nestled at their feet. Rising sheer from the water–high, steep, and misty–Umanarssuak was foreboding in the face of a rising gale. We gradually veered left, keeping its peak squarely aport–almost as if we were pivoting around its base–as we headed east then north into the big dark waters of the bounding North Atlantic Ocean.

Reportedly, the *Nevada* had been a Great Lakes cargo ship before being pressed into military service. This story seemed reasonable enough to us, as the vessel wasn't notably seaworthy, at least in the North Atlantic, though we never figured out how the ship got from the lakes into the ocean. (The St. Lawrence Seaway was only a dream at that time, decades away from construction.) The *Nevada* pitched and rolled in the heavy waters off southern Greenland, and as we stood ashen-faced on the slippery deck, our coast guard escort vessel disappeared from view behind each swell, only to reappear as both ships topped the waves. Early in the morning of the second day out Lieutenant Borden staggered unsteadily onto deck, and I asked politely how he had fared at mess: "Great," he replied, "I had five prunes for breakfast and only lost three of them." In a spell of particularly tumultuous weather, the ship's cook prepared greasy pork chops for dinner, a sort of maritime ritual, I judged, just to see our faces as we sat down to eat. Most of us didn't stay long, including me, although I had a stronger stomach than many aboard. Anyway, we were cruising up the incredible coast of Tingmiarmiut, where a hundred icy spitzhorns pierced the sky, and no right-minded person would be below deck voluntarily at a time like that. Tingmiarmiut means "bird people." Great rookeries must have lined the cliffs onshore. In the hidden shelter of the fjords, say early reports, there were native hunting camps, not often used, amid a profusion of dwarfed Arctic shrubs and wild flowers, but from our rolling deck we could see only the towering peaks and glaciers. The phalanx of mountains reached north to the horizon, but no single peak dominated the unbroken wall of sky-piercing giants. Now, biting cold gripped the air as the sun dipped below the mountains, backlighting their snowy north flanks in rosy alpenglow. We all turned in, and the snoring below deck was muffled by the noise from the engine room.

In the morning we were opposite Umivik–"the place to bring ashore your boat"–not many miles from our destination, and the aspect of the country was changing. The mountains were not as high as those down the coast, and the spaces between were buried in expanses of ice. Closing in on our goal, I found the *Nevada*'s approach in some ways anticlimactic, in other ways high adventure. From Eriksfjord down to Cape Farewell and north

Fig. 3-2. The angular peaks of Tingmiarmiut. Engraved by H. P. Hansen in 1888.

along the east coast, Greenland's spectacular skyline was dominated by countless rocky spires—whole chains of Matterhorns—but overwhelmed by snow, fog, and ice. In the words of the late, great explorer Knud Rasmussen, "Even a seasoned Greenland-farer, accustomed to the life in this harsh but beautiful Arctic land, cannot but be impressed by the east coast."

On August 26 we neared the end of our voyage, and I wished we could prolong the trip. The jagged pinnacles had thinned out, giving way to the glistening dome of the Ice Cap, which here sloped down to the shore and met the North Atlantic on a broad front. Awesome in its grandeur, it overwhelmed the coastal mountains, burying many almost to their summits. Even the biggest peaks here were subordinated by the crest of the cap—it loomed above them all—but I was just a bit disappointed at first by the change of scene and the preponderance of ice over rock.

Steaming north along the bounding main, rolling with the tremendous swells, the *Nevada* and its cutter escort stayed well out to sea, well outside the pack ice, but within sight of the rugged shore. We passed many solitary icebergs, but they were widely scattered and posed no threat to sailing. The biggest bergs lay still in the water, unassailable, unyielding to the onslaught of the largest swells, fortified by their enormous mass and great inertia. The waves simply rose and fell against their flanks.

At the latitude of Kjoge Bugt the cutter disengaged, and the *Nevada* turned west toward land. Here at 1300 hours we entered the pack ice head on, and the ship slowed to a crawl. We eased through a gradually thickening pack for five or ten miles, occasionally stopping dead against a large floe. The sea was calm; the swells were damped out by the ice. All of us landlubbers— wide-eyed and entranced–crowded the rail in a pitch of excitement. Then a thousand yards off the bow, a great white wall blocked our way. Dwarfing the ship, it looked impenetrably solid and utterly impassable. The skipper let up on the engines, reversed the propeller, and brought the ship to a stop. While the *Nevada* lay idle in the water, he ordered a boat over the side, and it soon disappeared into the pack. When it returned, heated discussion followed on the bridge, with much shaking and nodding of heads.

Suddenly a small aircraft buzzed the ship out of the north, a silver twin-engined A-26 attack bomber, and after circling a couple of times, it directed us on through the ice. It seemed an unlikely place to see an airplane, but the skipper's plea for assistance had brought a quick response from Bluie East-2. The A-26 peeled back up the coast, and as we made our way cautiously through the ice, almost at idling speed, the wall just opened up, wrapped around the ship, and closed behind us. We craned our necks at its towering white spires, nearly close enough to reach out and touch. The wall looked just as impassable as before, but now it was at our stern and we were inside, with an open lead all the way to shore. All this heavy ice, really a floe of closely packed but separate bergs, had come from the big glaciers pouring off the Ice Cap at the head of Kjoge Bugt. Our destination and landfall lay just ten miles ahead in fairly open water.

Kjoge Bugt is a broad, irregular bight in the coastline of southeast Greenland. As an aside, note the etymology of "bight" and its Norse ties: *bygt, byht* (old English), *bugt* (Danish), bight, bay. Our destination was one of Kjoge Bugt's lesser satellites, a small fjord called Igtip Kangertiva or Comanche Bay. Here we would debark, set up and secure base operations high above the fjord, install a coastal mountain weather station (Atterbury Dome), and begin our assault on the Ice Cap. Our main charge was to build and operate year-round weather/rescue stations on the Ice Cap itself, a plan that required that our base camp be eight hundred feet above the fjord for ready access to the Cap. A year before, another expedition had tried, but its best efforts had ended in disaster, and we were its replacement. We dropped anchor at 1800 hours.

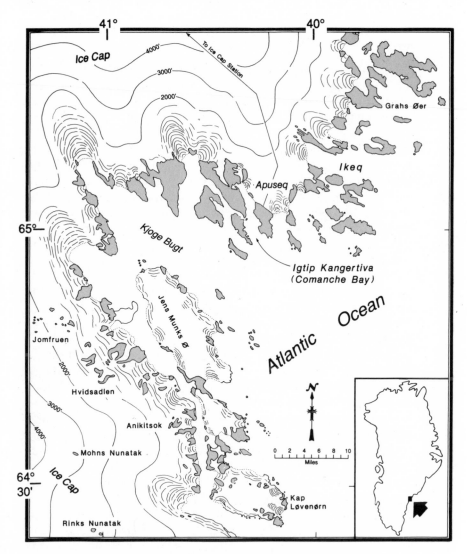

Map 3-1.   Kjoge Bay and vicinity.

Even before we dropped anchor we were greeted by the sight
of another vessel anchored just offshore. It was the *Izarah*, an
old four-masted whaler out of Newfoundland, run by a jolly crew
who called themselves the Goofy Noofies. The *Izarah* had been
hired to bring in our advance party, including our medic Mark
"Doc" Johnson, thirty-five sled dogs, some contract civilian construction workers, and a huge stash of building supplies. The
civilians and dogs moved ashore as soon as shelter was avail-

able, and the Noofies were glad to get the beasts off the deck—
the dogs, that is. Our officers took over a twenty-by-twenty-foot
shack, thenceforth called the beachhead station, built the year
before by the previous expedition. The rest of us stayed on board
the *Nevada*.

The Noofies were basic seafaring types, and they practically
never went ashore. They had frequent revelries aboard the
Izarah, though, and we often heard them screaming, cursing,
and brawling far into the night as they swarmed over the ship.
Their main job was unloading cargo, and during one prolonged
internal dispute everything came to a halt. With summer nearly
gone we had no time for their frivolities, so Captain Wade
grabbed our only tommy gun, commandeered the outboard motorboat, and hailed aboard. As he exerted his leadership, tran-
quility quickly returned, and the Noofies caused no more trouble
from then on. They just unloaded their ship and departed.
Though no shot was fired, the incident became known locally as
the Battle of Comanche Bay.

Meanwhile, we stayed on the *Nevada* until space became
available on shore. The contractors first built and occupied a
quonset-type warehouse next to the beachhead shack while they
worked on our base camp eight hundred feet higher up. Then
they moved up the hill and we took over the quonset. (A quonset
hut was a semicylindrical building made of corrugated iron,
looking something like a large half culvert closed at both ends
with bulkheads. Quonsets were widely used in the Arctic, but
they weren't very well adapted to the climate, and they made
miserable living quarters. The corrugated iron, for one thing,
tended to sweat from condensation.)

The *Nevada* stayed on until all essential construction work
was finished. Then we took over base camp and closed down the
beachhead station, and all the construction workers went aboard
the ship. Before its departure we had several strong wind storms
out of the north—our introduction to the *piteraq*. These were
what meteorologists call "katabatic" winds. They form during
periods of high pressure, when air over the Ice Cap is chilled by
thermal radiation and long exposure to the numbing cold; the
heavy, frigid air then flows downslope under its own weight as a
gravity current, gathering momentum as it goes.

These winds were mere breezes compared with what was yet
to come, but they were strong enough to alarm the ship's captain.

Comanche Bay offered poor anchorage, so lights were lit on shore, and under full steam the ship held its position as it faced into the wind. Without steam it would have dragged anchor, drifted ashore, and smashed into the rocks. When the ship raised anchor and steamed away on October 3, those aboard were happy to leave. Months later we heard that the *Nevada* had capsized in a winter storm off Cape Farewell, with loss of all hands. We tried to recall the faces of her crew, the people who so briefly had entered our lives, then were gone forever.

The beachhead station shack had been erected by Cpt. Alan Innes-Taylor and his executive officer, Lt. Max Demorest. Demorest was a promising young glaciologist from the University of Michigan and a protégé of the eminent geologist W. H. Hobbs, who had worked in West Greenland before the war. Professor Hobbs, through his considerable influence in Washington, had been instrumental in urging the army to set up American bases on the big island in 1941 even before the United States had officially entered the war. Lieutenant Demorest lost his life in November, 1942, in a series of tragic happenings during the protracted rescue attempt after a B-17 bomber crashed on the Ice Cap. The details of the tragedy have been documented by William S. Carlson (1962). Demorest, riding a motor sled, dropped into a hidden crevasse close to the site of the crash near the head of Kjoge Bay, about fifteen miles from the beachhead station. Four other men died in the try also—one in another crevasse and three in the subsequent crash of a small coast guard rescue aircraft.

Meanwhile, the remaining expeditioners at the beachhead station were nearly asphyxiated by a defective oil stove. As a result all survivors were evacuated, and we came in as their replacements—back to square one. We used their old task-force number, 4998-A, and Captain Innes-Taylor again arranged logistics. This time we were supplied with anthracite coal, shipped in gunny sacks by air transport from Pennsylvania to Greenland. At the outset we had top military priorities, even for shipping coal by air. Our high support was based on the army's very real concern that nothing prevent the successful ferrying of aircraft to Europe via Labrador, Greenland, and Iceland. Because of the treachery of the Greenland weather, the task force was a key unit in the plan.

Our charge also had high political backing, a plan conceived by Gen. Elliot Roosevelt, son of FDR himself. I flew to Greenland on a class 1 priority–usually reserved for senior brass and the general's dog–bumping a major off the plane at Goose Bay. Even our dog food was flown in under high priority, on one occasion bumping mail for the troops at BW-1. This caused sullen resentment, mail being regarded as sacred during WWII, but it also lent stature and grudging respect for our little nineteen-man expedition. Early on, we used our task-force number and "BICD" on our return mail address, but we were told by the Army Post Office that we would have to use the full name of our organization–Base Ice Cap Detachment–even though nobody was supposed to know our whereabouts or where any organizational unit was based overseas. Now, where else on Earth would there have been a Base Ice Cap Detachment during WWII except in Greenland? To avoid any errors in the use of the alphabet, particularly in radio transmissions, the military gave each letter an unmistakable code name: able, baker, cat, dog, easy, fox, and so on. BICD was "Baker Idea Cat Dog." Our call letters were "William Victor Howe Love." The base commander at BW-1 was a crusty navy admiral known as Able Dog Smith.

Our orders to set up and man three combined rescue/weather stations on the Ice Cap included the ongoing weather observations at Atterbury Dome. Logistical problems related to weather later cut our plans back to one Ice Cap station. Our first leader was a Maj. John T. Crowell, a softspoken downeaster sailor from Maine and a master mariner, soon replaced by Captain Wade, a geology professor who liked to be called "Hardrock Al." In Wade's several prewar Antarctic expeditions under Admiral Byrd, he had made the acquaintance of Sgt. Tony Colombo, a dog driver, and he brought Colombo along to Greenland. I had the feeling at the time, probably unfounded, that Major Crowell's healthy respect for the Ice Cap and its foul weather bordered on fear, and that was the reason for his transfer. More likely, he was just deeply concerned for the safety of his subordinates and was more needed elsewhere. Soon after leaving, he was placed in charge of all marine shipping to and from Greenland. During his short tenure with us, he allowed no one to venture outside the camp perimeter. Above all, we were to stay off the adjacent glaciers except for official duty.

4

Igtip Kangertiva

Igtip Kangertiva is a Greenlandic mouthful meaning "small fjord buttressed by a cliff." Uncle Sam, in his infinite wisdom, called it Comanche Bay after the U.S. Coast Guard cutter *Comanche*, which anchored there in 1942 during the disastrous rescue mission of the crashed B-17 bomber on the Ice Cap and most members of our predecessor expedition. Commander Atterbury, for whom Atterbury Dome was named, was skipper of the cutter.

As Greenland fjords go, Igtip Kangertiva isn't all that much, but it has a certain grandeur. A pretty little bay at the very foot of the Greenland Ice Cap, it is set off at its head by three stunning outlet glaciers, an outlet glacier being one that drains part of the Cap and empties into the sea, like a stream from a lake to the ocean. If Igtip were in the conterminous United States, say in Maine or California, it surely would be a national park. In

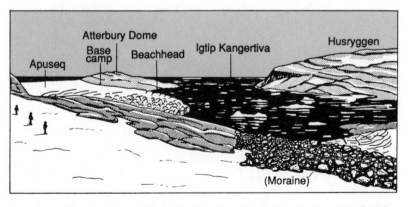

Fig. 4-1. Sketch view of Igtip Kangertiva, from the glacier at its head looking south toward the mouth.

Greenland it was just a small fjord buttressed by a cliff. Greenland has hundreds of such fjords. From head to mouth, Igtip
Kangertiva is about nine miles long and about a mile wide, flaring out to three miles at its mouth, where small embayments,
craggy islands, and rocky skerries add variety to its shoreline.
Low, rocky hills guarding its opening lack majesty, not *la grande
entrée*, but its inner west wall is more imposing. The Greenlanders didn't see fit to name its summit, at least not on maps, but
the Danes call it Husryggen, or "house roof," in allusion to its
gablelike crestline. Reaching a height of 1,810 feet, Husryggen
drops to the incredibly blue fjord in a series of glacially polished
rock ledges and sheer cliffs, utterly devoid of soil or vegetation
but highlighted by small perennial snowfields where the slopes
are not too steep to hold them. Our side of the fjord, on the other
hand, was buttressed by the rounded summit of Atterbury Dome,
1,100 feet high and the site of our weather shack. At the north
flank of the Dome was base camp, high above the fjord and right
on the edge of Apuseq Glacier, which merges north with the Ice
Cap and cascades west down to the fjord in a jagged aquamarine
wall three miles long. Two smaller glaciers at the head of the
fjord added just the right balance to an unforgettable scene, and
the scattered icebergs in the fjord provided extra punctuation.
One small berg lay grounded just off the beachhead for more
than a year.

From the time we arrived on the *Nevada*, Barry Borden and I
clamored to cross Igtip Kangertiva and explore the opposite
shore. Rearing above the water, the flank of Husryggen stood
cold and aloof, and we studied its details from our side of the
fjord every day that work and weather permitted. Barry–Lt.
Charles B. Borden, second-in-command–was a West Pointer and
a fine gentleman of natural good breeding and sensitivity, though
not typical officer material. He was from a military family, and
West Point had been his father's idea, not his own. Barry re-
signed his commission on graduation and went on reserve but
was called to active duty at the time of Pearl Harbor. He then
joined the ski-mountain troops and was training at Mount Rain-
ier in Washington when he learned of our task force and obtained a transfer. He later learned that his old outfit had been
shipped to a hellhole duty post in the South Pacific, Guadalcanal,
he said.

Barry and I were both avid skiers, and we spent a lot of our
spare time ski touring together, I a corporal and he a lieutenant

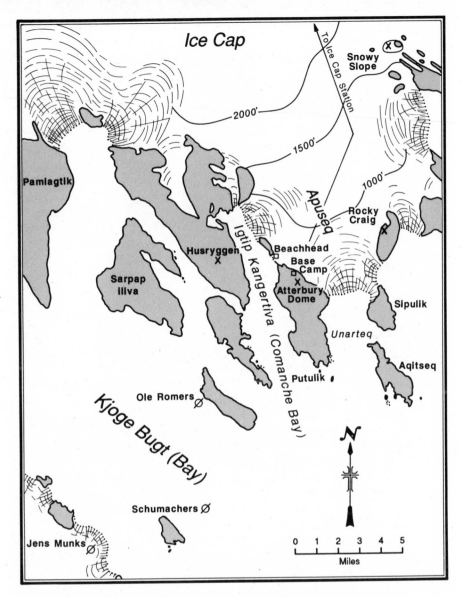

Map 4-1. Igtip Kangertiva (Comanche Bay) and vicinity.

ten years by senior. In the brashness of youth, I considered my Utah ski background superior to his from Vermont. His technique was a little unpolished, I felt, particularly his downhill technique. He may have regarded mine the same way, though in his heart he knew that I skied better. Barry hadn't fully learned to relax on skis. His weight shifting was a bit stiff, and his turns were a bit jerky, even for a man his age, but no one else in camp approached his ability.

From Atterbury Dome I scanned the far shore with the theodolite and binoculars, and as best I could from that distance I studied the rocks. They weren't quite like the rocks on our side; they were more monolithic, more massive, and they formed a more impressive outcrop. What secrets did they hold? How did they look up close? In reconnaissance years later, the Greenland Geological Survey speculated that the two differing kinds of rock juxtaposed across the fjord had been brought together along a large fault beneath the depths of the fjord. Abrupt changes in rock type often indicate faulting, though not always, and valleys or fjords are sometimes eroded out along zones of rock weakened by such faults. The rocks of Husryggen were coarsely layered—as were all the rocks in our part of Greenland—and they sloped gently northward beneath the Ice Cap. This fact was obvious even from a distance, and it jumped out to the eye. Here were rocks more than two billion years old, formed in the bowels of the Earth and exposed at the surface by eons of erosion, yet still sloping only gently. No convulsive deformations, no severe structural adjustments, unlike the much younger Wasatch Range, the Appalachians, or the Alps. These rocks just sloped north through eternity, and what secrets they held could only be disclosed by the patient, close-up study of a pedantic geologist.

Any early attempt to cross the fjord was out of the question, so the challenge grew stronger as the days turned into months. We wanted to climb Husryggen to view the big glaciers at the head of Kjoge Bugt. I wanted to set up cairns on top for survey and mapping purposes, and I wanted to sample the rocks. But in the summer and fall of 1943, every available hour of good weather and daylight was needed to secure camp and move supplies up the hill before the arrival of winter. We had a seaworthy German lifeboat, captured in an early engagement with the Germans in northeast Greenland and given to us by the coast guard, but when winter did settle in and there was free time for frivolities, our boat was deeply encased in solid ice. The only logical alternative was to ski across the frozen fjord.

As early as August, thin skiffs of ice began to form on Igtip Kangertiva on still nights, but they were quickly dispersed by the wind and waves. Ice didn't freeze on the fjord in earnest until midwinter and, even then, before a respectable thickness could

Fig. 4–2. View west across Igtip Kangertiva toward Husryggen from the snow slope above the beachhead station, foreground. The small island offshore was a caching place for supplies.

form, the piteraq would blow it out to sea. But each new coating was a bit thicker than the last, and eventually a solid base of hard black ice began to accumulate. As it thickened, it turned white.

In early winter the gang spent a day or two each week at the beachhead, running the winch line up the hill and wrestling a few drums and jerry cans of oil and gasoline up to base camp. Each time, Barry and I badgered Captain Wade about crossing over on the ice. Wade was cautious by nature, and in this matter he deferred to the judgment of Johan Johansen, our Norwegian civilian trail man, wartime expatriate from Nazi-occupied Norway. He had years of Arctic experience and a sixth sense about Arctic safety and danger. "The ice should be yoost a leetle bit thicker," Joe would say, and Wade would shake his head. Finally, in early March, we measured three feet of ice three hundred feet offshore, and Wade gave us the nod.

By then the beachhead station was completely buried by snow, even the top of the roof, and a great sloping drift reached out onto the fjord from the snowfield above. That night Barry and I packed our rucksacks with K rations, stowed extra clothing, and waxed our skis, and at first light we started down the hill. We guessed we could make the round trip in six or seven hours with plenty of time to explore, sightsee, and lay out plans for a follow-up trip. By now the days were lengthening rapidly. Dawn had broken to a high, thin overcast of cirrostratus clouds, but with a bright sun and distinct shadows it was the kind of sky that scatters the sun's ultraviolet rays and gives you a good sunburn. On a smooth, hard snow surface, and all keyed up by the spirit of adventure and the crisp beauty of the scene, we took just ten minutes and a long schuss to reach the beachhead. Across the ice, the shore–only a mile away–looked very close. We would be there in fifteen minutes.

In the short time it had taken Barry and me to ski from base camp to the beachhead and out an eighth of a mile or so onto the ice, however, the weather had taken an ominous turn. A gusty breeze had sprung up, blowing down the fjord. Wisps of snow were stirring at the head of the fjord, and a thickening film of clouds was moving across the sun. These portents gave us pause. We could press on, after months of frustrating anticipation, complete the crossing but cut short our stay, and easily return in an hour. Or we could turn back.

Discretion prevailed and we did turn back. Whether out of wisdom or fear, I don't recall, but we returned across the ice and up the long hill to camp, and in forty-five minutes we were in the mess hall, recounting our story to a relieved commanding officer. The wind had by then reached strong-gale force, and visibility had dropped off in a stirring ground blizzard. The storm lasted three days, reaching Beaufort 12, and when it died and the air cleared, the fjord was completely free of ice. Not a floe or ice pan remained, just dark gray water. Three feet of solid ice had vanished out to sea.

Barry Borden never did set foot on the far side of the fjord, but late in the summer of 1944, on the kind of sparking day that makes the Arctic summer memorable, Don Galbreath, Homer Loar, and I slipped quietly down to the beachhead, and with no one knowing of our daring plan, we pushed off the German lifeboat and rowed across. The far shore met the water in a near-vertical cliff, and we scrambled up a broken ledge with barely room to stand. "Gneiss," I said to myself, "granodiorite gneiss." This was just a guess; you can't really tell without a microscope

Fig. 4-3. Two views of the beachhead station. Top, in August, 1943, and bottom, March, 1944. Note the antenna pole on the roof of the shack in both views. In the bottom view, the snow hump with the ski poles on it buries a warehouse to right of center.

35

and, preferably, a chemical analysis. Most people would simply call it granite and wouldn't be far wrong.

Our side of the fjord, seen from afar for the first time, was an intoxicating sight. The tiny beachhead station, hardly visible, clung precariously to a mere foothold between the ice sheet above the water of the fjord below, and our antennae field high above the fjord looked like a collection of slender toothpicks on a block of white cream cheese. We drank in the awesome beauty of Apuseq's western front, a fractured blue wall of ice hundreds of feet high and three miles wide. No such view of the glacier was available from our side of the fjord. Then we reboarded the lifeboat, dipped our oars, and headed hurriedly back, lest Wade notice our absence. (Wade already knew; he had watched us all the way through his surveyor's transit, wishing no doubt to have been along.)

Qitsalivaq

If Igtip Kangertiva could be intoxicating, it could also be moody and unpredictable—by turns awesome, aloof, cold, somber, sunny and bright, tumultuous, gray, blue, black, or dazzling white. Firm ice finally covered the fjord late in March, 1944, and it stayed on until the June 10, when a piteraq cleared it out. With the ice came droves of seals, and from a high vantage point and aided by binoculars, I once counted about six hundred of them basking under the early summer sun. They were mostly small spotted seals—*qitsalivaq*—prized by the Greenlanders for their tasty flesh and attractive pelts. Also gathered at Igtip Kangertiva were bearded seals, *angneq* or *ukssuk*, ten to twelve feet long, and weighing several hundred pounds—their flesh wasn't cherished, but their thick, gray hides were used for covering *umiaks*, the women's boats; *saggaq* or *tordluluatsiaq*, the fjord seal; *nalinginaq*, the saddleback; and *neriniarteq*, the bladdernose.

In the water the seals were bold and curious, often approaching close to our boats or coming close to shore to watch the strange antics of the U.S. Army, but on the ice they were fitful and apprehensive. They liked to sun themselves, dozing head down on the ice for a few seconds, then glancing around quickly, head up, and dozing off again, head down. Nervous caution was their best assurance of safety from their one real natural enemy, *nanoq*, the polar bear. Each seal had its own breathing hole, and these were spaced rather uniformly apart. At the slightest hint of danger all would disappear beneath the ice with a quick swish of flippers. The Greenlanders depended on seals for their livelihood, and made heavy inroads near all their settlements, but Igtip Kangertiva was outside their normal hunting grounds.

I scanned the fjord from time to time in vain attempts to spot walruses, narwhals, and killer whales, but these beasts didn't seem to frequent our part of Greenland, at least not Igtip Kangertiva. My observations, of course, were limited to favorable weather conditions and short periods; at other times the fjord could easily have been crowded with all sorts of marine mammals. Old accounts do mention Greenland sharks—*aqaluviaq*—which the Greenlanders hunted by chumming the ice holes with rotted flesh. Sharks have highly developed olfactory organs and will gather from long distances to zero in on favorable scents. The Greenlanders would break loose a large slab of ice and shove it part way under the side of the ice hole to form a submerged shelf for stashing the bait and drawing out the sharks. Some sharks were large enough, according to the accounts, to dissuade the hunters from attempting to harpoon them, even through the ice, but the largest (and only) fish I ever saw in Igtip Kangertiva was a sculpin, or sea scorpion—*nagssugtoq*—six inches long, a fish so ugly that only another sculpin could abide it presence.

Since the fjord contained sculpins and shellfish, it presumably held other fishes also. We tried a rod and reel once or twice but never had the opportunity or inclination to test the waters thoroughly, since we spent ninety-five percent of our time up at base camp, Atterbury Dome, or the Ice Cap. When we were at the beachhead station, we usually were preoccupied with our assigned "rigorous duty in the Arctic" and lacked the luxury of leisure. The few native fish that may have skulked in the fjord also include caplin (*angmagssat*), sea perch (*agtarajik*), salmon (*aqaluk*), and cod (*sarugdlik*). Marine invertebrates among the local fauna would have been starfish (*avataussaq*), mussel (*kilijitaq*), crab (*pussugutilikasit*), anemone (*sunaunaq*), and snail (*uvavfaq*). Small barnacles clung to the rock, and small jellyfish were common in the fjord. Many lakes and rivers in southeast Greenland teem with trout or Arctic char. A small lake at the head of our fjord may have had them too, but we never found out. We just didn't manage to get there.

Glacier barriers and the rather sterile shorelines of Comanche Bay didn't encourage land animals to colonize our rocky little peninsula. We sometimes saw obscure tracks in the snow, mostly of hares and lemmings and perhaps a fox, but not the creatures themselves. Once we thought we saw bear tracks near base camp, but the snow was too deep and loose to be sure.

Quparneq, the guillemot

Birds were fairly common, not being hemmed out by the glaciers, and a good watcher could have compiled a respectable list. Down along Unarteq, in sheltered cliffy coves where tidal currents and winds kept the water open all winter long, there were always hundreds of noisy sea birds, especially the ubiquitous gulls (*quseq*), eiders (*ugpaterqorteq*), and guillemots, but also other species unfamiliar to me at the time, either by name or sight. A field guide would have helped. Ostermann (1938) mentioned about thirty-five species in southeast Greenland. Our local denizens, some of which probably bred elsewhere (possibly northeast Greenland) and just stopped off for a visit, were the arctic tern (*imerqutailaq*), black guillemot (*quparneq*), eider duck (*ugpaterqorteq*), Greeland falcon (*kigssaviarssuk*), ivory gull (*tingmiavarssuk*), kittiwake (*tateraq*), puffin (*sikutoq*), and snow bunting (*piseq*). We saw Arctic terns on the Ice Cap, out of sight of land, but any bird that had flown that far up from South America must have known where it was going. At Atterbury Dome we often saw ptarmigan (*erqerniangagssaq*), and at base camp we once enjoyed the sighting of a snowy owl in its fine white plumage. Our resident ravens were on hand nearly every day, at least when they weren't taking shelter from blizzards.

5

The Ice Cap

One of the great natural wonders of the world, the Greenland Ice Cap was the focus of all our lives for more than a year and a half. Aside from running the weather station at Atterbury Dome, our single purpose in being in the army and being in Greenland centered on the Ice Cap, on getting supplies up the long hill of ice onto the Cap, and on establishing a working station on the ice to send out weather reports. The Ice Cap station also was to be the takeoff point for any missions needed to rescue the crews of aircraft downed and disabled on the Cap.

Greenland is the world's largest island. Almost continental in size, it covers 840,000 square miles, most of it buried by ice. If you could set it over the East Coast of the United States, it would reach from Key West, Florida, to Halifax, Nova Scotia, and from New York to Chicago, or on the West Coast, from San Diego, California, to Ketchikan, Alaska, and from San Francisco to Grand Junction Colorado. About eighty percent of this area is covered by the Ice Cap—known to the Europeans as the "inland ice" and to the Greenlanders as by *Sermerssuak,* the "great glacier." The Ice Cap is larger than all of Washington, Oregon, Idaho, California, Nevada, and Utah combined. The "ice-free" borderlands of Greenland are about equal in total size to Norway, or about one and a half times the size of the state of Colorado. Thousands of local ice caps and lesser glaciers dot the borderlands, though the most northerly part, Peary Land, is ice free. Not that Peary Land isn't cold enough—it just doesn't get enough snow; the northernmost landmass on Earth, except for a nearby tiny island, Peary Land is a frigid polar desert.

At its center the Ice Cap is more than two miles thick. It rests on a bedrock base hundreds of feet below sea level near the center of Greenland and rises to an ice plateau more than ten thousand feet above sea level. The great weight of the ice has actually depressed the Earth's crust beneath the center of the island. All this has been proven by seismic profiling, using the same instruments and techniques applied to petroleum exploration elsewhere in the world. Scientists, moreover, are now using drill rigs to measure and sample the ice to depths of more than two miles—rigs that melt their way down through the ice and at the same time take ice cores for arcane analysis in low-temperature laboratories where glaciologists are suitably dressed for the polar climate. The air trapped in the ice cores, for example, reveals the composition of the atmosphere and its contained gasses, such as carbon dioxide and methane, at the time the air over the Ice Cap was entrained by succeeding layers of new fallen snow thousands of years ago. This information, in turn, provides clues to past climates in the rest of the world and, moreover, offers projections as to future climatic changes. Scientists also look for volcanic ash layers in the cores. Correlated with major eruptions around the world, or dated by isotopic analysis, these layers disclose the age of the enclosing ice. The best evidence presently available (based largely on analysis of deep-sea cores rather than on Ice Cap cores) indicates that the Greenland Ice Cap at about its present size has been in existence about three and a half million years. Its very beginnings may be nearly twice that old.

In describing a deep-drilling project high on the ice sponsored by the U.S. Army in the 1960s, Chester C. Langway provided some interesting statistics. Calculations placed the surface area of the ice cap at about 666,000 square miles, its maximum elevation at 10,800 feet, mean elevation is 7,000 feet, and mean thickness 5,000 feet. The total volume of ice was estimated to be roughly 620,000 cubic miles.

From base camp we could see about ten miles north onto the Cap. Our view west was partly blocked by Husryggen, the steep rock ridge across the fjord, and by a low, bare outcrop just west of our buildings. But looking west from Atterbury Dome we had an unobstructed profile view of the Ice Cap that reached sixty miles north to south. I spent many hours gaping at it, at all seasons of the year. Of course, it looked pretty much the same all year around, but with the seasonal shifts of the sun, the moods and shaded vales of the Ice Cap varied month by month, week by week, day by day, hour by hour, and minute by minute.

The surface of the Ice Cap is shaped like an enormous dome. Near its center it is as flat as a billiard table, a featureless plateau sloping only a few feet per mile, but toward the margins it slopes off at a gradually steepening pitch until in some places it drops several hundred feet per mile and terminates in a vertical ice cliff. At Comanche Bay, the Apuseq Glacier lobe of the ice Cap falls eight hundred feet to the fjord in about half a mile.

Actually, the Ice Cap has two main domes of ice, an enormous one centered at about latitude seventy-five degrees north and a smaller one at about latitude sixty-three, just southwest of Kjoge Bugt. Both domes are hemmed in by rugged coastal mountains that give rise to the name "inland ice." The southern dome is really just an appendage of the northern one, but both have several smaller (thought still large) satellitic domes in various places around their margins. The shapes of these domes approach a theoretical "equilibrium profile" that glaciologists have calculated for any large, outward-spreading mass of ice—what they call an ice sheet—pancaked out by its own great weight. This profile is a product of the accumulation of snow, gradually compacted to ice; glacial outflow caused by solid flowage of the ice under its own weight; and melting of the ice at its margins below the regional snowline, where melting in summertime exceeds the annual snowfall. At Kjoge Bugt, the equilibrium profile is oversteepened by the continuing calving of icebergs from the mouths of the big outlet glaciers.

Along our route onto the Ice Cap, the true profile of the glacier varied from the theoretical slope, with many changes of pitch between the ice margin and the crest. The steep pitch just above the fjord rose to a rolling bench at a height of about eight hundred feet, where slushy water ponded in a few spots at the end of the melt season in August. Above eight hundred feet, the summer melting, if any, was less than the yearly snowfall, so the ice was covered by snow all year around. Then the surface rose again in easy steps headed inland to a long, fairly steep pitch we called the fifteen-mile hill. Sixteen miles out at an elevation of 3,200 feet, the slope leveled off near where the expedition of 1942 had setup its small plywood weather station, soon buried by snow. Our route to this point was mostly north, but with a detour to the east to avoid crevasses. Then our trail turned northwest to the site of our own Ice Cap station and on to the crest of the cap itself. This route ascended gradually with one gentle roll and swale after another, rolls perhaps fifty to one hundred feet high and a fourth to half a mile or so across, until finally the crestline was reached.

In a larger sense the shape of the southern dome also differs from the theoretical model because of its uneven distribution of snowfall. The west slope of the dome is much drier than the east slope, so the snowfall is correspondingly less and the snowline is higher. The wet east wind–*ningeq*–after dumping its snow on the east slope blows down the west slope as a dry gale, thawing the surface as it goes.

In most places, the borders of the Ice Cap in late summer are bare, glistening ice up to six thousand feet above sea level, but on our side, bare ice reaches up only to about eight hundred feet, and then only in very late summer. Above that, all is drifting snow. Facing the stormy North Atlantic Ocean, accumulating seven hundred inches or more of snow annually, and having no real melt season above eight hundred feet, our side of the Ice Cap just had to have a steeper slope than the west side. This fact of climatology is what made Comanche Bay–Igtip Kangertiva– the best and strategically most attractive access point to the interior of the Cap in all of southern Greenland. Foul weather, yes, but smooth, hard snow obviously makes a better travel surface than rough, bare ice. And because of the high rate of snowfall, the Ice Cap reaches right down to sea level on the east side of the island were we were. At the same latitude on the west coast, the Ice Cap is hemmed in by nearly impassable bare-rock mountains a hundred miles across.

From Atterbury Dome the setting of the Ice Cap is a vista of untamed splendor, possibly one of the grandest views on Earth. When the weather is fair in coastal Greenland, visibility is limited only by the Earth's curvature. To the east and southeast the ice-choked Atlantic Ocean stretches to the far horizon. To the west is the Ice Cap itself, awesome in its grandeur, and from Atterbury Dome we saw its near two-mile height in one unbroken declivity, from its rolling crestline down to the sea. Though the crestline actually is almost flat, perspective plus irregularities in its contour make it appear uneven as seen from below.

You can get a rough idea of the scale of this view by looking west from Denver across the valley of the South Platte River toward the Rocky Mountains. In your mind's eye, superimpose the view from Atterbury Dome on the view from Denver. In both views the vertical relief from base to top is about the same. So are the horizontal distances. But as you'd scan the horizon from Pikes Peak on the south to Longs Peak on the north, you'd see none of the familiar landmarks. A shimmering plateau of ice would bury all the great peaks along the Continental Divide. Just a few isolated summits would emerge as nunataks. All the foreground from Denver to the foothills would be awash in a sea of floating ice. The foothills themselves would be sheathed in ice, and outliers such as the Rampart Range would support their own ice caps. Then try to imagine the same view in New Hampshire, looking from Belknap Mountain near Laconia northwest across Lake Winnepesaukee toward the White Mountains. Here, the entire Presidential Range, including Mount Washington, would be buried to twice its height by an unbroken wall of ice.

Our farthest coastal landmark was Kap Poul Løvenørn forty miles to the south, jutting east into the ocean. Fridtjof Nansen began his historic first crossing of the Ice Cap near there in 1889 at a peninsula now called Fridtjof Nansen Halvø. A zoologist and national hero who later became prime minister of Norway, explorer Nansen and his party hauled their own sledges across the Cap, completing the crossing to Godthaab, also called Nuuk on the west coast without the use of dogs.) Kap Løvenørn is on an island, Jens Munks Ø, but from our perspective it appeared to merge with the mainland, and for a time we thought it did. Behind it, towering nunataks pierced the Ice Cap sixty to seventy miles away. One nunatak carried the name of explorer Gustav Holm, who in 1884 had spent some months with the people of Angmagssalik—people unknown at that time to the outside world. Other nunataks include Jomfruen ("the maidens"), Hvidsadlen ("white saddle"), plus several named for other early-day explorers such as Peary and Whymper. Between Kap Løvenørn and Atterbury Dome is an expanse of uninhabited coast made of dark crags, shimmering glaciers, and ice-filled bays, all dominated by the Ice Cap looming high above.

At dawn for an hour or two or three, depending on the season of the year and hence the position of the sun, the entire sixty-mile-long scene is bathed in rosy alpenglow—the icebergs, pack ice, rocks, and most of all the Ice Cap itself. Greenland's alpenglow is not a momentary thing glimpsed and gone like Alfred, Lord Tennyson's faint flush of Monte Rosa ("How faintly flush'd, how phantom fair . . ."). It lingers on and on as the rising arctic sun skims low along the eastern horizon. Feasting my eyes from Atterbury Dome, I gaped in awe at its stark beauty, but it finally did fade, and in its place as the sun climbed its low arc into the crisp southern sky, the Ice Cap gleamed white as polished platinum.

Then the sun crossed the meridian, and the whole scene gradually turned to azure–yes, everything–the sky, water, icebergs, distant crags, and the snow underfoot. Most of all the Ice Cap. I never ceased to marvel at the color of the Arctic snow, even the dark blue holes punched out by my ski poles. In the dim light of the barracks, a faint blue glow filtered into the room through the snow-buried windows. Outside the barracks door, the piss holes in the snow bank had dark blue cores.

Bare glacier ice under a bright sun resembles aquamarine, if it's wet, or turquoise, if it's dry. First-time viewers are startled by its beauty. Deep crevasses are dark as indigo. I haven't seen this intense, all-encompassing blueness in the snows of temperate latitudes and am at a loss to explain it, but it too is ephemeral, and when the overcast moves across the sky, all is gray. (Old glacier ice, ravaged and ablated by the weather, is often chalky white.)

Due west of Atterbury Dome is Kjoge Bugt, named for a bay in Denmark where the Danes whipped the Swedes in a decisive naval battle in 1677. It is known to the Greenlanders as Pikiutdlek, meaning the "place where, when we first arrived, there was a bird's nest." Kjoge Bugt is a broad-mouthed indentation in the East Greenland coast, fully thirty miles across and fifty-five miles long, head to mouth. Within it are several big rocky islands, including Jens Munks Ø, itself thirty-eight miles long. Jens Munks, though, is almost totally sheathed in its own three-domed ice cap, even though its snowy crestline is hardly sixteen hundred feet above sea level. From Atterbury Dome I spent much time peering at it through the theodolite, admiring its flowing contours, ice cliffs, and crevasses. Kap Løvenørn, incidentally, is its southern spur. Studying it on aerial photographs, Wade and I noted things not visible from Atterbury Dome. Its west side, for example, is bounded by a long, narrow sound, Kagtertoq, largely covered all year around by perennial ice–*siko sujornarnisaq*–what the glaciologists like to call "paleocrystic ice." Some of this ice may have come from floating tongues of the adjacent Ice Cap–from "shelf ice."

Fig. 5-1.   Jens Munks ø (Island), seen from Kjoge Bugt. Engraved by
H. P. Hansen in 1888.

At Kjoge Bugt the Ice Cap slopes steeply down to the sea along
a broad front broken only by occasional rocky capes and headlands. At least two dozen outlet glaciers, some extraordinarily
large and active even for Greenland, pour countless thousands
of bergs into the water. On still nights the calving ice sometimes
rumbles like distant thunder. All this ice joins a long procession
of bergs that drift slowly south with the East Greenland Current
like a ghostly armada of silent white ships. Eventually they
swing west around Cape Farewell, then travel north with the
West Greenland Current as far as Davis Strait at about latitude
sixty-seven degrees north, but some disperse south into the shipping lanes off Cape Farewell, slip into the warmth of the Gulf
Stream, and disappear. In the Arctic seas, if you drift with the
current like the icebergs, land will be to your right. Exceptions
are few, and seafarers many years ago learned and applied this
rule–the Vikings surely among them.

6

Homer and the Winch Line

Cpl. Homer "By God" Loar from West-by-God Virginia might have been the most individualistic man at Comanche Bay. Of medium height and stature, with ruddy, roundish, undistinguished face and thinning dark blond hair, he was neither athletic nor uncoordinated. He came into the army from law school, and his idea of strenuous exercise was a good game of checkers, at which he excelled. I always wondered how he arrived on a weather expedition to East Greenland, especially in view of the formidable screening of each man being hired. Expedition members were selected from a long list of volunteers for "rigorous duty in the Arctic," brought together at Houlton Army Air Base in Maine for a final physical, mental, and psychiatric examination by a staff of military specialists with polar expertise. I had come to Houlton, for example, with twenty-five other volunteer weathermen from all around the country and was the only man selected from the group. I think the army was impressed by my Utah mountain background, my agility on skis, and by the fact that I had once built my own kayak. Besides, Captain Wade was a geologist, and I had a degree in geology and a year of graduate work.

But Homer? Homer's perfunctory winter survival training in Michigan included a few hours of crosscountry skiing, but he wasn't by nature the outdoor type, and his qualifications for rigorous duty in the Arctic were not overwhelming. A chronic griper, he was the most vocal and constantly outraged man on the expedition—in brief, a classic army latrine lawyer. Nevertheless, the military examiners were right: he proved to be one of the most productive and dedicated men in camp.

In the summer of 1943, in the big push to get base camp established before winter—and that meant getting hundreds of tons of supplies up there from the beachhead–Homer ran the winch station halfway up the hill. His pull was 3,600 feet long in two stages, using two 1,800-foot cables with which laden sledges were winched, uncoupled, recoupled, and rewinched in sequence. A second winch pulled the sledges the remaining 2,100 feet to the top of the hill, and a tractor then pulled them the final half-mile into camp.

We had half a dozen homemade cargo sledges, and we hoisted them up the hill one at a time on Homer's winch line. Occasionally we winched two or more in tandem as trailers. Since the winch held only 1,800 feet of cable, the line had to be reeled in twice to get the cargo up the first 3,600 feet of hill, by unbuckling the second length of cable and rereeling the first. A motor toboggan served as a switch engine to unreel and switch cables and return the empty sledges down the hill. This operation went on hour after hour, day after day, until halted by the frightful blizzards of winter.

The snowfield between the beachhead station and the site of base camp had a smooth, broadly convex brow, so that a man at the top of the hill couldn't see the bottom. We stationed a signalman at the brow–Max Morris, the smallest man on the team–to signal Homer when to start and stop the winch. The bigger guys loaded and unloaded cargo. Max's job was possibly the dullest in all of Greenland. At the proper moment he flailed his arms in a series of agreed-upon signals. In the meantime he just sat on a wooden box, bracing himself against the cold, reliving his college days in Michigan, and hating the army.

After a few days of bumbling trial and error, our operation ran like a finely tuned machine. We peaked out with about twenty-five loads per day. Larry Phillips, from Atlanta, Georgia, ran the toboggan, a primitive forerunner of today's recreational snowmobile. Our toboggan, officially the Eliason motor toboggan, was powered by a two-cylinder motorcycle engine. In 1943 what was called a snowmobile was a fully enclosed vehicle with tractor treads and a Studebaker-champion automobile engine; it was a close relative of a then newly developed amphibious contraption called a weasel, which was designed for use in jungle swamps but also worked on snow. We had several snowmobiles–"T-15 light-cargo carriers" in official army lingo–intended for use on the Ice Cap.

The Eliason motor toboggan had lots of problems. It was temperamental and undependable, hard to start, easy to stall, and

Fig. 6–1. After stalling on the long hill between base camp and the beachhead station, Larry Phillips patiently coaxes the Eliason motor toboggan to start.

likely to bog down. It was heavy and unwieldy, with the turning radius of a dump truck. Larry Phillips had the mechanical skill and patience to keep it going, and for that he rose from corporal to buck sergeant. Under the right snow conditions the toboggan ran smoothly and fast. On a good surface it could reach twenty-five miles per hour, but on loose, soft, or deep snow, it could go nowhere. We started out with six of them in August and by November three of them were abandoned and buried on Apuseq Glacier. Larry walked away from at least one of them himself.

The toboggan had a cleated, fabric-belted track coupled to the motor with a bike chain and sprocket. It had a dead-man throttle on a steering arm that resembled the tiller of a Vikingship. Two bucket seats in tandem were reminiscent of an early touring car, circa 1912. The starter was a stomp-down pedal, motorcycle fashion, and Larry spent hours adjusting the carburetor and stomping the pedal. Except on the winch line, we used toboggans mostly for play. We never took them up on the cap, depending instead on the dog team for reconnaissance and T-15 snowmobiles for haulage. The earlier Demorest group, though, relied heavily on them for their more modest transport requirements, and Demorest was riding one when he lost his life in the crevasse. Larry Phillips was a tinkerer, and he enjoyed his job more than anyone else in camp. He even rode and fussed with the toboggans on his time off, through any hours of daylight–which in early summer meant around the clock. His antics included racing over the roof of the barracks at two or three in the morning, much to the displeasure of everyone else.

When we were running the winch line and Larry was towing cable back down the hill, Homer had time to check over his winch. Homer dutifully and repeatedly lubricated all moving parts, including his parka, which surely was the best-greased rag in Greenland. But because of his diligence, the winch never stalled and never failed to start, and it ran like a Swiss watch, even in the spring after having been buried for several months under eight feet of snow. Actually, we used three winches to run the line: a short pull at the bottom of the hill to clear the loading area and get the sledges lined up for the long pull, and another link at the top to clear the last part of the hill. Just about anyone available ran the bottom winch, and Tex Fincher usually ran the one at the top. Tex was a radio technician but an otherwise decent chap who enjoyed being outdoors occasionally like the rest of us. Few places in Greenland were more dismal and gloomy than the inside of our radio shack.

The runners of a loaded sledge always froze to the snow, and before starting out up the hill they had to be broken free to get the load moving. Whenever the sledge stopped for whatever reason, they instantly froze in again. A steel cable 3,600 feet long had a lot of stretch, and as it slowly tightened on the drum against the resistance of the frozen runners, it quivered like a bow string before the sledge finally broke loose and took off like an arrow. This motion relieved the tension in the cable, and the sledge halted and again froze fast. The heavier the load, the greater the tension, and the harder the snap. After three or four jerks and stops, all the slack would be out of the cable, and the load would proceed smoothly on up the hill.

Late in the summer of 1943 some civilian contactors arrived at Comanche Bay, reportedly to install refrigeration (!) up at base camp. This was an act of closing the barn door after the horse had bolted, because all our fresh meat for the winter had already spoiled when it was unloaded from the ship before the cold weather set in. We buried it in a snow bank, but not quickly enough to save it. At any rate, the contractors wanted to hitch a ride up the hill on the winch line–understandably–rather than hike the mile and a half up to camp. We explained the jerky starting procedure and suggested that they might want to climb far enough up the slope to catch their ride on the run, but they demurred, preferring to board, they said, at the bottom. With their weight added to the already loaded sledge, they of course increased the tension needed to break loose the runners, and they were hurtled high into the air at the first snap, arms and legs flailing, to land in a heap in the snow. Wild-eyed, they picked themselves up, ran panting for the now stopped sledge, climbed aboard, and were pitched aloft once more. After the third flip, they took our advice, waiting for the next sledge, and caught it on the run.

The long pull up the hill was a diagonal traverse that caused problems when the surface was icy, particularly after a freezing drizzle when the sledges tended to sideslip. One time a slipping sledge got out of control, stalled out the winch, unspooled the drum, and careened at frightening speed all the way down the snowfield, over the ice foot, and into the fjord with a great splash. While airborne, as seen in profile from the beachhead, the flying sledge was a magnificent sight, but it was demolished when it hit the water, and we never recovered the cargo. Another sledge smashed in similar fashion into a pile of glacial boulders part way down the slope, but without loss of cargo. On yet another occasion a team of dogs and I began sliding down the same icy slope, straight for the ice foot, but the dogs had a strong instinct for survival and were smart enough to turn quickly uphill, flatten themselves on their bellies, and scratch into the ice with their claws. They and I shared a bad moment together, but we halted with room to spare. One's thoughts at such a time, when accelerating down an icy slope a thousand feet toward a fjord, are not easily put into words.

The last link of the winch line approaching camp was a near-flat stretch on the edge of the glacier, but in some ways it was the toughest leg of all. Late in summer it was rough bare ice, and it took a heavy toll of sledges. Narrow crevasses a foot or so across were cut deep into the ice by surface meltwater, and they sheared off the runners of any sledge that happened to slide into one sideways, occasionally dumping the cargo into the crack as well. Once, when these crevasses were bridged over with fresh snow and I was on foot, I dropped into one despite wary pussy-footing and foreknowledge of their general location. I caught my-self on my forearms without incident, even though I was car-rying a heavy mercurial barometer, but the sensation caused a flush of adrenaline.

All our sledges had names, mostly mild profanities like those of military aircraft in those days. Almost all bombers, for ex-ample, were given obscene names by their crews and their resi-dent sign painter. We had the "Fifth Avenue Express," which was innocent enough, but also the "Zowie Bird," the "Snark," the "Big-Ass Bird," and the "Blivot Buggy." A zowie bird, according to mililtary legend, flew in ever-diminshing circles at an ever-increasing rate of speed, until with a flash of lightning and a clap of thunder, *zowie*, it flew up its own behind and disappeared. A snark was an unsavory deviate who ate the crotches out of old underwear. A big-ass bird was an army figure of speech in a widely used simile: to take off like a big-ass bird was to leave in a hurry. A blivot was simply two pounds of scats in a one-pound bag. Do not try to fathom the workings of the military mind. Pro-fanity and obscenity were crutches to help the soldier cope with the boredom, fear, indignities, and humiliation of army life. Re-gardless of upbringing, nearly all enlisted men and most officers eventually acquired the habit.

I often used the winch line to get in a little extra skiing. Tying a fifty-foot length of rope behind a sledge, I hung on skijoring fashion while swinging to and fro up the hill in wide arcs, then cut loose at the top and schussed the mile or so back down to the beachhead, usually doing a few linked christies toward the bottom to impress the pedestrians loading cargo. Uphill, as I ap-proached the winch station, Homer or Tex would good-naturedly stomp down on the accelerator to try to dump me off my feet, but they never succeeded. I had ridden too many high-speed rope tows in pre-army days at Alta, Utah, to be done in by a mere winch.

I also built a small takeoff down near the fjord so that some visiting Norwegian seamen and I could polish our jumping tech-niques. They were much better jumpers than I and they gave me some good pointers. These men, like our resident Norwegian, Johan Johansen, had been caught in Greenland by the war, and were hired by the army to transport supplies from place to place in their cutter *Polarbjorn*–"polar bear." Jumping for them was a great diversion and a relaxing change of pace. They were old trapper friends of Johansen, and their meeting at Comanche Bay was a tearful reunion, celebrated with a ski meet up on the hill and a bottle of cognac out on the cutter.

My skis were seven-foot, six-inch hickories with bear-trap cable bindings. I could adjust the tension for jumping, downhill, or crosscountry, although the skis were basically downhill models. I had a wide assortment of waxes for all possible snow conditions: Captain Innes-Taylor, amazing planner, had thought of just about everything. I used the longest skis available, partly because they were more stable in the rough snow conditions of Greenland but mostly because they gave the greatest possible flotation on the snow. Less weight per unit area. Also they would span a bridged crevasse better than a shorter ski, and bridged crevasses were the worst kind. They were hidden and unexpected, and although some were outlined by subtle troughlike depressions in the snow, others were completely concealed. Some snow bridges were strong enough to support the weight of a person on foot, or even a snowmobile, but others would collapse under their own weight.

Two seven-foot, six-inch skis had about 540 square inches of surface in contact with the snow, so a 180-pound man weighed only about one-third of a pound per square inch. On foot, the same man weighed six to twelve times as much per unit area, depending on whether his weight was on one foot or two, and on his shoe size, but in walking, of course, all of a man's weight is alternately on each foot. So the skis provided a substantial margin of safety against hidden crevasses. Lieutenant Demorest, riding a motor toboggan, had had less weight per unit area than a man on foot but more than a man on skis, and the area where he died was a maze of large, hidden crevasses.

All the borders of the Greenland Ice Cap are crevassed and potentially dangerous, some more so than others, and in some places the crevasses reach far inland. Our route onto the Cap was relatively free of them, though we crossed many small ones and passed near to some very large ones. The extent of crevassing on a glacier depends chiefly on three factors, the foremost being the rate of ice movement–the faster the movement, the more the fracturing. Other factors include the shape of the subglacial floor, variations in thickness of the ice, and combinations thereof. Traversing the border zone, you cannot be too careful. Most bad accidents on the Ice Cap take place there, and long skis are just one form of minimal protection.

7

Weather Watching in the Frozen North

Our weather shack stood atop Atterbury Dome, the bare rock knob 1,100 feet high that the Greenlanders called Putulik – "the place with a hole," perhaps in reference to a small cove or niche in the southeast side of the knob, facing the ocean. Commanding an unobstructed view in all directions, Atterbury Dome rose like a broad sentinel above the entrance to Comanche Bay.

Following long-established international procedure, we encoded weather information in five-digit groups of numbers that covered all aspects of current weather for transmittal throughout the World. Each digit or pair or group of three digits stood for a particular weather element, such as air pressure, temperature, humidity, wind speed and direction, cloud type and cover, snowfall, visibility, and so forth. These things were listed in tables normally posted in every weather station using the international code, but they were also memorized by all weather people, who thus could instantly visualize any weather condition by looking at a sequence of coded numbers. Besides this, the Greenland Base Command had a supplemental weather series called the "Greenland special-phenomena code" that included things important to local weather analysis and travel, such as sea-ice and fjord-ice conditions, fog banks, snow plumes, and top wind speeds beyond Beaufort 12 (more than seventy-three miles per hour).

To keep all this coded information from the enemy, namely the Axis powers, and anyone else not privy to our data, we then enciphered it through a process called false subtraction, by subtracting each coded digit from a series of figures changed daily in a secret code book. Without the book we were told, the code was unbreakable, and we couldn't imagine that it wasn't, but that was before the days of electronic computers.

The three-man crew at Atterbury Dome had to record weather conditions every hour and fill out various forms required by the bureaucracy: hourly, daily, and monthly reports, the latter primarily for climatological detailing. If something unusual happened in the meantime—a sudden wind shift, the onset of a blizzard, or a rapid change in air pressure—it was duly recorded also, regardless of the time. Every three hours, the Atterbury Dome crew phoned down the latest weather report to the radio shack, where another weatherman enciphered it for shortwave radio transmittal to Greenland Base Command. GBC then broadcast it to receivers around the world. If the weather had been a bit unusual, Barry Borden always got on the line to ask if any records had been broken—usually wind speeds or temperatures. He wanted that information for his official journal. Most stations also made upper-air probes, such as pilot-balloon and radiosonde runs, to sample the speed, direction, pressure, and humidity of the upper air. A radiosonde was a miniature weather-reading and radio-transmitting device hanging from a balloon. Expendable, it was only used once. All this information was crucial to accurate forecasting and safe air travel.

The pilot-balloon run—PIBAL was its weather code abbreviation—was a simple way to measure wind speed and direction aloft, and cloud height. With a fixed rate of rise, the balloon was tracked through the sky with a theodolite. Through a telephone hookup to another weatherman in the office, coordinates were plotted at the same time on a board, and the speed of the balloon (equals wind speed) and wind direction were quickly computed graphically with the aid of trigonometric tables. It sounds complicated, but any idiot could learn to do it.

We didn't start balloon runs as soon as Greenland Base Command would have liked, and the more urgent business of establishing wintertime camp security triggered a series of acrimonious radiograms from headquarters. Our call letters WVHL, William Victor Howe Love, were used on the air with increasing derogation, but in due course, and after several false starts, we built a hydrogen shack to shelter the generator to make the gas to inflate the balloons. This shack had to be well outside the main camp area to minimize the fire hazard, hydrogen being extremely explosive. We put up a frame of two-by-fours eight feet on a side and seven feet high, anchored down with boulders, like an Indian tipi ring. We covered it with heavy canvas and were nearly finished when the weather turned foul, as you might guess, and we had to suspend operations. The storm lasted three days, and when it had blown itself out, nothing of the hydrogen shack remained—nothing. It had disappeared without a trace from the face of the Earth.

In response to further agitated queries, Wade sent out a testy reply to Greenland Base Command: "Hydrogen shack carried away by 90-mile-per-hour zephyr. Was last seen headed toward Skjoldungen. Has not yet returned." Chuckling with self-satisfaction, we visualized a puzzled cryptographer at BW-1 uncoding Wade's message and turning to his radio operator: "Do you suppose that captain really expects that shack to return?" We finally started balloon runs on December 14, 1943.

Most wintertime activities in southeast Greenland were chores, and making balloon runs was among the foremost. First, we had to generate the hydrogen, and that was a tricky job. We dumped a chemical called ferrohydride into a steel generator cylinder, added hot water, closed the valve, and presto—hydrogen. Simple enough, but as the chemical and water reaction set in, the temperature and pressure in the cylinder rose alarmingly, so we had to get well out of the area until the reaction was completed, the tank cooled down again, and the excess pressure dropped off. Then we skulked back to bleed off the gas into a separate storage tank and clean out the cylinder. We added more hot water and broke up the solid residue with a brass-tipped rod (no sparks, please), rinsed out the generator, and were ready for the next balloon run.

The hardest part of making hydrogen was heating the water outdoors in the numbing cold. We couldn't bring water out from the kitchen; it would have turned to ice in the distance from there to the hydrogen shack. But as soon as we poured the water on the ferrohydride, an exothermic chemical reaction set in, and the water temperature rose on its own. Then, after the reaction was completed, the excess water cooled down and froze inside the cylinder. We started out by melting snow in a plumber's pot, which was a gasoline heater that looked like an oversized Coleman trail stove. With a hand pump on the side of the gas tank, gasoline was fed into the burner through a needle valve. Perhaps our gasoline wasn't clean, because we always had trouble with the valve. Maybe it just froze up. At any rate, when Howard Sullivan and I had our turn at making hydrogen, we had trouble clearing the valve and starting up the pot.

Sullivan—Sully, for short—from Williamsport, Pennsylvania,

had a high GCT score and an imperturbable nature. GCT stood for the army's general classification test, similar to an IQ test. Sully had learned to minimize all needless motion early in his military career, to avoid scrupulously any precipitate action, and to move no faster than circumstances warranted. His idea of con-structive relaxation was to lie flat on his cot with ankles crossed, hands behind his head, and eyes closed or fixed on a spot on the ceiling. On Sully's day to cook, his idea of a good meal was sliced bread and bacon.

While Sully was on his knees in the snow diligently pumping up the gas tank, I was on my haunches worrying the needle valve, trying to clear the orifice. Experience told us that the valve on a Coleman stove would turn only so far, then stop. Not so the plumber's pot: as I slowly turned the valve, it suddenly was loose in my hand, and ignited gasoline was jetting like a flame thrower twenty feet out the side of the burner. Automatically I cupped it out with a snowball and looked up just in time to see the gray blur of Sully's rear disappear over the nearby hilltop. I was im-pressed by his animal-like grace and the easy fluidity of his un-wasted motion.

The balloon run itself was fun. An inflated pilot balloon was about three feet across, and it came in three optional colors for different sky conditions: red for blue sky, black for cloudy, and white for dark, heavy overcast. Experience had shown that these colors gave the balloon the best visibility for the conditions spec-ified. As we inflated the balloon, we balanced it against a pre-scribed weight to assure the correct rate of rise. Overinflation would make it rise too fast; underinflation, too slowly. At night we affixed a small paper lantern lit by candlelight. (Stateside, these lanterns in the sky were often mistaken for flying saucers.)

Though it may seem strange, a pilot balloon is easier to track by theodolite in a strong wind than in a dead calm. When the air is still, the balloon rises directly overhead in a lazy spiral, but seen through the theodolite its relative position changes rapidly in all quadrants of the compass. You have to be adept at handling the tangent screws and reading the verniers to keep the balloon in view, and if you aren't careful you'll kick a leg out from under the tripod as you circle it. Tangent screws are the little milled wheels that control the azimuth and altitude (that is, direction and pitch) of the telescope. The verniers read in fractions of de-grees.

During a strong wind, on the other hand, the azimuth of the

Fig. 7–1. Don Galbreath readies a pilot ballon in the hydrogen shack to measure the winds aloft.

balloon doesn't change much. You can line up your sights before the balloon is released, clamp the balloon in your field of view, and just watch—mostly with your hands deep in your pockets—as it slowly climbs the crosshairs. Usually the run is over when your balloon reaches the first cloud layer, but not always. I once followed a balloon into an altostratus layer at eight-thousand feet and didn't lose it until it had reached twenty-thousand—some indication of the thin, vapid nature of the overcast. That was the kind of sky that causes whiteouts on the ice cap but that eventually thickens, lowers, and brings snow. Nowadays pilot balloons are used mainly for measuring cloud heights. Knowing the rate of rise in feet per minute and multiplying the time in minutes until the balloon enters the cloud gives the height. More sophisticated probes of the upper atmosphere today are targeted by radar. They transmit their own signals, and they read out the data by computer.

The five-digit format of the National Weather Code and the need for brevity in military communication led to many interesting acronyms that were widely used during World War II. Most

of these have all but disappeared from the idiom, but four re-
membered and cherished by old soldiers deserve to be preserved
in perpetuity:

SNAFU – Situation normal, all fouled up;
SUSFU – Situation unchanged, still fouled up;
TARFU – Things are really fouled up;
FUBAR – Fouled up beyond all recognition.

A few others commonly used were:

NOTAM – Notice to airmen;
RADNO – Radio not operative;
FROPA – Frontal passage;
IFR – Instrument flight rules
VFR – visual flight rules;
PIBAL – Pilot balloon (observation);
CAVU – Ceiling and visibility unlimited;
RAOB FINO – Radiosonde observation not filed.

And one from the Navy:

CINCUS: Commander-in-Chief, U.S. [Navy] (Subsequently
    changed to COMINCH, for obvious reasons).

Many coded abbreviations were impromptu, made simply by de-
leting all but key letters in a phrase: SVR TURB ALFT SW – severe
turbulence aloft southwest. TSTM + 3 MI NE STN – heavy thunder-
storm three miles northeast of station. The possibilities were unlimited for the imaginative communicator, but the meaning had
to be unmistakable. The consequences of a misreading could
be serious.

8

Sparks in the Polar Night

The pride and showcase of Comanche Bay–that was the radio shack. Spacious but a model of efficiency, located squarely amid camp, it was the nerve center of the outpost. A transmitting and receiving room crowded with dials and black boxes, an electric shop, living quarters for four GI radiomen, separate accommodations for Captain Wade and for Lieutenant Borden, and the camp headquarters/office all were crowded within. There, too, was the armory–not that we had a lot of armament: just a tommy gun, three or four automatic handguns for the officers, and a few cases of ammo. (Back at the barracks, each weatherman had a carbine assigned to his own care, plus a few rounds of .30-caliber ammunition for blasting tin cans, icebergs, and any Nazi raiders encountered on the Ice Cap.) The weather barracks, though a trifle more Spartan than the radio shack, was really not all that bad either, but we were slightly miffed by the close proximity of the radiomen to the officers, and hence their unequaled opportunity to fraternize, polish apples, and brown nose. We each had a private stall about the size of the solitary cells at Sing Sing, separated from one another by four-by-eight sheets of plywood.

All the radiomen had come to the expedition from the Army Airways Communications Service and they had a high sense of belonging and esprit de corps, though like the rest of us, they were now under the Operations and Plans Division of the General Staff in Washington, not AACS. Scott Field near Belleville, Illinois, was the center of their technical training command and where they learned the army way by the numbers. They (1) learned their trade, and (2) learned the Scott Field cheer:

> Three dits, four dits
> Two dits, dah!

Scott Field, Scott Field,
Rah! Rah! Rah!

A "dit" was radio-operator lingo for a Morse-code dot. A "dah" was a dash. That's how dots and dashes actually sound on the telegraph key, like dits and dahs. Three dits is an "s," four dits is an "h," and two dits is an "i." Any good dictionary lists all other letters of the code as well.

Only one man, Sgt. Caryl Force, had really good access to Wade. A highly talented radioman and expert high-speed key operator, he was dubbed "QQ" because he received and decoded "secret" messages. "Captain," he would confide in a stage whisper at breakfast, or at any other time that he could be overheard, "I have a qq [communication] for you," and Wade would solemnly nod. QQ was a bit older than most men in camp, probably in his mid-thirties, and he projected a fatherly image. By his own admission he was a man of the world–widely experienced, knowledgeable about many subjects, able to meet and best any emergency, and master of his trade. Spending much time indoors glued dutifully to his transmitter and receiver, and tirelessly deciphering qq's, he stood aloof from his suntanned but adoring disciples whose jobs entailed occasional forays outdoors to string telephone wires up to the weather station or to climb antennae poles to adjust the tension on the cables. QQ's ghostly pallor was emphasized by a long, dark beard, which he stroked introspectively over a cup of coffee in the mess hall. He slightly resembled Lionel Barrymore's portrayal of Rasputin in the classic movie *Rasputin and the Empress.*

QQ's shining hour came with his receipt of a "Book message to all stations, TOP SECRET," signed by none other than General Ulio, the adjutant general of the United States Army. Tension mounted around camp as the word leaked out and the cipher came in–three hours receiving and three hours deciphering. Lieutenant Borden paced the floor as Captain Wade swilled coffee, both nervously awaiting the words of the adjutant general. Could the big push be under way?

Then it was out, "A message to all stations, repeat, to all stations: How to prepare carter spread for greater palatability in army mess halls." Carter spread was the army's answer to Wisconsin butter. Designed for all earthly climates and all theaters of military operations, it was a waxlike, heat-resistant substance, flavorless to all but the most discerning taste buds, but spoilproof and utterly indestructible in the hottest desert or the coldest corner of the frozen north. From that stirring moment on, after a belly-busting laugh from all hands, carter spread would be known as "Uliomargarine." I always wondered, but never knew, if General Ulio's secret message actually contained arcane instructions, a signal to alert the proper authorities to a hidden course of action. On the other hand, perhaps it was designed to perplex the Axis powers. Or maybe it really was meant to enhance the palatability of carter spread.

The end of the proud radio shack was ignominious and not long in coming. On October 6, 1943, at 1900 hours, fire from an overheated stove quickly flashed through the building. Most of us had moved up the hill from the beachhead station just a few days before, and most of us were at dinner in the mess hall when it started. Everyone just stood helplessly by and watched in awe as the flames raged out of control. Lieutenant Borden, as camp historian, wanted to duck in to retrieve his official journal but refrained under direct orders from Captain Wade. Good thinking, Captain. Quickly, the ammunition began to go, but not like the crack of a rifle nor in a great explosion. Each round just went off by itself with the dull pop of a small firecracker, first one at a time, then in staccato bursts like ladyfingers as we crawled behind rocks to duck the occasional ricochet. Then a great orange fireball lighted the night sky and swallowed the roof, and it was all over. By morning nothing remained, not the merest wisp of smoke. Even the embers had cooled. All expedition records normally kept in the headquarters office, all invoices, and Borden's official journal—as well as the worthy radio shack itself—were gone.

Fire out of control is one of the greatest fears in the Arctic, for its consequences can be tragic even after the embers are cold; lives are at risk with the loss of adequate shelter. We were briefly in a state of shock over our considerable losses, but no one was injured and we had other buildings, other options, and bounteous supplies of everything in our warehouses—we had complete furnishings, in fact, for a full year of operations for three more weather outposts, which we planned to erect on the Ice Cap. We weren't even cut off from the world. Our coding machine had been lost in the fire, but we still had the beachhead station, and before the day was out, our crew was down there starting up the generator and radioing Greenland Base Command for instructions and assistance. GBC's response was prompt and terse, calling our attention to the Articles of War and mentioning the penalties for sending messages in the clear (not coded) over the air in wartime. We shut down forthwith and didn't transmit again until a week later when *Giggle Peter*, the army's East Greenland supply plane piloted by a gallant Captain Shiffrin, buzzed down from Ikateq and dropped us a shiny new machine. Meanwhile, Wade and Borden moved into the mess hall with Cookie, and all available hands were called out to erect a new shack from one of our prefabricated modular prospective Ice Cap stations. Made of double-walled insulated panels, it went up fast and Comanche Bay was back in business, with QQ at the console.

9

Back to the Beachhead Station

After the radio shack fire, and into early winter, we continued to make frequent trips to the beachhead station to wrestle up supplies for camp and to augment our growing stash of gear for the Ice Cap. These activities ended only when we could no longer cope with the deepening cover of snow and ice. Eventually the whole beachhead station was buried without a visible trace, all except the very top of the flagpole. Working down by the fjord was a pleasant respite from the tedium of existence up at camp, and besides, I looked forward to the chance to do a little downhill skiing on the long slope between camp and the beachhead.

The beachhead station had no sanitary facilities except the rocky shore. The fjord, though, had a vigorous tide, with a range of about twelve feet between low and high water. By timing our movements with the ebb and flow of the tide, we preserved a modicum of sanitation and concomitantly augmented the diet of the few mussels and sea scorpions in the fjord.

The narrow, stony beach was hemmed in by the fjord on one side and a vertical ice foot *qineq* 30 feet high on the other, formed where a big perennial snowfield flanking our glacier reached right down to the water and where wave and tide maintained a vertical or overhanging ice cliff. An ice foot is land-fast sea ice attached to the shore, as distinguished from the more mobile floating pack or drift ice beyond. Usually there is a patch of open water or shore lead between the free-floating pack and the ice foot. Or there may be nothing but open water beyond the ice foot if the winds keep the pack ice out to sea, as they did at Comanche Bay. Our ice foot was interrupted at the beachhead station by an outcropping of dark granite (more properly, schist) an acre or so in size that provided the only land access to the shore, though you could walk a mile south along the narrow cobblestone beach during low tide, between the water on one side and the ice foot on the other. To the north along the shore, the ice foot merged with the glacier in an ice cliff two hundred or so feet high.

One breezy day, Barry Borden walked far down the stony beach beneath the ice foot, ostensibly to study barnacles. Barry was a private sort of person. As usual, the breeze blew out of the north along the fjord, straight down the beach. Barry looked up with a sideward glance just in time to see an object unfurled in the wind and headed straight toward him, spanning the width of the beach. Despite instant recognition, there was no escape, no room to maneuver. He was immobilized for an awful instant that seemed an eternity. It was a long strand of soiled toilet paper, and its embrace, he confided, was a nightmare. When he finally regained his composure, tore himself free, and retraced his steps, he confronted the smoking gun not far from the beachhead station, swashing gently in the waves of the rising tide, fully a foot long, but in two segments that resembled, he said, a giant exclamation mark. Barry was not pleased, but the mussels and sea scorpions must have been happy.

One day in about the middle of October, 1943, several of us were down at the fjord moving oil drums to the mainland from our cache on the small island offshore. We stored things on the island because it was roomier than on the mainland and because it was easier to unload cargo there from shipboard, even though it meant a second handling to get things to the mainland and up the hill. At low tide the island was a peninsula. We could walk across the fifty-yard cobble-bottomed isthmus, or snake an oil drum across with a winch stationed on the mainland. Normally, we winched things across with an overhead-cable arrangement held up by timbered A-frames and fitted out with a small home-made trolley car slung underneath. We pulled the trolley car back and forth across the channel with ropes and pulleys powered by the winch on the mainland.

Three men were working on the island terminal at low water, Howard "Sully" Sullivan, Larry "Scratch" Phillips, and Carl "Sandbag" Sanford, when a fast-rising tide swept in almost unnoticed and cut them off. Although the normal tidal range in Comanche Bay was about twelve feet, the channel to the island was rarely under more than three or four feet of water. Besides, we usually timed our work to take advantage of the low tide. This time, as the tide rose, the weather began to turn bad, and we judged it prudent to get back up the hill to camp. Snow had

Fig. 9-1. Ice foot at the beachhead station. The roof of the beachhead shack is almost hidden above and behind the ice lip, center of picture. Note figure for scale, lower right of center.

started to fall and the wind was whipping whitecaps on the fjord. Our German lifeboat by then had long since been encased in shore ice, mostly frozen spindrift from the fjord, and the only escape from the island short of wading was by way of the trolley. The capacity of the trolley, was just two men, and Sandbag stood gallantly aside as Sully and Scratch swung aboard.

Though rocking precariously, Sully and Scratch crossed over without incident, the wind blowing hard on their tails. Then the trolley car was returned to the island for Sandbag and he climbed aboard, but right in midchannel the lead pulley slipped off the cable, and Sandbag was stranded. No amount of coaxing could unjam the pulley, and with the wind rising to a stiff breeze, Sandbag elected to jump off and wade ashore.

Sandbag hung from the trolley and let go, and when he dropped into the water, he went right out of sight—he was in over his head. Unsuspected by anyone, an exceptionally high tide had filled the channel with more than seven feet of water, and Sandbag was less than six feet tall. Such tides occasionally came in when high water coincided with passage of an especially strong low-pressure system or when an onshore breeze backed water into the fjord. Sandbag of course quickly reappeared, though the wait seemed like an eternity to us. He looked around with just a hint of astonishment, then headed for the island, doing a strong left-handed sidestroke. When he stumbled ashore, slightly disoriented, he realized his mistake, hesitated for just a second, and struck out once more—this time for the mainland in a lightning crawl that would have made Olympian Mark Spitz gasp in envy. Had we had a stopwatch, Sandbag might have been immortalized in the *Guinness Book of Records.*

Salt water has a lower freezing point than fresh water. In equilibrium with the floating drift ice, it had a temperature of about twenty-eight degrees. That's why backyard picnickers are able to freeze homemade ice cream in a canister immersed in ice and brine: with the addition of rock salt, heat is extracted by the melting ice, and the canister becomes colder than the freezing point of the ice cream. The transfer of heat from the cream to the canister causes the cream to freeze. In Sandbag's case, the heat of his body was being transferred rapidly to the brine of the fjord, so his good time in crossing from the island was understandable. He reached shore before turning completely blue, urged on by half a dozen cheering soldiers who then half-dragged and half-carried him across the snow to the beachhead station, where he slowly thawed out, wrapped in blankets beside a well-heated stove. Everyone had a good laugh. Well, almost everyone. In his refined, genteel, Baltimorean way, even Sandbag chuckled a little bit, a week or so later. Hypothermia was still an uncoined word in those days, at least in the vocabulary of the masses, and its effects were not well known or taken very seriously. Few people realized that unchecked hypothermia was irreversible. Its poorly understood but ultimate effect was death by exposure. Many "drownings at sea" were in fact deaths by hypothermia.

On another occasion and on a brighter note, I went to the beachhead a few weeks later with Scratch Phillips and Homer "By God" Loar to see to some chores around the station. Scratch was a wild-eyed rebel from Georgia who cursed General Sherman and damned the day he took Atlanta. Scratch's nickname came from a fancied resemblance to Walter Houston's portrayal of Scratch, the Devil, in the movie *The Devil and Daniel Webster.*

Like Scratch of the movie, Larry affected a scruffy red goatee. Homer's nickname reflected his propensity toward profane oaths, worthy of any self-respecting West By-God Virginian.

The island was now bound tightly to the mainland by a thick wedge of solid ice, and we worked there for several hours without incident. But the weather again turned sour, as it now was doing with increased frequency, and I envisioned three days or more trapped in the beachhead shack with only those two for company. Playing checkers with two far better players than I, listening to Homer's diatribes, and reliving the Civil War through a protracted blizzard was not my idea of a pleasant interlude, so despite the warmth of our camaraderie and over their objections, I strapped on my skis and struck out for base camp a mile and a half up the hill.

By now we were into a full gale and visibility was about like potato soup, but the wind was at my back, blowing as usual straight out of the north down the fjord. By bearing about two points to the left of the wind, I figured I'd head right into camp. I was well aware that a few more degrees of deflection would put me out on Apuseq Glacier, but my navigational sense was reinforced by an occasional glimpse of the antennae field through the blizzard and, thus reassured, I hit camp dead center without so much as a midcourse correction.

Though I can't guess the wind speed, it was impressive. Uphill all the way, I hardly planted a ski pole, even though camp was eight hundred vertical feet above the beachhead. I simply spread my arms and parka like a scarecrow, leaned back into the wind, and sailed up the hill like an iceboat, or like an early-day windsurfer–altogether refreshed and exhilarated by the new experience. Elapsed time: ten or fifteen minutes.

Wade, however, was unimpressed. Homer had alerted him by telephone as soon as I left, giving the captain ample time to frame his remarks, and his vocabulary was noteworthy even for a college professor. I had no choice but to suffer his tirade in silence then skulk off to the barracks indignant at his unfeeling lack of empathy. After all, I thought to myself, it wasn't really a big deal: I had done a bit of winter mountaineering in the snowy wilds of Utah and was no novice to the great outdoors. But Wade was right, of course. I should have stayed at the beachhead. Arctic blizzards are not fun and games, and Comanche Bay was the big time. We soon would face the worst winter weather on Earth.

10
Piteraq's Rage

Even before the *Nevada* steamed away in October, 1943, the weather at Comanche Bay rapidly worsened. Winter-type storms grew more frequent, more intense, and lasted longer—each storm worse than the one before. In the mists of time, I may have mixed some parts of different storms together, but the events recalled were all real. The archetypal climax came on December 13. At 1000 hours the sky was very dark—not what most people would call angry, just dark. The overcast had moved in two days before as a flat, milky blanket, a real buttermilk sky that dulled the shadows and turned the sun to a pale disk. Then, as the cloud deck thickened and darkened, the sun, the horizon, and the snow-covered ground itself all disappeared in turn in an enveloping gray gloom. A fresh breeze out of the south brought in the first soft flakes of snow, and as the storm slowly intensified, the wind backed to the east and its velocity gradually rose. By 1400 hours the wind had risen to fifty miles an hour, visibility had shrunk to fifty yards, and the new snow on the ground was about two feet deep.

In winter the Arctic night falls across southern Greenland like a blackout curtain, even in fair weather. On this night of driving snow, our weather-instrument shelter was beyond the reach of a flashlight beam even though it was just a few steps from the weather station. After an earlier storm we had fashioned a lifeline of heavy manila rope spanning the twenty feet or so from the building to the shelter, but at 1600 hours, reaching and reading the instruments had become a chore, even with the help of a lifeline. Weather observations were recorded hourly on the half-hour, so at the half-hour I slipped into a pullover sweater, pulled on my mukluks, and struggled into my parka, tightening the waist, wrist, and face strings. "Mukluk" is an Alaskan term. In

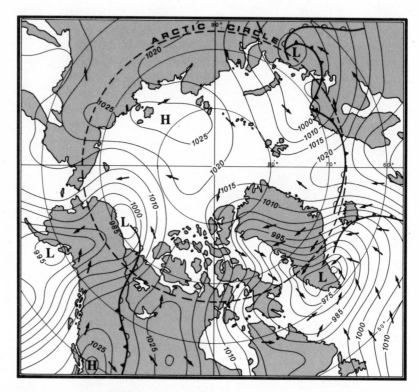

Map 10–1.   The big storm of December 13, 1943, 1230 hours, Greenwich time. With the great cyclone centered over southern Greenland, moisture-laden winds pounded the southeast coast. Snowfall six feet deep accumulated overnight at Atterbury Dome, followed the next day by winds of hurricane-force category 4 (present-day usage), blowing out of the north under a clear blue sky. Archival map data courtesy National Weather Service.

West Greenland, a sealskin or bearskin boot is called a *kamik* (plural *kangmit*). The East Greenland word is *atertaqag*. Ours were GI, made of canvas with leather feet. I turned on the flashlight, slid on my mittens, and shuffled out into the storm.

I never really got used to the buffeting of the wind. At fifty miles an hour it was very gusty, and walking was arduous. The now hip-deep snow was flying in horizontally, and it filled my tracks as fast as I made them. I turned my back and bent low to steady my balance. Despite its powerful thrust, the wind was strangely quiet, muffled by the thickening cover of snow.

Fig. 10-1. The weather station at Atterbury Dome. The rocky ridge in
the background is Husryggen, four miles distant across the fjord,
which is hidden from view behind the station.

A quick glance at the thermometer read nineteen degrees
Fahrenheit–minus seven degrees Celsius. The psychrometer, for
measuring humidity, indicated ninety percent, but at subfreezing
temperatures its accuracy was doubtful. A psychrometer consists
of a pair of attached thermometers, one bare, and one with a
muslin sleeve fixed over the bulb. When the muslin is wetted
with water, evaporation cools the bulb and drives the temperature reading down to the dew point; the humidity is then read
off a table, from the temperature difference between the two
bulbs. You can notice the same effect by baring two fingers–one
wet, one dry–to the cold and feeling the temperature difference.
The higher the dew point, the higher the humidity. At one hundred percent humidity the two bulbs read the same. The only
trouble is that when the temperature is below freezing, the wet
bulb immediately freezes, and the latent heat released by the
process drives the bulb temperature right back up to thirty-two
degrees. (Whenever water freezes, heat is released by the water
molecules at a rate of eighty calories per gram; that's why a re-

71

frigerator needs a fan to dispel the excess heat it generates when it makes ice. The compressor generates heat, also, as it compresses the coolant that freezes the ice–the same thermodynamic process that warms the katabatic wind on the Ice Cap.) To get an accurate reading of the humidity, I had to hang on in the pounding gale while the frozen bulb slowly crept back down from freezing to the actual wet-bulb temperature. Then I read and reset all the instruments in the shelter. The maximum and minimum thermometers yielded the spread between hourly readings; I checked the thermograph, which plotted a continuous reading on a drum; I shut and latched the shelter door–all by the numbers like a good soldier–and inched back along the rope toward the station. In the darkness I stumbled through a new drift that had formed across my path. I sprawled into the weather shack with eyebrows, beard, and fur-trimmed hood all matted with ice. Indoors, I read the wind speed off the anemometer, jotted down the barometric pressure off the mercurial barometer–also by the numbers (one, open the case; two, set the mercury level; three, read the vernier; four, record the reading, etc.)–and reset the microbarograph, which inked out a continuous record of pressure change to the nearest hundredth of an inch.

Each weatherman occupied the three-man weather station for three weeks, one man rotating back to base camp each week. Early on we tried a two-man, two-week arrangement, but it proved to be unsatisfactory. The week of the big storm I shared the station with Bob Grahl, from Wisconsin, and Max Morris, from Michigan. By evening, we decided to discontinue the outside readings until the storm abated. Going outside had become risky, and anyway, we had a remote-reading device called a telethermoscope that could be read from the comfort of the shack. Captain Wade had borrowed it from the Smithsonian Institution in Washington. The telethermoscope was intended for glaciological studies and was less accurate than a mercurial thermometer, but it was better than no reading at all. It was built around a device that picked up changes in electric resistance with changes in temperature at the end of a wire in the instrument shelter. Electrical resistance was read out as temperature on a dial back in the shack, and it was accurate to about one degree Celsius or two degrees Fahrenheit. Our mercurial thermometers, on the other hand, could be read to a tenth of a degree Fahrenheit by a trained weather observer. Our anemometer gave the wind speed in miles per hour and wind direction in every sixteenth turn of the compass; in other words, north, north-northeast, northeast, east-northeast, east, and so on.

Snowfall continued into the night. *Ningeq*, the northeast wind, was heavy with moisture from a thousand miles of choppy ocean whipped to a froth in the vortex of the storm. Now reaching about sixty mph, the ningeq spilled its burden on the frozen East Greenland coast in a great swath five hundred miles long and 150 miles across, hemmed in on the west by the ten-thousand-foot-high barrier of the Ice Cap. At our latitude, the Ice Cap was about 375 miles across from west to east, and the ningeq dumped all its moisture on the east slope. As it blew across the cap it wrung itself out over the chilled surface, and it descended the west slope as a "warm" dry gale, meteorologically identical with the chinook wind of the Rocky Mountains and the foehn of the Alps. A chinook or foehn gains heat by thermodynamic compression of the descending air at a rate of about five degrees Fahrenheit per thousand feet. That should mean fifty degrees of warming in its descent of the Ice Cap, but a lot of heat is extracted from the system by the billowing snow blown high into the air by the ningeq in its wild race down the west slope. Additional heat is lost directly to the chilled surface of the cap, so the down-slope ningeq in southwest Greenland, though warmed, remains cold.

Max Morris took his turn at fixing supper, gourmet fare featuring fried Vienna sausages à la army mess hall, rehydrated shoestring potatoes Julianehaab, canned corn d'hotel Atterbury, and fresh-baked bread sent up from camp by Cookie just before the storm. Dehydrated potatoes were a brand-new technological wonder in 1943. Bob Grahl cleaned up the dishes as I finished my shift and phoned the weather report down to base camp. It was only mid-December, but Sgt. Robert (the) Bruce, an ex-telephone lineman from Pennsylvania, had already strung three sets of telephone wires up to the weather station. The wind had repeatedly swept bare much of the rocky ground between camp and the station, and the whipping action on the rocks had flayed the insulation and shorted out the wires. Stringing new wires the three-fourths of a mile up to the station, Bruce said, was easier than finding and repairing all the flaws in the old ones.

Fig. 10–2. Inside the weather station Max Morris prepares a tasty concoction.

Down at base camp, Don Galbreath, from Oregon, enciphered my report, and radioman Bob Wiggins, from Tennessee, shortwaved it out to Greenland Base Command and the world. Then I hit the sack, and Max took over the night shift. Sound sleeping wasn't encouraged by the confines of the weather shack, and I tossed restlessly in the top bunk only feet from where Max sat at his desk. Bob in the lower bunk read *Studs Lonigan* far into the night by the low hum and flickering of the Coleman lantern.

All too soon I awoke to a strange stillness. The wind had died, and the only sound was the sizzle of frying salt pork. Bob was stirring oatmeal, Max was sleeping face to the wall, and a dim blue light was filtering through the window. "What time is it," I asked?

"Ten," replied Bob. "You slept like a goddamn baby."

"But it's still dark," I protested. "It should be daylight by now."

"Look again, soldier, we're buried. We're under six feet of snow–six feet in eighteen hours"!

Down at the bottom of the hill, base camp was digging out, and the first order of business was our thirty-five Greenland huskies. Staked out just beyond the buildings, each dog was chained individually to an iron pipe driven into the snow. A ring at the end of each chain, slipped over the pipe, let the dog circle the pipe without winding itself up, but if the chain should freeze to the pipe or ground, the dog might suffocate under the growing drifts. Dog houses were unfeasible for the same reason: they'd fill with snow and suffocate their occupants. Although leaving dogs out in an Arctic blizzard might seem cruel, the dogs were climatically adapted and didn't seem to mind.

Wallowing one hundred yards through six feet of loose snow to rescue dogs isn't easy, but the dogs had to be freed or face possible death. Experience in the two preceding months had taught us that the real blizzard, the *piteraq*, blowing out of the north, would follow the ningeq in minutes or hours, so we had little time to make ready. The piteraq blows with unleashed fury off the Ice Cap out of a clear blue sky, but it causes ground blizzards that reduce visibility to zero, and it carries away everything that isn't lashed down. Anticipating its arrival, four men walking in single file took turns breaking trail to the dogs, each man in turn struggling ahead eight or ten feet, then dropping back. Snowshoes were useless in that kind of snow; skis were worse than nothing. Loose dogs meant trouble too—there would be vicious fights—but the alternative was worse. Dogs would die on their chains.

Our respite from the blizzard was short-lived, like the eye of a hurricane, just as we had come to expect. The sky had cleared and the wind had dropped, but ominous portents appeared on the Ice Cap to the north and west. Snow plumes were building out from all the nunataks, the dark peaks that thrust their craggy summits through the margin of the Ice Cap far in the distance. Foremost of these was Anikitsok—"the tapered one"—a rocky spire shaped like the Matterhorn. Anikitsok rose four thousand feet out of the ocean at the edge of the Ice Cap about thirty miles southwest of Atterbury Dome, not far from Umivik.

All these native names are purely descriptive. In southeast Greenland they identify and describe uninhabited locales on an empty, hostile coastline, names that are likely to appear repeatedly on any map of Greenland. There was no permanent settlement at Umivik, though the Greenlanders sometimes set up hunting camps there and occasionally wintered over. Otherwise, Umivik was just bare rocks, ice, and magnificent scenery. The Greenlanders never named a landmark to commemorate a human being, and they couldn't understand the European propensity to do so. Their names tell something about a place, its chief attribute, or its purpose.

This was the coast where Erik the Red, according to tradition, made his first Greenland landfall. Although Erik is widely credited with having discovered Greenland in the year 982, the Icelandic sagas say the real discoverer was a Viking named Gunnbjorn Ulfson, who was blown off course on a voyage from Norway to Iceland in about the year 900. Gunnbjorn supposedly landed at a group of rocky skerries or islets near the present village of Angmagssalik, about 150 miles northeast of Comanche Bay. These islets became known as the Gunnbjarnar Skerries, but the actual position of Gunnbjorn's landing place is lost in the mists of antiquity, and he could just as easily have come ashore at any of the many small islands along our coastline visible from Atterbury Dome. Looking down from the weather station, I preferred to think so. Today the highest mountain in all the arctic also carries his name: Gunnbjorns Fjeld, 12,139 feet high and five hundred miles farther north on the Blosseville coast near Scoresby Sound. Gunnbjorns Fjeld wasn't discovered until the 1930s, hence its name is Nordic rather than Greenlandic. More recently, mountain climbers claim to have found a still higher summit in the same mountain complex. Until recently, guidelines for geographic names in Greenland have called for either Nordic or Greenlandic names. A European naming a landmark in the 1930s would most likely use a Nordic name rather than a Greenlandic one, though this was not always the case (but nowadays, the Nordic names are being phased out).

Erik the Red was banished first from Norway and then from Iceland for antisocial behavior (homicide), but before his banishment, the sagas say, he had heard about Gunnbjorn's exploit from old acquaintances in Iceland. If indeed he made shore near Comanche Bay, Erik could hardly have stayed very long. Eyeing the utter desolation and harassed by foul weather, he would likely have relaunched his longboats and turned south. His followers called the landfall Hvitserk–"White shirt" or "White mountain," or "Midjøkull–"midglacier." Steer due west two days from Snaefellsness (in Iceland) until you sight Hvitserk, then turn south, staying well outside the ice pack. The East Greenland Current will then carry you south around Kap Farvel–Cape Farewell–and back north up the west coast toward the Viking settlements at Eriksfjord. In hundreds of miles of mountainous coast, Midjøkull is the only place where the Ice Cap descends broadside into the ocean, broken but here and there by small knobs and rocky peaks. Atterbury Dome is such a knob, and Anikitsok is such a peak. Elsewhere, the Ice Cap is mostly hidden from the ocean by a broad barrier of rugged coastal mountains, and most visitors to Greenland never see it.

Our weather shack was a small plywood building about the size of an average household kitchen, about ten or twelve feet on a side, including work area, bunks, stove, and table. It was guyed down against the wind by steel cables stretched over the roof and anchored to bedrock with drill steel. Attached on the south side was a closet-sized vestibule that served as a sort of airlock between the indoors and the outside, and as a pantry cooled by nature. Here a soldier could brush off the snow before coming the rest of the way indoors. Here also we kept an assortment of empty tin cans for emergency use when the weather was too bad to go the full distance to our latrine, which was an open crack in the granite ledge a few steps from the door. Air-conditioned by nature at the lip of a cliff looking out over the North Atlantic, our latrine had a marvelous view of the distant pack ice and silent procession of great porcelain icebergs, a vista of misty blue islands, a brilliant morning sunrise, and a panorama of nearby Apuseq Glacier hundreds of feet below. The east front of Apuseq–"the snowy place"–faced the ocean with a wall of ice two hundred feet high and five miles long.

In the weather station, besides our instruments and office equipment, we had a shipmate's stove–a miniature bake oven with a firebox about the size of a loaf of bread and an oven just large enough to handle a small cake tin. Well fired with hard coal, the stove kept the station comfortably warm, considering the fact that we always wore woolen long johns and suitable outerwear.

Tapered Anikitsok, rising above Midjøkull, was a faithful weathercock that we watched from Atterbury Dome as a visibility marker and crystal ball. When the ceiling lowered, Anikitsok's sharp peak was first to vanish, and when the wind rose, the snow plumes appeared there first. These plumes reached out thousands of feet like great white banners unfurled in the wind. We viewed them from Atterbury Dome with awe and apprehension, just as Erik the Red might have seen them from shipboard 960 years before. Seeing such plumes on the sharp peaks above Narsarssuak, down on the southwest coast, Captain Strong at Greenland Base Command said they were erupting volcanoes. Maybe he was just pulling our legs.

Meanwhile, with six feet of new-fallen snow, the wind began to whip the surface of the Ice Cap into a whispy veil. From Atterbury Dome, where the air still remained calm beneath a clear blue sky, it was an incredible sight: horizon, peaks, and glaciers all disappearing in the billowy tempest—fuzzy, as if out of focus, and swirling hundreds of feet into the air. Our visibility from the dome extended about thirty-five miles onto the Ice Cap in the upwind direction, and we watched in stunned silence as the snow-laden wind first stirred high on the Cap, then poured down the slopes like a torrent of cresting waves. We had maybe an hour of lead time to watch the awesome scene and make ready for the onslaught on our station.

The wind that had brought in the prodigious earlier snowfall had gathered its moisture from the warm humid air above the Gulf Stream south of Iceland. As the storm drifted slowly northward in a great counterclockwise swirl, the wind shifted gradually from south and east off the ocean to north off the Ice Cap, so that now it was blowing cold and dry straight out of the north with a power and violence unbelievable to anyone who hadn't actually felt it. But even then the storm grew worse as the barometer continued to fall. East Greenland at such times has an uncommonly steep air-pressure gradient between the Ice Cap to the west and the warm Icelandic low-pressure cell to the east. As the storm cycle progressed, the barometer dropped from a high of about 31.5 inches of mercury to a low of about 28.5—a difference of about three inches. Sometimes it was more; I recall readings as low as 28.0. At most Stateside stations, by way of contrast, the pressure seldom varies more than a fraction of an inch, from about 29.5 to about 30.4.

Since our stock microbarograph could handle only two inches of pressure change, we had to deftly reset the inked pen arm and recalibrate it during each storm, before the fast-falling pen dropped clear off the drum and blotted out the record in a messy smear. We quickly raised the pen an inch just as the pressure began to plummet, and we reversed the procedure as the pressure bottomed out and started back up again. Once Bob and I stared spellbound at the barograph when the pressure rose an inch in fifteen seconds; we felt it on our eardrums. This meteorological spectacular resulted from the chilling effect of the Ice Cap. The heavy, chilled air drained off like a tidal wave pouring toward the warm, dilated airmass over the ocean. Chilled air is heavy because the slowed activity of the air molecules crowds more mass into a smaller space. More mass equals greater weight. Warm air is light because the more active molecules are farther apart.

As the wind rose, it began to pick up the deep loose fluff from the recent snowstorm. Horizontal visibility quickly fell to zero even though the sky overhead remained blue. The ground blizzard was now about forty feet deep at Atterbury Dome (and much deeper down the hill at base camp), and with nightfall, a flashlight beam carried about six feet. Then, as the last of the newly fallen snow was finally blown away–six feet of it blown clear out to sea–the air cleared, visibility returned, and the wind began to attack the old packed base.

The packed-snow base contained thin layers of ice, some perhaps half an inch thick, deposited by freezing drizzles in earlier storms. Even in the height of winter, many such storms began with freezing drizzles or rains that coated everything in a sheath of ice, especially along the East Greenland seaboard. As such storms progress, the drizzle gives way to snow. The drizzle freezes on impact, either because the droplets are supercooled below normal freezing temperatures or because they strike subfreezing surfaces. To the dread of seafarers, ships in the North Atlantic are often coated with such ice in wintertime. During this piteraq, as the air cleared, the wind began to erode the base, undercutting the ice layers and hurling sheets of ice through the air like panes of flying glass.

Fortunately the window in our shack faced east, away from the direction of the piteraq. We take credit for that measure of foresight, and we were able to watch the furious scene outside with combined scientific detachment and fear. It was rather like looking through the window of an airplane flying low through snow squalls in a stratus cloud. Soon bare rock reappeared around the weather station and we made contingency plans for the collapse of the building. Sheets of ice blasting the north side scarred and etched the plywood, and we wondered again whether the building would survive. If it began to fail, we planned to grab sleeping bags and K rations and make our way downwind to the lee of rock ledges on the south slope of the Dome, where we figured we could wait out the storm in comparative safety. A hatch door for setting up theodolite observations on the roof had torn loose and blown away in an earlier storm, but the rest of the building survived this time, and our abandonment plan remained untried. We felt a rush of adrenaline when one blast knocked stores of supplies off the shelves on the inside north wall—canned goods, tools, batteries, and sundry items needed only in a weather station. We didn't learn until two days later than the whole outer layer of plywood had been stripped from the north wall by ice and flying gravel. The pounding was frightfully gusty, and between gusts, air bubbles formed in the snowwater on the cabin floor, like spilled soda water. Inside the barometer the mercury shimmied like jelly, and across the drum of the barograph, the pen inked out an untidy track half an inch wide—half an inch of pulsating pressure change—resembling the seismogram of a strong earthquake.

Piteraqs of this sort on the heels of snow storm generally lasted about two or three days. This one lasted four, and the highest wind velocity we were able to measure—a sustained velocity, not a gust—was 154 miles per hour. A gust is a sudden brief increase in wind speed lasting only a few seconds, and that is what television weathercasters are generally talking about when they mention wind speeds on the evening news. Our instruments couldn't clock short gusts; we needed about a minute of velocity to measure speed accurately.

We measured wind speed with a Robinson three-cup anemometer, a reliable instrument that averaged peak speeds into the overall velocity. For twelve hours that day, the wind averaged eighty-eight miles per hour, and it blew without interruption. (Hurricane velocity begins at seventy-three miles per hour.) For ninety-six hours the wind averaged forty-five, pulsing up to a hundred, and the temperature bottomed at zero degrees Fahrenheit. For the entire month of December, 1943, the wind velocity at Atterbury Dome averaged twenty-five. I engraved all these figures in my memory. For mapping purposes in those days, the army and the U.S. Weather Bureau (now called the National Weather Service) reported wind speeds on the Beaufort scale—a scale no longer in use, though it lasted 150 years. It was devised by the British admiral Sir Francis Beaufort in 1805, originally for the use of ships under sail in the Royal Navy. Today, the wind is reported in knots–nautical miles per hour. One knot equals about 1.15 miles per hour, and both are shown in the accompanying table, modified from National Weather Service material.

Bodily functions don't stop during piteraqs, even though Atterbury Dome lacked developed sanitation. Our fractured outcrop, with a crack about a foot wide and ten feet deep, served as a ready, if breezy, open-air privy, but prudence precluded its use during severely inclement weather, despite its other advantages.

Passing water in the wind presents few problems at the lower velocities, and a seasoned outdoors person experiences little difficulty below about thirty-five miles per hour. Between about thirty-five and forty-five one can face directly downwind with one's back to the gale, but at about forty-five miles per hour a troublesome back eddy carries spray onto the hands and face. The problem can be averted by turning crosswise to the gale so the spray just atomizes downwind. This trick fails above about fifty-five, owing to increased turbulence, so we learned to lean close against the building, lee side, dog fashion, and pee directly on the plywood. At about sixty-five miles per hour, the jarring and buffeting tense the body to the point where even the loosest bladder cannot relax, and venturing outdoors in the piteraq becomes foolhardy anyway.

For such occasions we kept empty tin cans in the vestibule; we favored number ten grapefruit-juice cans, and we kept a few empty five-gallon dogfood cans for solid waste. We also ate a lot of cheese, which causes constipation. Between gusts we simply tossed the accumulated frozen cans outside, and the next blast of wind carried them off. Nowadays, such behavior would be condemned as unspeakable littering, but at Atterbury Dome in the winter of 1943 we lacked other options during the piteraq. Once during fair weather, out of curiosity, I searched downwind on my skis all the way from Atterbury Dome to the ocean, a distance of about four miles, but found no trace of refuse, not a single tin can. All had blown out to sea.

Primarily, though, I was outdoors just for the sheer pleasure of ski touring in the brilliance of the Arctic landscape, exhilarated by the crisp air, and communing with nature away from the stuffy weather shack and my unwashed GI comrades.

Beaufort Wind Scale

Beaufort number	Miles per hour	Knots (mph × 1.15)	International designation	Description
0	less than 1	less than 1	Calm	Smoke rises vertically.
1	1–3	1–3	Light air	Wind direction shown by rising smoke but not by wind vane
2	4–7	4–6	Light breeze	Felt on face; ordinary vane moved by wind
3	8–12	7–10	Gentle breeze	Extends light flag; leaves and twigs in constant motion
4	13–18	11–16	Moderate breeze	Small branches in motion; light drifting of dry snow
5	19–24	17–21	Fresh breeze	Light swaying of trees; ripples on ponds; considerable drifting of snow
6	25–31	22–27	Strong breeze	Large branches in motion; whistling in overhead wires
7	32–38	28–33	Moderate gale	Whole trees in motion; inconvenience felt in walking against wind; heavy drifting
8	39–46	34–40	Fresh gale	Twigs broken off trees; difficulty felt in walking
9	47–54	41–47	Strong gale	Light damage to buildings (chimney pots, slates removed); ground blizzards
10	55–63	48–55	Storm	Much difficulty felt in walking; trees uprooted; heavy ground blizzards

Beaufort Wind Scale (*continued*)

Beaufort number	Miles per hour	Knots (mph × 1.15)	International designation	Description
11	64–72	56–63	Violent storm	Very rare in inland areas; heavy loose objects blown away; extensive damage; loud moaning of overhead wires
12	73–82	64–71	Hurricane	Extreme difficulty in walking; widespread damage to unprotected structures; severe ground blizzards

Weather and work permitting, I skied nearly every day all year around. I generally carried a carbine for protection against marauding polar bears and for target practice against miscellaneous icebergs. I also carried a small piton hammer as a make-do geologist's pick, and saw many interesting rocks, but met no bears. Whether or not a carbine would drop a sixteen-hundred-pound polar bear, therefore, remained unanswered. I'm fairly sure I hit several icebergs, though a direct hit from a .30-caliber carbine slug makes little impression on a piece of ice the size of HMS *Queen Mary*.

The chances of meeting *nanoq*, the polar bear, on the rocky flanks of Atterbury Dome were really rather remote–on the shore, perhaps, but not high above the fjord. Nanoq is basically an aquatic predator, eating seal meat almost exclusively, and not straying far from the vicinity of such quarry. At Hudson Bay in Arctic Canada, the polar bear has turned to digging and browsing inland for roots and berries in summertime, when the bay is free of ice and seals are unobtainable, but elsewhere in the Arctic the bears reside mainly on the pack ice beside the leads of open water, where the chances of finding red meat are optimal. Females come ashore in early winter to den up and bear their young while hibernating in the shelter of snow caves, but big males don't hibernate and seldom leave the ice.

Nanoq, the polar bear

Nanoq is uniquely adapted to a cold, watery habitat, having branched from the brown-bear family tree during the Great Ice Age. Long, glossy guard hair backed up by thick underfur and a heavy layer of insulating body fat together deflect the Arctic cold. Aside from a white camouflage suit, nanoq has huge paws padded with fur underneath to add nonslip traction on the ice. In the water polar bears spread their toes to assist their dog-paddle style of swimming, which isn't fast but is strong; the skin between their toes almost forms a webbing. Unlike their long-clawed grizzly and brown bear cousins, whose thick, straight claws are adapted for digging earth and overturning rocks, polar bears have shorter, retractable, catlike claws designed for seizing and holding prey. Brown bears catch fish when they can, mostly seizing their catch with their jaws, not their claws.) Nanoq hunts with stealth, patience, and cunning, and strikes with lightning speed. While not averse to stalking and attacking a warm-blooded soldier if the occasion arose, nanoq wouldn't stray far from the pack ice looking for one. Up at the weather station, we had little to fear, though the winter darkness offered slight reassurance to the lone weatherman shuffling outside to read his instruments or check the anemometer while his colleagues snored through the night.

The Robinson three-cup anemometer, widely used in those days by the army and the Weather Bureau, had a dial that tallied up the speed and total miles of wind, much like the odometer in a car. Each turn of the cups measured a short increment of wind. A vane on top veered with the wind direction. Both the cups and the vane contacted a series of battery-charged electric points that lighted a dial inside the station for direct readout. A light flashed and a buzzer sounded every sixtieth of a mile of wind, so one minute of buzzes and flashes converted directly to miles per hour. Sixty buzzes per minute meant sixty miles per hour.

We followed procedures set forth in a document published by the Weather Bureau called "Circular N," the weather observer's bible. Circular N called for cleaning and oiling the anemometer every thirty days or every thousand miles of wind, whichever came first. But in a big Arctic storm, a thousand miles of wind would pass our station in just a few hours. At eighty-eight miles per hour, for example, we would record a thousand miles of wind in just a little more than eleven hours. So we spent a lot of time climbing the anemometer pole and dismantling anemometers. We kept one instrument serviced and ready, and we learned to replace the one on the pole almost between gusts. Early in the winter of 1943–44 we lost a set of cups in our first really bad blow, velocity undetermined, and we never found them again. The lubricating oil had congealed in the cold, the bearings had overheated, and the cups had simply sheared off. After that we used powdered graphite for lubricant and had no more problems.

Predictably, the Greenlanders have an extensive vocabulary for winds. As recounted by Ostermann (1938) and mentioned earlier, in southeast Greenland the northeast wind, called the *ningeq,* is the hard-driving wind that brings in the heavy snows of winter. It also causes high seas that push the pack ice close in to shore.

The *piteraq,* the north wind, usually follows the ningeq. Blowing straight out of the north at Atterbury Dome, this cold, dry, violent wind brought the most stupendous ground blizzards we experienced, beneath clear blue skies. It clears the fjord of ice and scatters all the pack ice out to sea, leaving only the big bergs behind. The *kanangnaq,* the east wind, is wet but not usually violent, and crowds the pack ice toward shore. The south or southwest wind, *avangarsarneq,* is a gentle wind of fair weather, but it drives pack ice into Comanche Bay. *Anore* is the generic West Greenland word for wind, widely familiar to us now in its derivative *anorak,* a pullover garment worn as a windbreaker; *anoritok* means "windy place." Other terms elegantly condense wind effects into a single word: *anorassuaq*–(West Greenland) "big wind," used for a gale with gusts; *pitoralikaseqaoq*–"it is storming"; *qerneraq*–"wind blowing across the water, making ripples"; and *suportoq*–"place that has many winds."

Many of our winds reached hurricane force, defined by international agreement as greater than seventy-three miles per hour. In southeastern Greenland, winds might exceed that speed at any time of the year. They often did so several times in a month, particularly in December and January, which were the windiest months, but we also had winds of hurricane force as late as May. These winds weren't classified as hurricanes, because they didn't originate in the tropics and weren't structured like hurricanes. They had "warm" and cold sectors separated by fronts, like ordinary cyclones and unlike hurricanes, and the airmasses involved were much colder. Even so, the Saffir/Simpson hurricane scale used by the Weather Service is a useful way to view them for comparative purposes.

Saffir/Simpson Hurricane Scale

Hurricane category		
	Winds (mph)	Central pressure (inches)
1	74–95	28.91 or more
2	96–110	less than 28.91
3	111–130	less than 28.47
4	131–155	less than 27.88
5	more than 155	less than 27.15

Most of our big blizzards reached category 1 or 2. Several reached 3, and a couple reached 4 or 5, although the air pressures were generally higher than in comparable hurricanes. During a big storm in November, 1943, however, Don Galbreath recorded a pressure of 27.45 inches and falling. The great danger of these wind storms was the reduced visibility in the blowing snow combined with the low temperatures. Most such winds blew with temperatures in the teens or the low twenties, but our big wind clocking more than a hundred miles per hour in December was accompanied by a temperature of zero degrees Fahrenheit. Although the wind chill factor as a measuring category hadn't yet been invented in 1943, the effect of the wind was the same. At zero degrees, even a fifty-mile-per-hour wind takes the chill factor below minus fifty. We knew perfectly well that the piteraq would quickly suck the life out of any GI caught unprotected from its wrath.

Chill Factor

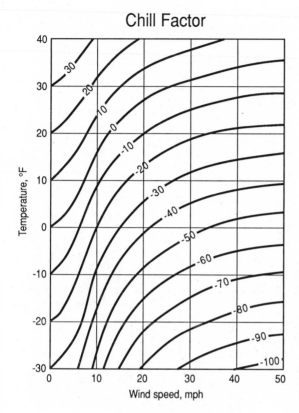

Fig. 10-3. Graph showing the chill factor, based on temperature and wind speed. Note that the intensity of the factor begins to level off at wind speeds beyond about fifty miles per hour. Modified from National Weather Service.

11
The Venturi Effect

Unlike our weather shack on Atterbury Dome, exposed to the full blast of the piteraq, our base camp was built in a slight hollow where there was less of an impact from the wind but more of a problem with the snow. Camp was just north of the Dome, about four-fifths of a mile from the weather station and a few hundred feet lower. Like the dome, it also was on bedrock, a kind of rock called garnet schist, but it was just yards from the edge of Apuseq Glacier. "Apuseq" is a common name for glaciers in East Greenland. It means "the snowy place," and that should have given us a clue about what to expect. Our Norwegian polar expert and advisor Johan Johansen, who had been at Comanche Bay with the ill-fated previous expedition, had urged the army not to locate camp at this particular place, but his advice was ignored. Camp stood high above the fjord, just off the head of the mile-and-a-half-long snowfield that sloped diagonally down the hill between the glacier and the water's edge. All our supplies came up this snowfield via Homer's winch line, and it was a well-chosen route, the master plan being to have a convenient staging area near the ice for ready access to the Ice Cap itself by way of Apuseq Glacier. Camp was at the top of the short, steepest part of the fifteen-mile-long glacier ramp that led inland toward our planned operations of the coming summer. Our charge from Washington was to erect our three Ice Caps stations strategically beneath the flight path of planes being ferried to Europe (at least before the long-range planes came on-line). Camp therefore was placed next to Apuseq for good strategic reasons, but our nearness to the glacier meant an unlimited supply of wind-driven snow to plague us through the winter. Atterbury Dome always blew clear, but base camp was another story.

At base camp, the early snows of autumn did blow clear of the buildings, because turbulence around the buildings set up a sort of rotary wind motion that kept drifts away from the walls and formed a moatlike trench around each building, each trench encircled by a sharp-crested cornice. Even though the snow was five or six feet deep by October, we didn't have to shovel out the entryways to the buildings; they blew clear. But with each passing storm—by then coming in every few days—the moats grew smaller and the drifts crept closer. Finally, the moats filled up, the drifts moved in, and the buildings were buried. Only the peaks of the gables blew clear. Eventually the snow leveled off at a depth of about twelve feet, covering all the buildings in camp, but in the hollows the snow was more than twenty feet deep.

One incident of early October, 1943, bore witness to the legendary smarts of the American soldier. Like the weather shack, all buildings in camp had vestibules to serve as stormlocks, but the prefabricated doors shipped up from the States all had keyholes, just like any army barracks in Georgia, Texas, or Louisiana. The front door of the weather barracks faced due north, catty-corner toward the mess hall about a hundred feet away, and directly into the path of the piteraq. Thus the north wall of the barracks took the full brunt of the wind, and the impact pressure against the wall was astonishing. According to an old textbook of mine, wind pressure against a flat surface rises in direct proportion to the square of the velocity, so at the higher speeds the pressure on a large surface increases dramatically; the back turbulence kept our "moats" temporarily clear of snow.

As the wind blows over the top of a building, though, the air path is lengthened and air pressure is reduced correspondingly, in a sort of standing wave like water rushing over a boulder in a mountain stream. This action causes suction underneath, much like the lift of an airfoil on an airplane, and it reduces the pressure inside the building. This is the well-known venturi effect. Because of the high pressure on the windward wall of the barracks and the reduced pressure inside, a stream of impalpably fine snow jetted through the keyhole into the vestibule, and it filled the little room with snow from the floor to ceiling. The vestibule, in fact, filled up three times in two weeks in three successive storms, each storm more violent than the one before, each one blocking egress from the building, and each trapping the occupants inside. After each storm we had to (1) open the inside door, which luckily opened inward, (2) shovel the snow from the vestibule into the main room of the barracks, (3) open

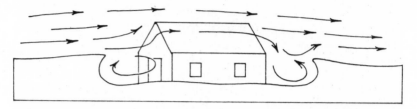

Fig. 11–1.   As the snows of early winter accumulated, the eddies and turbulence of the wind kept moat-like trenches open around each building, but as winter progressed, the moats gradually filled in, and the buildings finally were covered.

the outside door, which also opened inward, and (4) shovel the snow back outside. After the third blizzard, it occurred to us in a flash of pure insight to plug up the keyhole, and the problem disappeared.

In a similar incident, an unthinking dogface half-wittedly opened the same door during another piteraq. A real no-no. Seeing his mistake as the snow streamed in, he tried to force the door shut–it was opened just a crack–but the snow filled in too fast to clear the jamb, and with the wind pressing on the door, the vestibule quickly filled again to the ceiling. He suffered intense verbal abuse from all other hands, but a few storms later the building covered over, and we lost the use of the door anyway.

Burial of the buildings was a growing concern and challenge. For practical reasons, we couldn't simply tunnel out like moles after each blizzard. Storms were now blowing through about every six days, and they lasted three or four days each. For safety reasons–for example, in the event of a fire–we needed quick escape, so we built closed, vertical hatchways around the doors of all buildings, and as the snow deepened, we built them higher. By mid-December our entryways looked like mine shafts–ladders inside and all.

One nice day when someone left the hatch lid of the barracks ajar, a big Norwegian sled dog named Svarten–Blacky–who usually wandered loose around camp, fell down the shaft into the building. Only Svarten's pride was hurt, and a couple of sea biscuits quickly healed that, sled dogs being almost brutishly invulnerable to injury. Although sea biscuits could hardly be smashed with a hammer and were insipid and unappetizing,

90

Fig. 11–2. Howard Sullivan stands beside the barracks vestibule filled with snow blown in through the outside keyhole. Note that the outside front door is still closed.

they made a big hit with Svarten, who happily wolfed down anything remotely like food. Svarten was always hungry, and he hung around the barracks hatchway a lot after that.

Svarten weighed about 120 pounds and was nearly as tall as a man when he had his front paws on your shoulders. Although he had the appearance of utmost ferocity, he was gentle as a lamb—an affectionate pet, if reluctant sled dog, beloved by everyone in camp. Very intelligent, he had learned to push the ring of his chain over the top of his pipe with his nose. Then he would bound cheerfully to the mess hall, where he usually stood guard above the hatchway, awaiting handouts from Cookie or anyone else leaving the building. Occasionally he paid a visit to the boys up at the weather station, scaring the daylights out of them as he scratched on the door in the black stillness of the winter night.

Camp area was dominated in some ways by our radio antennae field, the only objects in camp visible from down at the fjord.

Each of five large wood poles was guyed down with steel cables anchored into bedrock, and the radio antennae were stretched between. Every big windstorm set the whole rigging to howling like banshees–poles, cables, and the antennae themselves, in a sort of high-pitched moan. Inside the barracks, the sound of the storm was even more awesome; roaring through the stovepipes, it was a deeper-throated sound overprinting the howl of the antennae field, and when combined with the rain of flying objects blasting the walls (before the buildings covered over), the effect was quite alarming. Even though the early autumn blizzards weren't as violent as later winter storms, they were more frightening, because we little knew what to expect of them and we were unsure of the safety of the still-exposed buildings themselves. With false bravado, we stood around the stove and hassled one another good-naturedly, or we sang a little, like small boys whistling past the cemetery. As the winter wore on and we knew the buildings would stand, we came to welcome the rising rattle of the stove pipes as a signaled respite from outdoor camp chores, especially when the sound arose at night. We just snuggled down deeper into our sacks.

The barracks had two stovepipes, one connected to our potbellied stove, and the other one empty, open to the roof to assure ventilation. The army was understandably paranoid about fresh air after the crew of the earlier expedition had nearly been asphyxiated when the beachhead station was buried under the deepening snow the year before. Their problem had been exacerbated by burning fuel oil, whereas we used anthracite. In any event, our building was always adequately ventilated; the roaring venturi suction up the empty stovepipe not only assured good air circulation, but it coincidentally blanked out all other sounds to the extent of hampering polite conversation.

Everyone smoked in those days, because Uncle Sam kindly provided free cigarettes in the rations. Some men suffered the habit the rest of their lives. Even then, cigarettes were called "coffin nails," although nobody had yet linked them to lung cancer or heart disease–they just caused smokers' hack–and even emphysema was unheard of in most circles. Growing up in Utah, I understandably never heard of emphysema until after the war, but otherwise I was as well informed as most soldiers. During a big wind it was fun to hold cigarette butts under the empty stovepipe and let the suction snap them up the chimney. We never were troubled with dirty ashtrays either; we just held them up beneath the stovepipe. One night when the roar of the wind in the pipe was so loud that no one was able to sleep, and we all tossed restlessly in our sacks, Tony Colombo, a burly dog driver from Brooklyn, stuffed a suit of dirty woolen underwear up the flue. Tony's inspired act stopped the roar instantly, and everyone relaxed–but only for a moment. In the next instant the suction pulled the underwear right up the chimney, and it was never seen again. Everyone upbraided Colombo for not hanging on. (Colombo was heavyset and muscular, but despite his consider-able bulk, he elected to let go rather than risk being pulled up the chimney with his underwear.)

12

When the Roll
Is Called Up Yonder

During the piteraq, camp chores would stop more by tacit agreement than by direct order. No sane person ventured needlessly outdoors into an Arctic blizzard, least of all into the piteraq. The weather station and the radio shack, of course, operated around the clock regardless, and the radio operators spent long hours furtively receiving and deciphering coded messages, most of which were much ado about nothing. When, with a knowing smirk and a backhanded whisper, they slipped messages to the CO at lunch or evening chow, everyone stopped, watched, and listened.

Outside, the dogs normally were fed every other day, so they suffered little hardship if they went three or four days in a blizzard without food. It merely sharpened their appetites. The dogs were quite capable of surviving the severest weather, having been selectively so bred for generations. We just turned them loose in a piteraq to shift for themselves at the start of the storm, and they never strayed far, because food was uppermost of their wants and they were totally dependent on their masters for sustenance. We lost a dog or two to fights during the winter, but we would have lost more if we hadn't freed them. Because at other times they were always chained up, the huskies never established group dominance or servility, and vicious fights broke out whenever they were loose. When a dog got down in a gang fight, all others would turn on it, biting and grabbing wherever they could—on the throat, ears, back, legs, or tail. We beat them off with boards and shovels.

During one particularly furious blizzard, when we heard the dogs fighting on the roof of the barracks, we were helpless to intervene because no one dared, or could, go outdoors. Going outside would mean risking our own lives, and opening the hatch lid even a crack would mean not getting it shut again and filling the shaft with snow. Dog fights broke out repeatedly, and when the blizzard ended, we had lost a fine German shepherd–Greenland husky crossbreed named Prinz, a handsome brute of a dog with honey-blond fur tipped with black. Something of a pet, Prinz had earlier been loose around camp much of the time and had serviced a few bitches in estrus while his chained-up rivals watched and brooded. When the storm ended and we crawled outside, all that remained of Prinz was his head and left forepaw; the rest of him was gone–eaten. A grisly sight, yet despite their savagery toward each other and general fear of humans, most of the dogs craved the attention and love they never got. They wanted to be petted, but in Greenland there was a general taboo against petting or affection: dogs were draft animals, we were told, and could not be both pets and good sled dogs. A driver's life could depend on them.

In the barracks during blizzards, the stove became the social gathering place where we could revile the army, exchange jokes and banter, or take a sponge bath. We had no bathing facilities beyond a wash basin and an old canned-ham tin which, we found, was good to rinse your feet in one at a time. We went fourteen months at Comanche Bay without a real bath or shower.

The temperature in the barracks didn't encourage fastidiousness. It varied inversely in rough proportion to the square of the distance from the stove. You could see your breath in the farther corners of the room all year around–not the cosiest environment for a sponge bath. Nail heads on the inside of all the outer walls grew little white frost flowers during the winter, but resilient young soldiers soon became acclimated, and there were few serious complaints. Of course there was nearly continuous inconsequential griping, occasionally vehement, and mostly about ratings, in the spirit of good soldiers everywhere. The weathermen griped about the radiomen and, I suppose, vice versa. During blizzards we sometimes stood around the stove harmonizing our favorite refrains, like fraternity boys. Don Galbreath, six feet, two inches tall, 145 pounds, and hard as nails, carried a good tune and liked to take the lead. Hailing from the backwoods of Oregon, Don leaned toward cowboy music, what is now called country western, such as "I don't worry, 'cause it makes no difference now." He also liked hymns.

Fig. 12–1. The back door of the barracks. The rear vestibule and the hatch shaft were filled with driven snow when persons unknown left the hatch lid ajar.

Don Galbreath's favorite:

> When the trumpets of the Lord shall sound
>> And times shall be no more,
>> And the morning shines eternal bright and fair,
> And the saints on Earth shall gather
>> Over on the other shore,
>> And the roll is called up yonder, I'll be there.

Max Morris's tastes were more ribald, possibly influenced by his Midwest-college background; he had attended a university in Michigan before being drafted. To the tune of "Reuben, Reuben":

> Caviar comes from virgin sturgeon.
>> Virgin sturgeon's a very fine fish.
>> Virgin sturgeon needs no urgin',
>> That's why caviar is my dish.
> I've got a gal from Kansas City.

She can shake and she can shimmy.
She can sing and she can dance.
She has a mustache in her pants.
I don't care if it rains or freezes,
I am safe in the hands of Jesus.
I am Jesus' little man.
Yes, by Jesus Christ, I am!

Bob Grahl's renditions leaned toward the sentimental: "Old soldiers never die, they only fade away," or, "Bless them all, bless them all, the long, the short, and the tall. There'll be no promotions this side of the ocean, so cheer up my lads, bless them all." He also liked "Lili Marlene." In fact, we all did. Captain Wade, quartered in the mess hall, occasionally burst forth with a rendering of "Rufus Rastus Johnson Brown, watcha gonna do when the rent comes round." One from my early childhood was "Jesus wants me for a sunbeam." I didn't carry much of a tune, but I went along anyway, and everyone joined in.

Barracks talk at Comanche Bay, as in army camps around the world, sooner or later turned toward sex, and it often involved the varied attributes of the female film personalities of the time. After a year of isolated duty in Greenland—nineteen men out of contact with the rest of the world except by shortwave radio—we perceived the actual existence of women as a theoretical concept cloaked in unreality. Most of the men in the barracks expressed no preference in their fantasies for any particular celebrity over any other, but a few individuals had strong outspoken biases for or against certain movie starlets, and they cherished whatever pinups of their favorites they were able to glean from old fan magazines. Doc Johnson, bunking in the solitary splendor of his dispensary at the far end of the building, treasured a magnificent full-page, three-quarter view of Rita Hayworth, a classic pinup known around the world. Bob Grahl jealously guarded a copy of the famous Chilly Williams pinup, clad in a polka-dot bathing suit, admired by frenzied GIs from Australia to Archangel. Bill Cadigan preferred the wholesome beauty of Donna Reed. My views were electic; I liked them all, but gangling Don Galbreath was partial to Betty Grable, and he defiantly pressed his views with an outspokenness bordering on hostility. Given his testy short fuse, Don was an easy target of good-natured abuse, and we often rebuked him for his narrow perceptions and lack of good taste. Years later he confided his feeling that I at times had ridden him more unmercifully than was called for by the circumstances. I pleaded *nolo contendere*. Interestingly enough, the favorite pinups of GIs all across the globe were drawings, not photographs, by two artists of *Esquire* magazine, originators of the famous Petty girls and Vargas girls. Though more voluptuous than Vargas girls, Petty girls were anatomically less well proportioned, with certain unrealistically oversized attributes.

Before winter was far advanced soft-spoken Lieutenant Borden felt that morale around camp was visibly sagging, particularly in the barracks. Weather permitting, he made daily rounds from his lair in the mess hall to arouse each man from his slumbers at an appropriate time of the morning–usually before 0800 hours, during pitch darkness–to deliver low-key lectures on military bearing and conduct. We should not, for example, make jokes about FDR. "After all," Barry said, "FDR is our Commander-in-Chief, and our disparagements could be viewed as disloyalty." In fact, we disparaged everyone in the public eye and out. It was a GI's prerogative, along with cursing and griping. Barry was from the green hills of Woodstock, Vermont, and Vermonters in those days were not widely known for raising either their voices or their emotions. Barry was archetypically Vermont. Once when he gently tiptoed into the dispensary to awaken Mark Johnson, Doc sprang from his sack shouting, "Is somebody hurt?" and Barry just hung his head and shuffled off. To commemorate his eagerly awaited morning visits, I composed a limerick and an accompanying cartoon, then posted them surreptitiously on the mess hall bulletin board:

A man of the world was he
    This Simon McBorden Legree.
Asked no quarter of his men
    Though he sacked until ten.
But he terrorized BICD.

13
Tea for Two or Three

Fixing appetizing meals for two or three people with the marginal cooking facilities at the weather station was a challenge to a concientious cook. Anyone could warm a can of stew, but more imaginative cookery with the ingredients we had available took a bit more planning. When Sully Sullivan was doing the cooking, no one counted on a sumptuous meal. Just bread and bacon, please, or possibly canned beans. But Max Morris was more resolute, and all hands could count on palatable food at his table. He even baked a cake or two in our tiny shipmate's stove.

We did have an official U.S. Army company cookbook, and it contained recipes for any number of epicurean satisfiers, but they all called for things like one hundred pounds of flour, ten dozen eggs, three-fourths of a pound of salt, twenty-five pounds of granulated sugar, or four gallons of milk, and before the day of the pocket calculator, converting such proportions to servings for three men exceeded the arithmetical prowess of your average weatherman. Fortunately for us, Captain Innes-Taylor, the polar expert who had organized our expedition, planned out all the logistics, and ordered all the supplies, also included a copy of *Fannie Farmer's Cookbook*. Its menus met or exceeded all our needs, though we still had the problem of making acceptable substitutions for the many ingredients missing from our pantry.

Everything in our larder was either canned or dried, food drying being part of a newly emerging technology that still had a long way to go. Dried sliced onions rehydrated better and more easily than anything else we had, and combined with powdered eggs, dried milk, and chopped cheese, they made a nourishing omelet. Our shredded julienne potatoes–"Julianehaab," we called them–were almost delicious if carefully and slowly rehydrated in ice-cold water, of which we had plenty, but our powdered mashed potatoes never quite achieved their intended potential. Smothered with gravy, and with a rare T-bone steak, they might have been acceptable, but not with U.S. Army Vienna sausages. A dear aunt of mine saved up her meat-ration stamps to send me a small can of elegant Vienna sausages for Christmas in 1943, and I was the butt of sarcastic humor for about two months afterwards. We had a whole warehouse full of Viennas, and all hands referred to them with an unprintable epithet. The prime target of most soldiers' obscenities in WW II was canned Spam—it was hated around the world—but to us it was outranked hands down by Viennas.

During one fleeting moment of inspiration at Atterbury Dome I created a culinary sensation that was soon called "Ice Cap ice cream." Everyone grudgingly conceded it was good—at least, all who tried it condescended to having seconds. Starting with about two cups of powdered milk, its complex recipe called for about a cup of powdered cocoa, several tablespoons of powdered eggs, maybe a quarter-cup of powdered confectioner's sugar, and a pinch of salt, all stirred together with a teaspoon of vanilla extract. Exact proportions didn't matter. All the ingredients were then thoroughly mixed with a bucketful of new-fallen snow. If available, a half-cup of compass alcohol was added before the snow. Then the concoction was set out briefly to harden in the instrument shelter and, *voilà*, creamy smooth delicious Ice Cap ice cream! A ladle of canned fruit cocktail per serving made an acceptable fruit sundae, although I preferred mine straight. For really auspicious occasions, hot fudge syrup could be made by following the directions on a cocoa can.

For drinking water at Atterbury Dome we kept a five-gallon aluminum pot as a snowmelter, always topped off with fresh snow to assure a continued supply. The pot had to be about half full of water at all times to satisfactorily maintain the ongoing melting process. Once, after some weeks of uninterrupted refilling and use, the water acquired a slight off taste, a slight turbidity, and a thickening iridescent film in a water glass. In the close quarters of the station we couldn't be too careful about stringent rules of sanitation, particularly with respect to water supply, so after due deliberation we wasted the five gallons and drained the pot. As soon as we ladled off the unmelted snow the cause of the problem became clear, though not the water: at the bottom lay three small turds—dog turds. Unsavory, yes, but surely benign in the aseptic environment of Igtip Kangertiva. Loose dogs up from camp were fairly frequent visitors to the station, particularly Svarten, but no one ever showed any untoward symptoms as a result of their presence. In fact, no one in the entire camp ever got so much as the sniffles all winter long, despite frequent drenchings in freezing drizzles and long hours of work in subfreezing temperatures. Even so, we took greater care thenceforth with the snow we collected for culinary water and for making Ice Cap ice cream.

Our experience at Atterbury Dome was an object lesson for base camp, where the loose-dog problem was an order of magnitude larger, inspection of the snowmelter was ten times more difficult, and water consumption was forty times greater. The snowmelter at base camp was at the mess hall. It was a built-in, galvanized-iron reservoir with a capacity of several hundred gallons, filled from the top and drained from the bottom. It relied on building heat for melting, which proved to be ineffective, so we turned to bailing water from a nearby pond, which, of course, was frozen over ten months of the year and was deeply buried under snow. We dug it out periodically to fill a sled train of water barrels pulled by a T-15 light-cargo carrier, our version of a snowmobile. The pond area was far enough away from camp and far enough upwind to escape much pollution from the dogs.

A potential corollary problem involved human-waste disposal. The only real latrine in camp was a little anteroom off the barracks, dubbed the "NCO Club," containing a three-holer with fifty-five-gallon honey barrels. Doc Johnson, as base sanitation officer, was nominally in charge, and he soon concluded that we would overtax the facilities unless we observed strict conservation measures. Doc decreed that the NCO Club was to be used only in dire emergencies, as during a dangerous blizzard, for example. At all other times more Spartan facilities were available in the rocks across the hill, in an area outside the immediate wind and drainage catchment of camp. That area was compensated by a good view of the fjord, and it was kept policed up by loose dogs, so that the men and dogs enjoyed a sort of symbiotic relationship. You couldn't trudge through the snow toward the rocks without a file of dogs trailing along behind. You felt self-conscious as they circled you at a respectful distance, patiently awaiting your completion of the business at hand.

Even so, the honey barrels did fill up, and emptying them was

Fig. 13–1. Doc Johnson goes in the hole digging for water at our snow-covered, frozen-over water-supply pond. Water was then pumped into steel barrels and hauled back to the mess hall where we had a galvanized-iron storage tank. On a still, sunny day, Doc could work shirtless briefly, without discomfort, even at low temperatures.

a memorable chore heightened by the bad news of first having to shovel out a ten-foot-deep snow shaft to reach the business end of the clubroom. The barrels were then hoisted up to a waiting T-15 and hauled over the hill to a designated dump site. The good news was that the contents were frozen. At times like this, I steadfastly tried to be on duty at the weather station.

Shoveling snow was an activity that we all learned well. It was an essential element of camp life, and we spent more wintertime man hours shoveling than doing anything else. We shoveled to keep the building entries open, to provide water, to uncover buried supplies and materiel, to make camp on the trail, to free stalled snowmobiles, and to dig out fuel. When we moved base camp up the hill from the beachhead station, we cached our coal and gasoline on a rocky ridge just outside the camp area in a place that nearly everyone figured would blow clear. Johan Johansen said it wouldn't and urged a higher location, but he was disdainfully overruled. By November, 1943, the ridge was covered, Joe's judgment was vindicated, and from that time on we had a mining operation going to recover the buried fuel.

Luckily, Captain Wade had shot in the location with his transit—in other words, he had precisely located the coal with reference to fixed camp landmarks. We shafted down through six or eight feet of snow until we struck coal then we drifted laterally to mine out the gunny sacks. That was when I acquired the coffee habit. Until I was twenty-two years old I had been a milk drinker. Having a cup of coffee was a good excuse for a respite in the mess hall, and we all caught on quickly, including the captain, an inveterate coffee drinker who swilled several cups per day. Back in the mine, the gunny sacks were often frozen together, and tearing them apart led to a lot of spilled anthracite. Our gasoline mine was a similar project, but most of the gas was stored in five-gallon jerry cans that were a lot easier to handle than hundred-pound coal bags.

We couldn't keep the shafts open during blizzards. They just blew full of snow, so each operation was a totally new dig and, I might add, a democratic one. Nearly everyone participated except the radio operators and weathermen on duty. Cookie didn't participate; he had more pressing obligations in the kitchen. Neither did Johan Johansen; chances were he would be down in the lower warehouse readying trail gear and attending to other matters such as adjusting the compasses, which were emersed in ethyl alcohol. Besides, his contract with the army didn't include digging for coal. Big, burly Captain Wade was a formidable shoveler, having gained early experience in Antarctica, where he had been a senior scientist with the Byrd expeditions. The even bigger Bob "Lardass" Johnson moved more snow yet, more in fact than any other man in camp. Lieutenant Borden was a steady, determined shoveler but a lightweight by comparison.

The winches we had used for hauling supplies up the hill from the beachhead station were buried early in winter, too, and finding them again in the spring was an exercise in snow removal. We ran the winch line as long as we could in the fall but eventually had to quit when we were overwhelmed by the storms of winter. We deliberately left the cables partly unreeled, even though Wade had shot in the winch locations with his transit. By trenching across their paths, we first uncovered the cables, then simply followed them back to the winches. A mine detector would have worked as well, but that was one of the few things Captain Innes-Taylor had failed to order. A trenching machine might have been even better.

14

The Northern Lights

During the summer months the nighttime sky in Greenland never gets dark enough to give visibility to one of the world's most awesome sights – the northern lights, the aurora borealis. It's there overhead, but you can't see it. Winter is another matter. The "northern lights," the term preferred by the Norwegians, was first called the "aurora borealis" by Galileo, back in the year 1619, according to geophysicist George L. Siscoe, who carefully researched the matter in 1978. Previous workers attributed the term to a contemporary of Galileo named Gassendi. During rare sightings in central Europe and northern Italy, as noted by Galileo and Gassendi, the aurora emits a deep red glow low on the northern horizon, giving the appearance of the dawn's early light – but in the north, not the east – hence the name aurora borealis or "northern dawn." In fact, the aurora has nothing to do with the dawn, but "aurora borealis" sounds tonier than "northern lights" and is the preferred term, therefore, in most of the scientific literature.

We saw our first display early in the fall of 1943, when the sun set low behind the Ice Cap, and the deep purple twilight fringe rose to the east in the penumbra of the earth's own shadow. A long, pleated drapery appeared quite suddenly, ethereal and glowing, undulating slowly across the still-light northern sky. Its sharp leading edge was watermelon red, grading upward into fluorescent green, fading gradually toward the zenith. Pulses moved wavelike across the sky. Then it was gone, and in the stillness of the darkening night we felt a deepening chill rising off the ice. As the nights grew longer and darker, the auroras became brighter and more frequent until, by winter, a night rarely passed without one or several luminous displays, except of course when the sky was hidden by clouds.

The aurora borealis is most common and most intense in a broad belt stretching across the Arctic regions through northwestern Alaska, northern Canada, southern Greenland, Iceland, northern Norway, and northern Siberia. This belt is called the "auroral zone," and it was first identified in 1860 by Professor Elias Loomis of Yale University, after a careful analysis of all available documented sightings. Loomis thus explained why the aurora, contrary to popular belief, is seldom seen overhead at the North Pole. The auroral zone in fact centers over the geomagnetic pole rather than the geographic or rotational pole, and at a radial distance of about twenty-two degrees. (The north geomagnetic pole is at the northwest corner of Greenland about 780 miles from the geographic pole.) During rare times of exceptionally strong sunspot activity, auroras may be visible as far south as Mexico. I've seen excellent displays in Colorado at about the latitude of the fortieth parallel. Another belt encircles Antarctica, the aurora australis, and satellite probes of the last few years have shown that displays in both hemispheres are simultaneous counterparts, alike even as to form and pattern.

Auroras form when bursts of solar radiation in the form of electrons and hydrogen nuclei penetrate the upper atmosphere. Traveling at immensely high speed—as much as six-hundred miles per second—the particles reach the Earth's upper atmosphere just a few hours after the explosions of intense solar flares. There they are drawn into the Earth's magnetic field, where they collide with molecules of oxygen and nitrogen, ionizing the rarified air and making it glow like a neon tube. Our auroras were seen best from Atterbury Dome, where we had an unobstructed view in all directions and where, besides, we kept a twenty-four-hour vigil of the sky. Many of our nicest displays were in the southern sky, because the auroral zone passes south of our part of Greenland. In aggregate, though, the band of lights encircling the geomagnetic pole at any given moment is oval, not round, and is often called the "auroral oval," as distinguished from Loomis's statistically computed auroral zone. In contrast with the auroral zone, which has a position fixed with respect to the Earth, the auroral oval shifts southward from evening until geomagnetic midnight, then retreats again to the north.

All this is less complicated than it seems. The auroral oval shifts south then north because it is stationary with respect to the sun, rather than to the Earth, and the Earth rotates beneath

Map 14-1. The auroral zone, where the aurora borealis is directly overhead most often and has the highest average intensity. Note that the zone is centered over the north geomagnetic pole in northwestern Greenland, not over the north geographic pole. This pattern is a long-term statistical average; any single auroral display may depart widely from it, both in shape and in position in the sky.

it. Its oval form is caused by distortion of the Earth's magnetic field by the solar wind, the solar wind being the constant stream of subatomic particles radiating out from the sun. The solar wind flattens the magnetic field on the "upwind" (daytime) side of the Earth—the side facing the sun—and draws it out like the tail of a comet on the downwind (nighttime) side. So the oval reaches farthest south at geomagnetic midnight as the Earth rotates beneath it, and a viewer on Earth sees the display gradually shift its position in the sky throughout the night.

Our brightest and most colorful auroras were generally the

most fleeting. Fast-moving draperies or curtains pulsed and undulated in tints of red, violet, and green. At times they lashed across the sky like giant bull whips, but more often they appeared as long white or greenish white streamers, looking very much like banks of searchlights playing across the sky. My credibility was strained once when I phoned down to the radio shack in the middle of the night, awed by an especially fine display, only to have it vanish before the boys in the shack could get outside to see it. Occasionally we found ourselves looking at a whole skyful of convergent rays, thousands of them focused on the zenith in a brilliant domelike corona. Coronas form when an auroral band is directly overhead. The rays follow the flow lines of the Earth's magnetic field and really are parallel to one another, but perspective makes them seem to converge.

The color and brilliance of the display depend on (1) the intensity of the solar outburst, (2) the gases being ionized, (3) the wavelength of the resulting radiation, and (4) the depth of penetration into the atmosphere. The more intense the outburst, the deeper the penetration. Oxygen may glow in either green or red, depending on the wavelength of the radiation. Nitrogen emits blue, violet, and deep red. Hydrogen also emits red. Hydrogen is very rare in the atmosphere—having so little mass, it readily escapes the Earth's gravity—but many of the incoming particles from the sun are hydrogen nuclei that pick up electrons as they collide with the outer atmosphere.

Before the days of orbiting satellites, scientists measured the height of auroras by triangulating from two or more ground stations aiming at the same band. Early work in this field was done mostly by the Norwegians and was much less precise than the work being done today. Part of the problem was identifying the same spot in the aurora from separate transit stations miles apart. The lowest bands of a display were found to range in height from about thirty-five miles above the Earth to about fifty miles, or about five to eight times the height of a cruising airliner. The tops are hundreds of miles high, and the length of a single curtain can be several hundred miles west to east. Because the aurora reaches its southernmost position at around midnight, which means it is then farthest above the horizon in temperate latitudes, television weathercasters tell their listeners to go outside at midnight right after a solar storm for the best viewing.

Strong auroral activity is accompanied by intense electrical storms caused by the solar wind "blowing" through the outer atmosphere. Investigators now know that such "auroral sub-storms" may generate billions of volts and that the steep potential gradients are capable of disrupting electrical and radio transmissions throughout the Earth's middle latitudes. Electric fuses and even transformers have been heavily damaged, although protective devices nowadays forestall most such problems. Today the study of solar radiation, geomagnetism, and the aurora borealis is a fast-growing field of research, stimulated by advances in rocketry and the geophysical exploration of space. Scores of learned papers are being published annually in scholarly journals. In 1943, the science was in its infancy.

From Atterbury Dome, I photographed some nice auroral displays over the Ice Cap in the winter of 1943–44, but I never got the pictures back from the army censors. Military censorship in those days was inscrutable, especially in backwaters such as Greenland. Regulations forbade photographing buildings, aircraft, ships, or mountains, on the chance that any such pictures in the hands of the Axis powers might be turned to their advantage. In Greenland? The fact that nothing of a sensitive nature appeared on my prints may itself have aroused the suspicions of the censors: "Why did that soldier take those pictures?"

15

Shine On, Shine On, Arctic Moon

The best place and time on Earth to view the full moon is under the Arctic sky in wintertime. Everyone knows the moon is full only when its orbital position is 180 degrees from the sun–what astronomers call opposition or syzygy. Only at such times is the side of the moon facing the earth fully lighted. Other orbital positions yield gibbous, half, quarter, or crescent phases. When I was young, all these phases of the moon were shown on the calendars that local merchants handed out to their customers, calendars that you seldom see any more. My dad always got one from Union Pacific Railroad with a magnificent color picture of a big engine under full steam, belching pollutants into the sky. In winter, when the Arctic sun is below the horizon, which is most of the time, the full moon is above, and it circles the sky in a low, lazy arc, timeless hour on hour. Combined with the starkly clear nighttime air and the chalky winter snowscape, the Arctic full moon illuminates landmarks near and far in ethereal detail easily seen from many miles away.

On still, moonlit winter nights some of us in the weather barracks occasionally forayed outdoors for a crisp nighttime stroll, to view the icebergs, the aurora, or the silent specter of the Ice Cap, or just to stretch our legs on the rocky ridge above camp. Another destination was Atterbury Dome, where after a fifteen-minute hike we could pay a courtesy call on our duty-bound colleagues in the weather station, there to exchange banter, jokes, and gossip. Within fifty yards or so of the shack we would good-naturedly lob a few rocks at the blind side of the building to alert the dozing occupants to our friendly approach. With only the low hiss of the Coleman lantern to break the silence of the night, the first stone cast was guaranteed to stimulate the nervous systems of the men indoors and assured a spirited conversation to follow.

From Atterbury Dome I studied the crisp outlines of Kap Løvenørn, Anikitsok, and the long line of dark nunataks leading onto the distant Ice Cap itself, aloof in its ghostly white splendor. At two o'clock in the morning I could distinguish the pattern of big crevasses twenty-five miles distant in the icefalls above Kjoge Bugt. Far below, in the frozen expanse of the North Atlantic, each silent iceberg stood apart in bold relief, altogether like white-on-white skyscrapers in a fairyland city of white. Icebergs, in fact, are best viewed at night: all the baroque details of their alabaster forms—lost in the harsh glare of the sun—are enhanced by the soft light of the moon.

Day or night, everyone who has seen icebergs—*ilulissat*—marvels at their solemn grandeur. Wrapped in an aura of stolid invincibility, they stand imperturbable against man, wind, or wave. Icebergs have a sculptural look of infinite variety, stately, sometimes bordering on grotesque, but carved out by a combination of simple physical processes.

Icebergs are born in the outlet glaciers of the Ice Cap from the fallen snows of the centuries. As the snow settles slowly under its own weight, it gradually transforms into ice, retaining in a compressed state the air initially entrapped. It differs in that respect from ice frozen from standing water, whether fresh or salty, which lacks interstitial air. Intermediate in character between the new snow and the glacier ice is a partly recrystallized form of snow called *firn* (German, from the old High German word for "old"). After the snow has been on the ground for a time, it starts to turn into firn—what skiers call "corn snow," though most hydrologists insist that the snow must be at least a year old to be properly called firn. The French call it *névé*. Like snow, firn contains interconnected pores filled with air. When the weight of the accumulating snow/firn overburden closes the pores, the firn becomes glacier ice, by definition, and it begins to flow under its own weight by plastic deformation. The entrapped air is largely responsible for the occasional, almost explosive spalling of ice from the sides of tall bergs.

The snows of the centuries, moreover, accumulate in distinct layers, and the layers survive in the ice of a glacier like pages of a book, despite thousands of years of tortured flowage. Each layer is a bit of earth history literally preserved in nature's deep freeze, where avid glaciologists study them for clues to the prehistory of the planet. In an iceberg, each preserved ice layer adds to the visual splendor and beauty of the floating block.

About nine-tenths of an iceberg lies below the waterline, its density being about nine-tenths that of water. (Salt water is a bit heavier than fresh water, so a berg would float a bit higher in the ocean than it would in a lake.) The ice is eight or nine times its original density as new-fallen snow, which averages only one-tenth that of water. The tip of the iceberg, therefore, is only the tip of the iceberg; most of it is out of view. Hidden projections below the waterline sometimes reach far beyond the visible parts, as many a skipper has learned to his dismay. As the ice above the waterline slowly melts in the summer sun, it assumes bizarre shapes, and the submerged part rises gradually in the water to preserve equilibrium and compensate for the mass lost to melting. Old waterlines engraved in the sides of the berg like inverted bathtub rings slowly rise above the surface, one after another, and they tilt and rotate with the shifting of the block's center of gravity. Underwater melting releases streams of escaping air bubbles that flute the sides of the berg with striking architectural patterns. Each time the melting iceberg shifts in the water, all the patterns shift also–the flutes, the old waterlines, and the layering of the ice itself–adding to the complex facade of the berg's superstructure. Sometimes a berg completely loses equilibrium, due either to deep melting or to a sudden sloughing of ice, and eyewitnesses are treated to the great spectacle of seeing its enormous mass churn and roll tirelessly in the water like a colossal sea monster.

Iceberg Sizes (International Ice Patrol)
Small: less than 50 feet high; less than 200 feet long
Medium: 50–150 feet high; 200–400 feet long
Large: 150–225 feet high; 400–700 feet long
Very large: more than 225 feet high; more than 700 feet long

Tabular bergs:
Small: less than 20 feet high; less than 300 feet long
Medium: 20–50 feet high; 300–700 feet long
Large: more than 50 feet high; more than 700 feet long

Some bergs contain dark streaks of pulverized rock, "dirt bands," that hark back to their glacial origin, dirt that the glacier picked up as it scoured its bed beneath the Ice Cap. As the far-traveled ice eventually melts in the warm waters of the Gulf Stream, perhaps off Newfoundland, this dirt settles out and be-

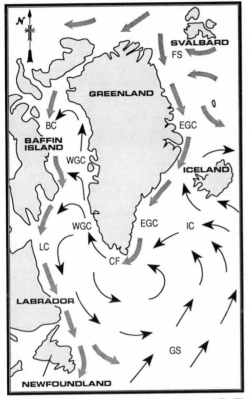

Map 15-1. Ocean currents, cold (heavy arrows) and warm (light arrows). Icebergs from the glaciers in southeast Greenland travel south with the cold East Greenland Current (EGC), which flows out of the Arctic Ocean through the Fram Strait (FS) between Greenland and Svalbard. Most of these south-flowing bergs then circle north around Cape Farewell and up the west coast in the West Greenland Current (WGC), where they gradually melt in waters warmed by the intermixing Irminger Current (IC), a branch of the Gulf Stream (GS), southwest of Iceland. Note the great counterclockwise gyre. Nearly all the ice that threatens shipping lanes east of Newfoundland originates in northwest Greenland and drifts south in the cold Baffin and Labrador currents (BC and LC). West Greenland ice has even been sighted southeast of Bermuda. Some bergs that probably originated in southeast Greenland, though, have been seen as far southeast as the Azores.

comes part of the bottom sediment where, years, centuries, or millennia later, oceanographers may discover it in cores taken by their research vessels as they probe the ocean floor. Its presence in the core is unmistakable evidence of glaciation at the time of its burial, though the glacial source may have been thousands of miles away. The larger rock fragments are called drop stones, and the process of their delivery across the sea is appropriately called rafting. Most of the dirty ice comes from the basal part of the glacier, where the bulk of the rocky debris is entrained, although dirt is sometimes lodged high up in the body of the ice by thrusting actions related to glacier motion. Medial and lateral moraines carry debris along on the surface, but many of the big outlet glaciers of southeast Greenland have no moraines. They have scoured their sides and beds so thoroughly down through the centuries that little removable rock remains, and they emerge from their source in the ice cap as pure as the driven snow. Conspicuous moraines form only where steep mountains abut a glacier—where the moving glacier loosens rock directly from the mountain flanks or where avalanches hurtling down the steep mountainsides dump rocks and boulders onto the surface of the ice.

Most bergs gain added character from conspicuous bands or layers of dark blue ice. These also were formed in the parent glacier, when the shifting ice recrystallized and densified as it flowed over its bed. You can see them in any glacier below the regional snowline, where the ice piles upon itself as it resists the thrusting pressure of the ice upstream. The basal ice is the densest and bluest, being the most highly recrystallized.

Countless icebergs form out of ice that collapses down the face of a glacier in splashy avalanches. Though spectacular in birth, most of these small bergs are mere "growlers," and they invariably are accompanied by showers of still smaller "brash," much of which is suitably sized for a Scotch on the rocks. Brash ice also forms during the spring breakup of the ice pack, or when the pack grinds itself to pieces in the heavy swells of a storm. Much larger tabular blocks may be released when the floating snout of a glacier breaks away along well-spaced intersecting crevasses. The basal ice of a glacier, on the other hand, may well up alarmingly from below under its own buoyancy, often as colossal blocks broken free from the cantilevered snout, perhaps on a rising tide and a full moon. In earlier times, and probably still, the Greenlanders feared such unexpected releases for their danger to boaters. *Puisortoq*, they were called—"rising to the surface like a seal." Imagine facing the debacle in a fragile skin boat. Bob Grahl and I were fishing down by the fjord once when we heard a loud but low boom from the direction of a nearby glacier. Puisortoq! We had presence of mind enough to scramble to the safety of higher ground just as the waves crashed on the rocks below. The bad news was that we caught no fish. Perhaps they fed only at night by the light of the Arctic moon.

16
Potato Mojo and Cookie's Sad Saga

One day in October, 1943, shortly after we had moved up to base camp from the beachhead station, Homer Loar approached me in the barracks with a twinkle in his eye: "I have something for you to try." My reaction was guarded and he repeated, "Try it, it's potato mojo. I made it myself from an old West Virginia recipe." Then he grinned broadly as I took a tentative sip. It wasn't bad: light, but nice balance. Smooth, but powerful. When I asked how he made it, he explained that he had fermented some potatoes under his (goddamn) bunk. "If Wade won't allow us a ration of barbed wire, by God, we can make it ourselves." "Barbed wire" was our code name for the expedition's store of liquor requisitioned by Captain Innes-Taylor, liquor so named to throw off track the sailors and stevedores who loaded our supplies aboard ship down at BW-1. When I suspiciously pressed Homer for details, he admitted that his mojo was merely banana extract filched from the warehouse.

Banana extract isn't drinkable as it comes from the bottle; some processing is required. The methodology developed in the Arctic outposts was to push a bottle into a snowbank overnight. By morning the flavoring would have separated from the alcohol as a waxy coagulate. The remaining essence was then poured through a thick slice of bread to filter out the wax. Lemon extract wasn't too bad either, but separating the residue from the alcohol was for some reason more difficult. Any kind of canned fruit juice made a suitable mixer, and we had no shortage of ice. All the extracts, I soon learned, had already disappeared from the warehouse, reportedly ending up mostly in the radio shack. Nothing official was ever said about the extracts incident, and it is uncertain whether Captain Wade was even aware of it, but Cookie's cuisine in the mess hall suffered a setback that intensified as the winter drew on.

Cookie–Sgt. Clevis Nallett–had the hardest job in camp, and the loss of his flavorings didn't help. Fixing three meals daily, months on end for a gang of grumbling malcontents would have been a challenge for a four-star chef under the most favorable circumstances. At an isolated outpost in the stormiest part of Greenland–make that the world–it deserved a battle star. Our menu revolved around the tin can, chiefly canned bully beef, Spam, and Vienna sausages. A whole generation of American men still rails at the mere mention of Spam, which was a sort of canned ham loaf and really not too bad if not taken in excess. Powdered mashed potatoes didn't help much, but Cookie baked excellent bread, which did help a lot. Breakfast was mostly powdered eggs in various guises, salt pork, and pancakes. Salt pork came in ten-pound slabs that resembled bacon but consisted almost entirely of hard fat still attached to the skin–no lean. It had to be cooked crisp to be palatable, and it had to be soaked in water before cooking to leach out the salt. The salt was a preservative that kept the "pork" from spoiling without refrigeration. Once when we were readying a convoy for the Ice Cap, persons unknown left the door ajar to the machine shop, where a T-15 was being loaded with supplies. Our dog Svarten went in to check things over and proudly emerged with a large slab of salt pork in his gaping maw. He chewed its corner contentedly for a few minutes, then yielded it to another dog, and yet another, each abandoning it in turn. All three dogs were then seen dragging their chins through the snow, gulping copious quantities for the next half-hour.

I liked peanut butter on my pancakes, plus Karo syrup, and generally had a table to myself at such times, shunned by the others, who got up and moved across the aisle. We had a few canned hams, some canned chicken (which was tiresome), and canned pilchards. All these entrees were actually quite good taken in moderation, but after a time they all became hard to look at. Pilchards are a sort of herring or large sardine; Boston Bill Cadigan said he had eaten a lot of them before the war, especially on Fridays. A Roman Catholic from Dorchester, Massachusetts, he referred to himself as a "mackerel snapper." In the military service, the customary fish dinner on Fridays was suspended by the church for the duration of the war, and later was abandoned entirely in the country at large, but the cognomen hung on. We also had large stores of chewy, straw-yellow canned asparagus that in color, texture, and palatability resembled short lengths of bamboo. One thing we didn't have was S.O.S.—"shit on a shingle." S.O.S. was standard breakfast fare in army mess halls around the world, made from hamburger cooked in milk-and-flour gravy served on toast, but at Comanche Bay we had no hamburger, no fresh meat, no fresh anything. On Doc Johnson's orders, all expedition members took one ascorbic acid pill daily—with no fresh food in our diets, we needed the vitamin C to avert any chance of contracting scurvy. More Arctic expeditions have fallen prey to scurvy than to cold or starvation. Even so, an army doctor later said we all showed early signs, such as the incipient withdrawal of the gum lines around our teeth.

Cookie was a talented and diligent mess sergeant. Before the war he had been a chef, he said, in a famous French restaurant in Montreal, but after a time his credibility and ingenuity waned. There were only so many ways to fix Spam, canned bully beef, or powdered eggs. Cookie became depressed and eventually was evacuated. He had held out for nearly ten months, and we all felt a little guilty. Cookie was a lonely, introspective person, a gentle soul who wanted to be one of the boys but never quite succeeded. For some reason he had slipped past the intensive psychological screening of the rest of us. He was just assigned to the expedition from the cooks-and-bakers pool of the Greenland Base Command. He was a shy, retiring sort and rather intimidated amidst a bunch of loud, assertive, intellectual slobs, mostly ex-college-boy draftees who felt they represented an elite minority in the army of World War II—elite corporals and sergeants, weathermen and radio operators.

Cookie had aspired to be a dog driver, and one day after baking a batch of particularly tasty bread, he thoughtfully decided to hitch up a team and take a few loaves to the boys up at the weather station. Cookie was just a little guy, maybe 110 pounds, and two strong dogs should have been able to haul him and his cargo up to the station. He picked Svarten—Svarten who had fallen down the barracks hatchway—and a young but big pup for his team. Svarten was good-natured and immensely strong, but a bad choice. Cookie hitched both dogs to a Nansen sled, broke the runners loose, and took off like Blitzen, straight for the mess hall. Svarten dragged the sled, the pup, Cookie, and the bread all the way into the kitchen. Never mind his best intentions, we all had a belly laugh at Cookie's expense.

After the radio shack burned down Cookie shared living space in the mess hall with Captain Wade and Lieutenant Borden. The nearby barracks was chiefly the domain of the eight weathermen, although three of them were always at the weather station and we shared the space with Colombo, the dog driver; Johansen, the Norwegian; Sanford, our supply sergeant; and Johnson, our medic from Denver. Doc Johnson was also our official photographer. He had a darkroom setup in his dispensary at the far end of the barracks, and he spent most of his time there printing photographs or snoozing in his sack. The four radiomen lived in the new radio shack, and our two mechanics lived in the machine and generator shack. Cookie and the two officers were not social equals, and despite the personal warmth of both officers, they and Cookie had disparate backgrounds and interests. The mess hall was also our recreation room, and other men usually were there after hours to socialize, read books (our rather good library included background information about Greenland, its people, and its language), listen to the phonograph, or play chess, acey-deucy, or Ping-Pong, but despite the company, Cookie spent many lonely hours by himself in his room next to the kitchen. During blizzards, moreover, no one but Wade and Borden might show up at all, even though Cookie had prepared food for everyone. The mess hall could be the center of social activity at Comanche Bay, or it could be the loneliest place in Greenland.

Our phonograph was a hand-wound portable, and we had a fair assortment of 78 rpm records provided by the Red Cross. Doc Johnson had his own clarinet and was our local music expert. He favored Helen O'Connell in the vocal department and Count Basie in his rendition of "I'm gonna move way out on the outskirts of town." Wade enjoyed Beatrice Kay and "She was only a bird in a guilded cage." Borden rather liked Jose Marais and his quaint songs of the veldt, such as "Road to Kimberley." Larry Phillips was partial to "Rabbit in the pea patch pickin' on peas."

When Wade finally decided that Cookie should be evacuated at the earliest opportunity, another man also began to develop health problems. Sergeant Sanford, our softspoken, gentle Baltimorean, had increasingly frequent abdominal pains. Sanford was the most fastidious man in camp, and he shaved and sponged off regularly. Because he kept a stash of toiletries, deodorants, and other sundries including razor blades neatly arranged on a shelf above his bunk, he took a certain amount of ribbing from his barracks mates. On at least one occasion, razor blades apparently fell to his bunk, and Sandbag half seriously accused persons unknown of putting them there. "Who's been putting razor blades in Sandbag's bunk" quickly became a widely used conversational gambit.

After Sandbag and Cookie had been flown back to Bluie West-1 and had been hospitalized for a time for medical observation, Wade received a radiogram to the effect that Cookie was OK and had been transferred out; the other man, it said, still had a few vague symptoms but did not have appendicitis. We wondered if he told the doctor that someone had been putting razor blades in his bunk.

Cookie's replacement, like Cookie, was assigned out of Greenland Base Command's cooks-and-bakers pool, and he took a rather dim view of life in the outposts, in keeping with his big-city, New York background and his lack of proper indoctrination into the solemn traditions of the far north. He didn't like the Arctic at all, he complained, and moreover, he had difficulty breathing, he said, because of the high latitude. When the army agreed to evacuate Cookie and Sandbag, it also decided that a medical officer should visit the outpost to check the physical and mental health of the rest of us. The man chosen was a young doctor fresh out of Little Rock, Arkansas, Dr. Huie Smith, a recently commissioned lieutenant new to the rigors of army life in the vastness of the Greenland outback.

Lieutenant Smith and our new cook were to come in on the same PBY flying boat that would take out Cookie and Sandbag. A PBY was a high-winged, twin-engined amphibian, a very reliable if awkward-looking bird of great stability and low stalling speed, and the workhorse of the far-flung Arctic lifeline. PBYs were used widely for antisubmarine patrol, but they served other masters as well. They were derisively but affectionately called "goonie birds," a name expropriated by later generations of servicemen for the aging C-47, or commercial DC-3, another reliable aircraft, but the original goonie bird was the PBY, Peter Baker Yoke, not the DC-3. Actually, the name was well deserved—a PBY could soar effortlessly, almost tirelessly, for endless hours above the storm-swept Atlantic Ocean, keeping constant vigil above the breaking swells, much like a real live goonie, the black footed albatross. A PBY, incidentally, was the patrol plane that spotted the Nazi superbattleship *Bismarck* in the North Atlantic off Iceland and led to its interception and sinking by the British navy.

To set a PBY down in Comanche Bay, the army wanted three miles of ice-free water, which was an outrageous stipulation even in summertime, but Wade assented, asking only that Greenland Base Command watch the weather closely (as GBC of course would have to do anyway) and be prepared to fly in right after the next big blow out of the north and before the succeeding high tide. When the wind soon arose, it lasted about three days, and when it stopped, Igtip Kangertiva was completely clear of ice–seven miles of ice-free water, except for a few large bergs out toward the mouth where they may have been grounded on a submerged reef. The big bergs, in any event, were insensitive to the wind: with most of their bulk submerged, they were virtually invulnerable and responded only to tides and sea currents.

After a flurry of radio exchanges, in came Peter Baker Yoke, and it settled quietly like a giant white goose on three hundred yards of smooth, blue water just off the beachhead station. All free hands came down to greet its arrival and wish well our departing buddies. Then a rubber raft was put overboard, and the landing party paddled toward shore in exchange for our evacuees. Lieutenant Smith had heard grim stories of sanitary conditions in the Greenland outposts, and he thought he was prepared for the worst possible eventuality, but with a gentle offshore breeze blowing toward the raft, he was unprepared for Comanche Bay. The Innes-Taylor expedition of 1942 had cached a large pile of dried fish at the beachhead, to be used as dog food through the following winter. When the expedition folded, the fish cache remained behind, and in the ensuing Arctic summer it rotted down to a great formless mass of malodorous obscenity covering an area the size of a suburban ranch house. The fish pile by then was nearly two years old, and on warm summer days the loose dogs in camp liked to trot down to the beachhead and roll in it. They'd hunch down on their elbows, push with their hind legs, and plow up a furrow with their half-buried noses. Sheer ecstasy. Or they'd wriggle over on their backs and grin contentedly as only a happy dog can. Then they wanted to be petted.

Lieutenant Smith hadn't heard about the fish pile, and as the raft drew closer to shore, his face grew longer, grayer, and more somber with each stroke of the oars. What abomination, what depravity, he wondered. Why hadn't he been warned? Why hadn't this case been reported in the medical journals?

Lieutenant Smith was much relieved on landing to learn that the offending odors emanated only from the point source of the fish pile and that the beachhead station was otherwise acceptably unsanitary. After a brief exchange of pleasantries between Wade and the pilot, the PBY departed, leaving Lieutenant Smith with us as the ice drifted back into the fjord on the rising tide. Then came the long hike up the snowfield to base camp, and one more surprise for the good doctor, who began counting the hours until his scheduled departure.

By now spring was advancing into summer, and the twenty-foot-deep snowpack of winter had melted down to only two or three feet of old granular ice. With summer came an astonishing concentration of all manner of camp refuse that had accumulated during the previous ten months. In some respects it resembled the ablation moraine of a melting glacier. Although our dogs had been tethered well away from the main camp area for sanitary reasons, we always had a few loose animals, camp pets and work dogs that had escaped their tethers. These dogs wandered freely about camp, but they congregated near the mess hall where the chance of a gratuitous morsel or two was optimal.

Throughout winter the camp area had looked clean as the driven snow itself, pristine in the purity of the trackless polar landscape, but as the snow wasted down, the scene steadily deteriorated. Outside the door of each building the snow had an ugly yellow discoloration; in the dim Arctic light it looked green. The whole camp area, perhaps three or four acres, was decorated with a mantle of concentrated doggy-do, and when Lieutenant Smith first saw it he was visibly shaken. Blanched, he asked Bob Grahl if any of it could be human excrement.

"Ah gee no, Doc," protested Bob, "the dogs eat all that."

17
Lardass and Bisson

The biggest man in the Base Ice Cap Detachment and also the most essential was a heavy-equipment operator from Texas named Sgt. Bob Johnson. Six feet, two inches tall, weighing maybe 230 pounds, Master Sergeant Johnson had the strength of two ordinary men. Most of us were skinny as rails, but Bob was heavily muscled and had an ample spare tire. We called him Lardass.

Before enlisting in the army, Bob had worked for the famous Texas equipment maker, R. J. LeTourneau, who specialized in the manufacture of colossal earthmovers and huge tractors that had a lot to do with the success of American construction battalions around the world. Just before joining our detachment, Bob Johnson had been awarded the Legion of Merit, which was the army's highest noncombat decoration. Everyone at BW-1 turned out for the formal ceremony. One of Bob's charges, unfulfilled so far as I know, was to design a large-wheeled crosscountry snowmobile, after the fashion of a LeTourneau Turnapull. Turnapulls had rubber tires as tall as a small house, but track or belt tread was the trend in oversnow vehicles at that time and still is. Tracks have better flotation on snow than wheels have, regardless of size. A few years earlier, propeller-driven sleds had been tried with mixed results, especially by the Germans. Alfred Wegener, for example, the eminent German meterologist and father of the concept of continental drift, had used prop-driven sleds on the Ice Cap in the middle 1930s. The fact that Wegener died of a heart attack while returning afoot from his Ice Cap station probably had little bearing on the utility of the propsled.

As our chief mechanic and troubleshooter, Bob Johnson looked after our T-15 snowmobiles, serviced our electric generators and winches, and did most of the rigging for the winch line up the margin of Apuseq Glacier. But if in some ways a paragon, Bob had one unforgivable fault: he snored. In the close confinement of an army barracks, his thunderous rumbling was devastating to all present. Not even a deaf man could have handled it. Bob didn't just snore like an ordinary mortal; he roared like an Olympian god—relentlessly, hour on hour, both inhaling and exhaling. Many an army barracks was emptied to a man when all hands fled outdoors as if his rumblings signaled the onset of an earthquake. We quickly exiled him to the machine shop, appropriately we thought, because our unmuffled, six-cylinder, gasoline-powered electric generator raised about the same number of decibels. He'd have languished there by himself in abject isolation through the winter but for the fortuitous reappearance of another mechanic, the thick-accented Maurice J. Bisson, from Brooklyn, New York. Bisson had been with the expedition at the outset but, because of an illness, had been reassigned in the fall of 1943 to duty at Ikateq, only to return later to share Bob Johnson's vigil. Like Bob, he was a consummate snorer in his own right, one who competed on equal terms decibelwise both with Bob and with the generator.

Our machine shop was a corrugated-iron–roofed quonset hut that vibrated badly during high winds, particularly the bulkheads fore and aft, and after a blizzard of three or four days' duration, both mechanics would emerge wan and shaken from their enforced confinement, their hands trembling and chins quivering. Several cups of coffee in the mess hall helped them gradually regain composure. When the machine shop finally was buried in the snow, the vibrations stopped, but then the building sweated from the condensation of moisture against its metal shell.

Bisson was a highly skilled mechanic also. He was a skinny little guy, maybe five feet, eight inches in his army boots, and except for his mechanical prowess and snoring, therefore, he was the antithesis of Bob Johnson. In his late thirties, he was an old man among us. I could hardly believe anyone that old could still be a soldier. Captain Wade was even older, forty-two, but he was an officer and his antiquity thus was to be expected. Johan Johansen, at forty-eight, was an elderly but well-preserved civilian who would have been in an old-folks home, I reasoned, had he not been caught in Greenland by the war. Bisson rated high marks for diligence and for the quality of his work, despite his advanced years, and he and Lardass made a great team. My sole gripe against Bisson, one that still rankles, was that he spoiled a roll of film I had taken on a once-in-a-lifetime trip to Rocky Craig, when he carelessly opened the back of the camera after I returned to camp.

In matters mechanical, Bob Johnson was both methodical and inventive. Coupled with his physical strength, he was a man of formidable talent, and an incident at the beachhead exemplified his adroit if unpolished manner. In August, 1943, the cargo ship *Nevada* still lay at anchor in the fjord as we unloaded cargo at the beachhead station. We were using a large steel barge to float supplies from ship to shore. Even heavily loaded, the barge rode high in the water, and with one end of it aground, Bob had started to ease a big gasoline-driven winch ashore under its own power down a makeshift ramp of wooden planks. His scheme was to unwind the cable a few turns from the drum, anchor it to a "deadman" buried ashore in the snow, then slowly skid the winch forward down the ramp as the cable was rewound.

At this point a radioman emerged from the beachhead shack shouting instructions and calling for a halt until he could take charge. Bob applied the brake. Having run many winches in the past, Sparks said, he would oversee the operation to make sure the winch was brought safely ashore without further delay. Sparks and Bob were not on close personal terms, but Bob said nothing as Sparks grasped the taut cable, placed one foot on the ramp, and swung himself up toward the barge. Instead Bob just lifted his own foot off the brake, the cable went slack, and Sparks dropped into the fjord. Nothing further was said. The soaked radioman sputtered back to his shack, and Bob finished unloading the winch. Laurel and Hardy couldn't have had better timing.

18
Johan Johansen, Trail Man

Johan Johansen, the oldest man in camp, was a weather-beaten Norwegian and a sailmaker by trade, a seafarer whose work had taken him to bustling and sleazy seaports on both sides of the Atlantic and the Mediterranean, but he had also ventured into the fur trade, and when the war broke out he was caught in northeast Greenland trapping the Arctic blue fox. His wife and seven-year-old son were in occupied Norway under the heel of the Nazi boot, and he had heard nothing at all about them for three years. After the fall of Denmark, American forces took Greenland into protective custody, and Johan–Joe, pronounced "Yo"–joined up as a civilian advisor to the U.S. Army. Joe had run traplines in the high Arctic near the supply station of Eskimonaes on Clavering Island in the ruggedly beautiful wilderness of northeast Greenland known as the fjord country.

All of coastal Greenland is indented by great fjords, but the fjords of northeast Greenland are the greatest in the world, the longest and most complex being Scoresby Sound and its rugged tributaries. The Scoresby Sound region is a dissected plateau six or seven thousand feet high, cut by the fjords into discrete blocks and islands mantled by local highland ice caps ten or twenty miles across. Nearly all the main fjords head in the Greenland Ice Cap itself or in its outlet glaciers. Although the heights of the fjord country are thus covered by ice, the fjord walls are tremendous cliffs of bare rock exposing their geologic structure on a scale so stark and sublime as to make a grown man cry–at least if he is a geologist. Geologically, northeast Greenland is part of the East Greenland Caledonian Fold Belt–once the west half of a great chain of mountains that reached hundreds of miles across Greenland, Scotland, and Norway four hundred or so million years ago when the North American and Eurasian crustal plates were joined as one. Continental drift finally tore the plates apart, but the internal mountain structure of the Caledonian Fold Belt is still grandly displayed in the precipitous walls of the fjords. Many of these walls are cliffs more than a mile high.

With a length of 280 miles, Scoresby Sound is more than twice as long as famous Sognefjord in Norway, the greatest fjord in Europe. Clavering Island is about 250 miles north of Scoresby, but Joe trapped much of the inland fjord country between, particularly an area called Myggbugt, "Mosquito Bay." The prime time for trapping was winter, when the fjords were frozen and the surface was hard and smooth for easy sledging. The winter night in northeast Greenland is long and brittle cold, but according to Joe it lacks the foul weather, heavy snowfall, and powerful winds of Kjoge Bugt and Igtip Kangertiva. The summer up there is longer, warmer, and drier than in southeast Greenland— in short, more equable, more habitable—because its twenty-four hour days of full sunshine brighten the skies and warm the air and because few cyclonic storms penetrate that far north.

Joe trapped foxes with a simple, homemade, deadfall trap baited in the figure-four configuration that every boy scout knows. It kills instantly, hence is inherently more humane than the steel-jawed traps still used by American trappers. Not that Norwegian trappers are (or were) less barbaric than Americans— the figure-four deadfall was just easier, cheaper, and more convenient to use than a steel trap, especially in the subzero temperatures of the fjords. All you needed was a few sticks of wood and a heavy boulder.

Arctic foxes have a brown coat in summer. Most turn white in winter, but some have a bluish hue, and these are the most prized. Joe once told me, however, that the very best pelt is that of a fetal muskox, though I shuddered to think that a trapper would deliberately kill a pregnant cow just for the pelt of her unborn calf or that a woman, however vain, would wear a fur thus obtained. Joe was sure that trapping would be especially good right after the war. Foxes should be abundant, he said, because there had been no trapping for six years, and he urged that we form a joint venture to trap them out. I graciously declined, being philosophically opposed to killing animals for their furs or for sport. Today the fjord country has been set aside as a national park where hunting and trapping are prohibited. Besides fox and muskoxen, the area is home to Arctic hares, lemmings, caribou and Arctic wolves (at least formerly), seals, walrus, narwhals, and polar bears, and seasonally, many species of birds.

Joe was a polar expert who knew every trick of Arctic survival. He had a special sense about the outdoors, the vagaries of the weather, ice conditions, the snow surface, and Ice Cap travel. He knew the best way to rig a sledge, handle dogs, repair a harness, pitch a tent, maintain a primus stove, prepare trail food, and navigate by compass, and no one questioned his judgment, at least after his vindication in the matter of siting base camp and the fuel dumps. He had great strength, quick reflexes, and astonishing agility for a man his age, but he had a weakness for alcohol.

Not that liquor was easy to come by in southeast Greenland. Wade kept our small stash of barbed wire, requisitioned by Innes-Taylor, well secured. Nobody saw or heard much about it until Wade was promoted to major a year after our arrival at Comanche Bay, even though Innes-Taylor had intended that everyone should receive a regular ration.

But Joe had sources of alcohol other than the barbed wire, and he guarded them as carefully as Wade guarded his. Two of the buildings in camp were quonset-type warehouses. One was stocked with food enough for three Ice Cap stations plus base camp and the weather station. The other held trail gear under Joe's management. It contained skis, snowshoes, ice axes, ropes, leather thongs, sledge parts, tents, sleeping bags, caribou hides (for ground cloths), bamboo trail wands, red nylon flagging, trail compasses, countless other small items, and ethyl (grain) alcohol. The compasses were a mariner's type used on small vessels and were well suited for Ice Cap navigation. They were leveled by two axial rings and were suspended in alcohol.

Joe often went down to the warehouse to repair dog harnesses, cut thongs for shoelaces, assemble a Nansen sledge, or attend to other chores, and he sometimes invited me along to help out, I being his confidant and closest friend in camp, though less than half his age. We shared a Viking heritage and often played chess together (he seldom lost). I was fascinated, moreover, by the cornucopia of outdoor equipment and mountaineering gear stashed in the warehouse. Joe would fire up the pot-bellied stove, fill a pan with snow, and put it on to melt. Then as it came to a boil he would add sugar and with utmost gentility just enough compass alcohol for a proper balance. "Hønsen, would you care for a little drink?" It being Armistice Day, November 11, 1943, or some other suitable occasion, a small drink and toast seemed appropriate. I have no recollection as to how many thongs were cut on Armistice Day, but when we climbed out of the warehouse hatchway, I recall falling to the ground three times en route back to the barracks. The snow, of course, was very slippery.

Joe binged for three days, and in that time he neither ate nor went to bed. All hands recognized his special problem and empathized with the emotional stress of his long separation from his family, but we lived three days of hell before he finally conked out. All hands feigned sleep as he stumbled through the darkness of the barracks, shaking first one man and then another as he staggered about. Being his nearest friend, I was singled out for special attention: "Hønsen, wake up, Hønsen, talk to me!"

We suspected that Joe's problem was the main reason Wade held back the barbed wire all those months when everyone could have used a little cheer. Once when Wade was readying a trip to the Ice Cap and Joe was in his cups, Wade just looked the other way as Joe cursedly berated his efforts, a behavior that was inconceivable when Joe was sober. But Joe's main target that day was Barry Borden, and his verbal abuse was merciless. Though all of us had heard much profanity since joining the army and had acquired a certain flair for vile language ourselves, and though the Norwegian language supposedly lacked inherently profane expletives, Joe's command of a whole spectrum of appropriate English alternatives included many words that were new to everyone else. Basically, Joe was just venting his withdrawn rage at the Nazi oppressors of his homeland and his perceived inability to do anything about it. In his own way he served his country well doing what he did best in the desolate isolation of southeast Greenland. He was a great man to have as a friend—loyal, honorable, intelligent, and hard as steel—but a man few men would want to face in a barroom brawl. When he finally sobered up he apologized contritely to everyone in camp.

When Joe and his fellow trappers left Clavering Island, he brought along his own team of dogs. (Actually he was evacuated from the wireless station at Scoresbysund, where he and his fellows were ordered to report by the Danish governor general of Greenland after the fall of Denmark.) Clavering Island had been

Fig. 18-1. Johan Johansen, Norwegian trapper and polar expert, at Comanche Bay, Greenland, April, 1944.

the site of a skirmish between a small force of German invaders and the Danish operators of the weather-radio station at Eskimonaes back in 1942. Germany recognized the importance of Greenland weather information to its war planning in Europe and wanted Eskimonaes for itself. Much of Europe's weather shaped up in the interplay of meteorological forces over Greenland and the adjacent North Atlantic Ocean. Not many shots were fired, but a Dane was killed before the Germans were routed. Joe recounted the story to me from the shelter of our tent on the Ice Cap.

Down at BW-1 Wade had occasion to talk to a German captive. They were scientists, the German said, not Nazis, interested primarily in meteorological research, not in fighting a war. Their capture, he added, was a loss to science, not a military setback, but their capture was a strategic loss to the German High Command: for want of a nail, a shoe was lost. The German scientists were the former owners of our lifeboat down at Comanche Bay, seized as a prize of war and given to us by the coast guard. Don Galbreath, Homer Loar, and I could thank the Germans for our voyage across the fjord one memorable day in August, 1944.

Joe's dogs were magnificent animals bred from a Greenland husky-German shepherd cross. They thus had the best qualities of both breeds, the brute strength and endurance of the husky and the intelligence of the shepherd, but they understood only Norwegian, and to drive the team I had to learn a few Norwegian commands: *heire*, right; *venstre*, left; *ligge ned*, lie down; *stop* meant stop, even in Norwegian.

Each dog had a distinctive temperament. The lead dog and dominant male of Joe's team, Poul, was a tough, savage animal who had fought polar bears. He bore a long scar across his nose where Joe had wired his mouth shut as punishment for attacking his master. Joe brooked no nonsense from his team, and he meted out punishment with a blind rage that I thought exceeded reasonable bounds of decency. When Poul was younger, Joe said, you didn't turn your back on him. Poul still bullied all the other dogs of the team, even though he had passed his prime and could have been beaten in a fair fight, but no other dog would challenge him.

Most of Joe's other dogs were less sinister and even craved affection, though petting them was discouraged, as a good sled dog was supposed to fear its master. Some cowered even if approached with a hint of kindness. They were draft animals, not pets, Joe said, and men's lives depended on their performance under stress. Today's drivers get far better performance from their teams through affectionate encouragement and rewards than Joe and his contemporaries ever got through brutal intimidation. Joe granted only two exceptions to his code of canine discipline: to Lizabet, queen mother of the team, and to Svarten, her son. Lizabet was a big honey blonde with a magnificent face, body, and regal carriage. Occasionally she was admitted to the barracks where she sat up, shook hands, spoke, and danced for tidbits. A word of caution: when hand-feeding a sled dog, hold the food low in an open palm, not between the thumb and fingers. Huskies will snap reflexively if they have to reach for food, and they may unwittingly take your fingers with it, but they will mouth it softly if it's offered from an open hand.

Svarten, the clown, liked to put his paws on your shoulders and lick your face, a habit that could be disconcerting if he had

Fig. 18–2.   Lizabet nursing her puppies.

just eaten something unmentionable. Svarten always talked back when spoken to. Few dogs have this talent, though I have owned two lovable mutts who both spoke readily and well. The secret is to talk often to the dog, for how else can he learn? Dogs are a lot like children in that respect—they learn from example. Like other Greenland huskies, though, Svarten did not bark, but he and all of them howled melodiously before meals and for ten or fifteen minutes just before settling down for the night—a primal, forlorn compulsion handed down through their genes from their lupine ancestors.

Most Greenland huskies don't lift their legs, either, having been bred for countless generations in a land with neither trees nor fireplugs. In harness on the Ice Cap, and flushed with the excitement of the trail, Poul would sometimes try to lift his leg against yours at rest stops, and he would wet on your boot if he got a chance. Often I skied a few yards ahead of the team to set trail and urge the dogs on, but Poul occasionally would spot a trail wand off to one side, perhaps a hundred feet off our course, and he'd turn the whole team away, despite my lead, to check it out and leave his mark. Then he'd savage the neck of the nearest dog perfunctorily a few times before resuming the march.

Joe hitched his team in the traditional Greenland fan hitch, an efficient arrangement in which each dog is on a separate trace that allows for a direct pull on the sledge by every animal. It also allows the lead dog to leap across the traces to cow any dog that gets out of line. The tandem hitch used in Alaska is better in the loose snow of the Alaskan forests, because the dogs up front break trail for the dogs behind, but on the smooth ice of a Greenland fjord, the fan hitch is superior. Also, the fan hitch is easier to use if the dogs tangle their traces in a gang fight.

The strongest and hardest worker in Joe's team was a dependable, dappled black and white beast named Truls, a smaller dog than Svarten. Truls strained at his traces all the time; Svarten usually kept them just taut enough to give the appearance of pulling when he was being watched. When he wasn't, they would go slack. Coming into camp, though, with visions of food and rest, Svarten pulled very well. Second in strength was Big Red, another animal of doubtful intelligence but great power. Big Red and Truls together pulled nearly as much load as the rest of the team combined. Besides Poul, Svarten, Big Red, Truls, and Lizabet, Joe's team included Wolf, Tufty, and Prinz.

At day's end, Joe would unfasten the harnesses and traces and check all leads for tears and breaks. Each dog was then chained to a separate snap on a longer chain anchored at either end in the snow. Leashes were spaced far enough apart to prevent fighting, and the rawhide harnesses would be put out of reach to keep the dogs from eating them. Then the ceremonial howling would start before feeding and bed. "Talk to me, Svarten," Joe would call from inside the tent, and Svarten would oblige with a long, low, tremulous woof.

19
More about the Dogs

Besides Joe Johansen's aristocratic team, the rest of our dogs were a mixed bag of lesser animals, including a few Siberians, bought by the army from people in West Greenland. We had about thirty-five dogs in camp, including pups. Joe also had a weird little short-haired, black and brindle fox-terrier sort of dog named Bella that he had picked up on a dock somewhere in Italy in his prewar travels. Bella was partial to her master and growled at everyone else, but she was attracted to male huskies and twice bore puppies at Comanche Bay. A union between a fifteen-pound terrier and a ninety-pound husky taxes credibility, but not as much as the resulting pups. The first litter, three beautiful little fur balls, resembled Pomeranians; one died at birth, one was run over by a snowmobile, and one was adopted by Larry Phillips. This dog at maturity weighed about eight pounds. She had thick black fur, a curly tail, erect ears, a sweet disposition—unlike her mother—and she liked to sit up and beg for food. I suspected that Svarten was her father.

Bella's next pup was adopted by the radiomen and named Butch, possibly the scruffiest animal in all of Greenland. Butch was a miniature also, weighing ten or twelve pounds. He looked like a terrier, with mid-length, wiry, light gray hair. Stiff, erect hair covered his nose and face on a head a bit too large for his body. His ears tipped over at the top, and his tail curled over close to his back, husky fashion. As a pup Butch would playfully try to couple to Svarten's nose as the big black dog lay basking in the snow, but Svarten would tolerantly bunt him aside. Butch also liked to stand on the roof of the radio shack and bark at the world, which in his case meant the few acres around base camp. He must have inherited this trait from his mother because, as mentioned, Greenland huskies don't bark. When they howled before feeding time or before bedding down, something in Butch's genes compelled him to join in, but not very convincingly. From the top of the radio shack he would lean back on his haunches, tilt his head high, and emit a sound more like a squeaky barn door than a wolf call.

Butch

Tingmiakajik, the raven

About 150 yards from the radio shack, down in the direction of the beachhead, was our garbage dump. This small mountain of frozen delights was soon spotted by a couple of ravens that lived year round at Comanche Bay and normally survived on a ration of carrion and crowberries. Neither of these commodities was very bountiful in our part of Greenland, so the birds spent many happy hours at the dump, and they soon waxed fat. Ravens are intelligent creatures who know a good thing when they see it. Butch, however, had a proprietary interest in the dump himself. He especially liked to roll in the freshly dumped, unfrozen garbage, and one day when en route from the mess hall he was enraged to see the dump preempted by the birds. His easy trot turned to a blind charge, and a low growl rose from his throat as he bore down on his feathered adversaries. The ravens, however, were undeterred by threats from such a small creature and they weren't about to yield their bonanza without a fight. When Butch was about fifteen feet away they just faced him down, half-raised their wings, and opened their heavy black beaks in a threatening stance. Butch's reflexes were fast, but he was only two feet away before he could check his forward motion, skid to a halt, reverse direction, and retreat to the safety of the mess hall. Butch never went near the dump again. He even detoured widely around it en route to the beachhead station with the other loose dogs and the work gang.

Another habitué of the mess hall door was Big Red who, like Svarten, abhorred confinement but, unlike Svarten, lacked the finesse to slip his chain. Big Red also lacked Svarten's endearing charm and ennobling intelligence, but he made up in brute strength what he lacked in wit. Svarten escaped his tethers by pushing the ring of his chain up over the end of his pipe with his nose. Big Red just put a strain on the tether, eventually pulling chain, pipe, and all out of the snow, and thus entrained, bounded off for the mess mall. Joe's dog Truls worked out a scheme halfway between: he jumped up and down, snapping his chain until the ring finally slipped over the top of the pipe and we had one more dog at the mess hall.

I once had an abasing experience involving Svarten and the garbage dump. On a balmy day, I had readied Joe's team for a trip to the beachhead. Several hands were outside the mess hall filling the snowmelter on the roof. I knew all Joe's dogs well, and they acknowledged my authority, so we generally functioned smoothly together. Using the Greenland fan hitch, I harnessed up the team and adjusted each dog's traces. Then I broke loose the runners, cracked the whip, and took off at breathtaking speed past the cheering crowd, the mess hall being right on the line of my route to the beachhead. But in an unforgiving error, I had given Svarten too long a trace. He was a shoulder length ahead of the lead dog, Poul, and despite my curses, shouts, and lashing whip, he broke into the lead and turned headlong toward the dump, followed reflexively by the entire team (and still within seeing, hearing, and cheering distance of the crowd at the mess hall). I swallowed my pride, but from that day forth, Svarten's rein was short and tight.

The savage reputation of the Greenland husky is well deserved, even among the pups. Unlike other breeds of dogs that cuddle and romp as puppies, ours fought almost from birth. It was disconcerting to see five-pound pups fighting fiercely among themselves, even drawing blood with their sharp little milk teeth, when to our minds they should have been playing happily in the snow. Savagery had somehow been instilled into their genetic makeup. Two particularly aggressive dogs from Tony Colombo's team usually worked together, having been littermates. They had sloe-eyed Oriental features and we called them the Soong brothers, Elmer and Charlie Soong. Young people may not remember the original Soong Sisters; they were a potent force in the politics of China before World War II, strongly tied in with the Koumin-

Fig. 19–1. Elmer Soong.

tang, the regime of Chiang Kai-shek, then president of China
(whom the GIs of the China-Burma-India theater called "Chan-
croid Jack."). Madame Chiang was one of the sisters. At any rate,
Charlie and Elmer Soong were young, rangy, and muscular
fighters in their physical prime and real troublemakers who always fought side by side whenever they got loose.

Both Charlie and Elmer occasionally serviced a rather
wretched bitch named Lady, from the west coast village of Egedesminde. Lady seemed nearly always to be in heat, and she kept
the male dogs in a state of constant frenzy. Either Charlie or Elmer sired a pup by her called Navy, named by Colombo for an
Antarctic dog from his Little America days under Admiral Byrd.
The genetic combination must have been just right. Navy was a
handsome beige pup who grew up to be the largest and most
powerful brute in camp, and though he had a lovable disposition
around people, he had his father's aggressive instinct and was
quick to pick a fight with other dogs, even as a yearling pup.

For a sled dog, savagery is not necessarily an undesirable trait,
provided the animal doesn't misbehave in the harness and
doesn't challenge the driver's will. A dog seriously injured while

fighting in harness might jeopardize the success of a whole trip. On the other hand, a good lead dog must be aggressive and must dominate the rest of the team. Lead dogs seem to sense this. Navy surely had the potential to be a superior sled dog and possibly a good leader, but he never was harnessed during our expedition, and I know nothing of his fate afterwards. Army rescue teams elsewhere in the Arctic used dogs, and Navy may have ended up with such a team, or maybe the army gave him to the Greenlanders. Navy had one noteworthy experience while still in our charge: on reaching sexual maturity he was mated to one of the bitches, and the whole camp turned out to cheer him on.

Other dogs whose names I remember were Nero, Libby, Owens, Ford, Blizzard, Marjorie, Cici, Brownie, Pinhead, Jackie, Walkie, and Talkie. Some were never named, because besides the work dogs, we had a semipermanent pack of loose dogs around camp all the time. Mostly they were adolescent pups that seldom fought, having established their own order of dominance early in life. Svarten, though hardly a pup, was a part of this coterie and was a reluctant Ferdinand who never picked a fight. He would lie complacently in the snow during the hassling by the younger animals climbing over him, nipping his ears, and biting his rear as they tried to incite him into action. The dogs we had to beat off with boards and shovels to break up their fights were the accidentally loose work dogs that, in violent bursts of fury, unleashed all the smoldering frustrations of their chains and confinement.

Another nonaggressive loose dog was named Slinker, so called because he would slink around the periphery of camp just out of reach, the nearest you could approach him being about twenty-five feet. Slinker was one of Tony Colombo's dogs. He had escaped his tethers while being unhitched from his trail harness, and we never were able to catch him, though I once nearly grabbed him from behind a rock after having baited it with food. I'm not sure what or when he ate, but I suspect that Colombo fed him surreptitiously when he fed the rest of his team. Or perhaps Slinker lived off the dump. I can still see him slinking around camp, skulking behind rocks like a lone wolf, head held low, one floppy ear, and his tail between his legs.

Colombo's lead dog was named Zero, and few animals have been more aptly named or less aptly qualified for leadership. In a Greenland fan hitch a more aggressive team member would surely have taken over. Zero was old and skinny, a shy, cowering beast who had lost most of his teeth, but in the Alaska tandem hitch used by Colombo, he seemed to work out acceptably. At least, he understood the commands. Finally, though, some of the men in camp decided Zero's time had come. Had I not been on duty at the weather station, I'd have tried to forestall what happened. They dragged Zero to the dump and ended his days with a shot through the heart. Then they propped up his frozen carcass to stand guard in grisly silence over the dump. Only the heavy wet snows of spring covered his wretched body and lent dignity to his passing. Eventually, with the coming of summer, he was eaten by the ravens.

20
Airplanes under the Ice

On an early sledge trip to the Ice Cap, Joe showed me the site of a massed forced landing of eight airplanes a few miles from Max Demorest's Ice Cap station. The landing had happened about a month before Demorest's station was erected and about a year before our arrival at Comanche Bay. By some accounts, this was the largest forced landing of World War II. Joe related the story as we lay in our sacks at bedtime on the ice; it was retold in the book *Lifelines through the Arctic* by William S. Carlson, ex-air force colonel, geology professor from Michigan, and old Greenland hand of the 1930s. At the time of my visit in the fall of 1943, the former Ice Cap station and all the aircraft were completely buried by snow, but the station and the tail sections had still been visible earlier in the summer when Joe visited the site with Captain Wade. On July 15, 1942, or July 17 according to some accounts, twenty-five men in two Boeing B-17 Flying Fortresses and six Lockheed P-38 Lightnings took off from BW-1 in fair weather bound for Keflavik, Iceland. Over the Ice Cap, according to Carlson, they got radio orders to go instead to BW-8 at Sondre Stromfjord because, they were told, bad weather had closed Keflavik Air Base. But when they neared Sondre Stromfjord, they were told it was now closed by weather, and they were ordered on to Iceland, which had opened again. According to Carlson's account they had been misled by false orders from a clandestine German radio station somewhere in northeast Greenland. Some reports suggest that the transmission came from a Nazi submarine or that radios were jammed by a submarine.

By this time, at any rate, the P-38s were low on fuel, and when one started a forced descent the rest of the flight elected to go down also. The first plane—wheels down—nosed over, but without serious injury to the pilot. The rest belly-landed without difficulty. Fortunately the weather was good, the planes were soon located, and all twenty-five men were led safely off the Ice Cap. They hiked out to Comanche Bay and were picked up by the coast guard.

This incident, and several more tragic ones, helped crystallize the idea that a weather/rescue station was needed at Comanche Bay, and work to that end soon began, led by our predecessors Captain Innes-Taylor and Lieutenant Demorest. Colonel Carlson organized the expedition but was reassigned before really getting started. Demorest had been one of Carlson's students at the University of Michigan. Joe had joined their group in September, 1942, before Demorest's death.

Another Arctic veteran, John W. Marr, a civilian botanist, also joined up but soon left. On contract to the army, John had located Comanche Bay as the site for future operations by carefully scanning trimetrogon aerial photographs of the southeast coast. Trimetrogon was a camera that took sets of left- and right-oblique and vertical frames simultaneously, thereby reconnoitering a great swath of country in one flight. Thirty years later in a remarkable coincidence, John and I met and exchanged stories. Subsequently he and I worked together for the U.S. Geological survey on some maps of the Denver metropolitan area in Colorado. In 1942 John had visited the B-17/P-38 crash site by motor toboggan and helped salvage radios and the like from the planes before they were buried under the snow. A Norden bombsight, a much ballyhooed but carefully guarded device of World War II, was removed from one of the B-17s by Maj. Norman D. Vaughan, who also had led the rescue of the flight crews.

In the early 1980s interest in the crash site was rekindled. World War II aircraft had become very rare, especially pursuit planes, and well-funded aviation enthusiasts were willing to go to great lengths to recover well-preserved specimens from the cold storage of the Cap. When word got out that I had been there during WWII, I began getting inquiries: What was the exact location? I really couldn't pinpoint it more closely than a few miles, largely because of a lack of landmarks and the planes having been buried at the time of my Ice Cap travels, but partly because I knew the ice had moved some undetermined distance in the forty years since then. In a mood of urgent rivalry, inquirers hoped to salvage eight mint-pure World War II aircraft preserved in the deep freeze, and they were put off by my vague and pessi-

Fig. 20–1.   P-38 Lightning and B-17 Flying Fortress (right rear) down
on the ice cap, July 15, 1942. Only the propellor of the P-38 is damaged.
Photo courtesy Greenland Expeditions Society.

mistic outlook. Being some 3,000 feet above the regional snowline in an area of heavy snowfall, I said, the planes should be
under a deep cover of hard, compact snow (or firn). I guessed
that 180 feet or more of burial was likely, and at that depth the
density of the snow should be close to that of ice. The annual
snowfall in that part of Greenland was around 700 inches, but as
it fell it settled to an annual accumulation of around 10 feet. In
forty years that would meant 400 feet, or about the same amount
as the height of a thirty-story building, except that the snow
would continue to settle under its own weight as it accumulated
down through the years.

The gradual compaction of the snow through the years should
have squashed the planes themselves, closing all voids and flat-
tening them like pancakes. They wouldn't be something you
could just fill with gasoline and fly off the Ice Cap. I also cautioned about the bad flying weather, the summer blizzards on
the Ice Cap, and the related problems of keeping a deep excava-
tion open on the Cap at such times. All the urgency about salvaging made me wonder if the planes carried gold bars and uncut
diamonds instead of chocolate bars and nylon stockings, but despite my caveats, competing plans went ahead to the extent of
getting salvage permits from the Danish government and pub-
lishing press releases in newspapers across the country.

Airborne magnetometers were considered early on for finding
the buried airplanes. Then one salvage operator reportedly lo-

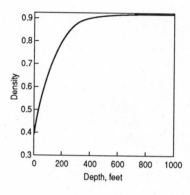
Fig. 20-2. Graph showing snow depth vs. density: snow to glacial ice.

cated them with airborne radar, which easily penetrates snow or ice. They were under forty feet of snow, he said, which is only about the height of a telephone pole. I was astounded. Later unconfirmed but seemingly more reliable scuttlebutt said the depth of burial was about sixty meters, or about two hundred feet. At that depth, as much as eight-tenths of the total compaction from snow to ice should have taken place, as you can see from the accompanying graph.

The curve in this graph was first plotted by Chester G. Langway, Jr., of the Army Cold Regions Laboratory, from measurements he had made of ice core taken in Greenland in the 1950s. The shape of the curve depends partly on the temperature and surface conditions at the times of snow accumulation, but the chief factor is simply compaction or "load metamorphism," in glaciologic lingo. Technically, after its first year of metamorphism, the snow is called firn. At a depth of about two hundred feet, more than eighty percent of the compaction had taken place at Langway's drill site, the pore spaces between ice grains had ceased to interconnect, and the firn had by definition become glacial ice. If those conditions held for the airplane crash site, the planes after forty years of burial would be encased in solid glacial ice under an overburden pressure of about five or six tons per square foot.

In the summer of 1990, in a marvel of technological sleuthing, searchers organized as the Greenland Expedition Society and headquartered at Epps Air Service in Atlanta, Georgia, precisely pinned down the site after a decade of searching. Using ice-penetrating radar and heated snowmelting probes, they located

142

a B-17 at a depth of 250 feet. From newspaper accounts I learned their address, and after a hurried phone call I received a bundle of informative letters and file material. From a five-foot diameter vertical shaft, they had extended a large ice chamber part way around the bomber and were already bringing relics and artifacts to the surface. Unfortunately, but not surprisingly, the plane was damaged beyond repair by the weight and flowage of the ice. The plane was slowly being pulled apart, and the roof of the cockpit was flattened clear down against the floor. In the words of Richard L. Taylor, coleader of the discovery group, "The control yokes, throttle quadrant, and seatbacks projected absurdly up through the thin aluminum skin." Although dreams of flying mint-pure aircraft off the Ice Cap thus quickly vanished, the story was not yet ended.

Shaken but undaunted, earnestly seeking more funding, the Greenland Expedition Society decided to probe for the six P-38s, hopeful that the smaller, more robust fighters would be less damaged than the thinner-skinned bomber. They were right. In the summer of 1992 the society returned to the Ice Cap with improved, newly designed hot-drilling equipment. Penetrating 257 feet of firn and ice, the team uncovered, dismantled, and retrieved a surprisingly well preserved, fifty-year-old P-38. Pat Epps, society president, believes the plane can be rebuilt, and he hopes to restore it to flyable condition. In early 1993 the plane was at Middlesboro, Kentucky, being disassembled, repaired and reconditioned piece by piece, and reassembled. (Of nearly ten thousand P-38s built in WWII, only five are known to be still flyable.)

Meanwhile, the society is scouring the countryside for more funding to pay outstanding obligations and to retrieve the remaining fighter planes. Success comes only to those who try, and one can but urge on and applaud their efforts. Set down over a wide area, the planes would all require separate excavations into an increasingly thick overburden of ice.

Any unrecovered aircraft will eventually emerge on their own, perhaps in about two hundred years. Although the annual accumulation of hard ice is about five feet, and the overburden pressure on each plane increases proportionately with depth, the slow but relentless flowage of ice—about one hundred to two hundred feet per year—will eventually carry them to the marginal zone of the glacier somewhere west of Grahs Øer (see map

3-1), where the loss of ice to summer melting exceeds the increment of new snow. There the planes will emerge, if somewhat
the worse for wear, either at the desolate border of the Ice Cap,
or from icebergs calving unseen into the cold waters off Greenland's rugged coast. But I'm betting on the Greenland Expedition
Society to get them first.

21

Communication with the Outside World

By late spring of 1944 the weather in Greenland had improved enough for the army to make fairly frequent air drops at the outposts along the southeast coast. These missions were flown by visual flight rules. Instrument flight was rather primitive in those days, especially in the Arctic, and air drops couldn't be made by instruments anyway. A flight normally took off from BW-1 at Narsarssuak and made a pass over each camp en route to BE-2 at Ikateq, a flight distance of about six hundred miles. Ordinarily an attempt was made about once a month. Mail and other packages were viewed as important morale builders, and the army took their delivery seriously, but we were demoralized more than once when local bad weather kept the planes out or pilots couldn't find us, despite ground-to-air radio contact.

Occasionally an aircraft circled within three or four miles without completing its drop because it lacked the time or extra fuel to search us out. Such a time might be when the weather was deteriorating and the pilot had to head on to Ikateq before the landing strip socked in. Two days before Thanksgiving in 1943, a drop was aborted by bad weather even though we could see the aircraft circling above. We weren't easily seen from the air: all our buildings were buried in the snow. But after our location was pegged down, pilots would sometimes come in low without warning like a strafing mission, almost buzzing the rooftops without even making radio contact. They'd drop off a few parcels, thoroughly scare the dogs, and be gone, as the startled animals—yelping and jumping, jerked wildly at their chains, some even defecating in the air. We'd rush outside in time to see the aircraft banking away in the distance, then we'd spend the next hour playing hide and seek in the snow, searching out packages. Deliveries were nearly always freefall, so if no one was outside at drop time, we could only look for the telltale craters in the snow. We had no real idea whether or not we had found everything they had dropped.

When fast food-freezing techniques were developed late in the war, the army began dropping frozen meat. By June of 1944, we hadn't eaten fresh meat for nine months except once in November when a cutter made a call at Comanche Bay, and at Christmas when the army dropped a fresh turkey. The meat drops were easy to find, because the loose dogs in camp quickly scented them out and chewed the corners off the cardboard cartons before we could chase them off.

Once we urgently needed a differential for a T-15 snowmobile—the T-15 was a lemon when it came to differentials. To steer it you used two handbrakes, one for each track, like a bulldozer, and the strain of turning was often too much for the differential. To turn, you pulled back on one of the brakes, locking the track underneath and transmitting the power of the engine to the other track through the differential. By priority prearrangement, the new differential was parachuted out on Apuseq Glacier, where the unbroken expanse of snow was far from any rocks. The parachute opened in a beautiful burst of red cloth, but the sudden jerk snapped the guy ropes, and the crated differential plummeted to the snow from a height of several hundred feet. Though buried six feet down, the crate wasn't too hard to find, but when we towed it out behind another snowmobile, we learned that the differential had continued down an additional six feet below the shattered crate. The whole gang spent the rest of the day digging it out.

Another airdrop was a smashing success. A loose package of phonograph records thoughtfully sent by the Red Cross just missed the mess hall and landed freefall on the rocks. Loosely packaged phonograph records landing freefall on any surface aren't apt to survive without serious deformation. Even soft snow is a bit too hard. Third prize was for two bushels of Idaho spuds wrapped in chicken wire. Try to imagine their condition after impact. And we hadn't tasted fresh potatoes for ten months. We had no doubt about the sincerity and good intentions of our delivery people, but they little realized how hard a surface could be that looked so soft aloft.

Our delivering angel at first was an army C-45 Beechcraft code-named *Giggle Peter*, a hot little two-engine aircraft piloted

Fig. 21–1. Parachute drop at base camp, Comanche Bay, Greenland. Mess hall hatchway is just to left of men on ground. Note chimney of the buried building at far left. Airplane is barely visible as speck below and to right of parachute.

by the good Captain Shiffrin. Heavy items like differentials were dropped by a C-47. Later on, all deliveries were taken over by a navy PBY patrol bomber that came over low enough for us to see the grins on the faces of the crew as we dove for cover and the dogs yanked at their chains. One of the men on board was Sergeant Bisson.

Besides those shattered phonograph records, the Red Cross once sent a bunch of dog-eared magazines that must have been salvaged from an NCO club, because all the pinup pictures had been cut out. We enjoyed the magazines even so, having had no "current" reading material for several months, but we were dismayed by one particular magazine essay by a famous travel correspondent named John Gunther, who had authored several best-selling books about conditions inside one country or another around the world. Here he described his stopover at Ascension Island, a volcanic mount rising from the submerged Mid-Atlantic Ridge halfway between Natal, Brazil and Dakar, French West Africa. Ascension, he noted, was a key ferry stop en route to the European theater, and many big transport planes and bombers stopped there every day on their way from the United

States, the "Arsenal of Democracy," to Europe and Africa. The several thousand men stationed at Ascension to guard the airfields and service the aircraft were rewarded with such cultural amenities as USO clubs, PXs, bowling alleys, athletic fields, restaurants, swimming pools, and movie theaters showing the latest releases from Hollywood. The brass didn't want any morale problems. Three or four times monthly, bevies of ravishingly beautiful young Hollywood starlets stopped off to entertain the troops.

Meanwhile, awestricken by the unspeakable hardships of the place, our travel correspondent went on to describe Ascension as "the most isolated outpost in which our men are called upon to serve." We of course took umbrage, all nineteen of us–but we were frustrated by the irony of our situation, by our inability to communicate a protest to either the author or the publisher. We had sent out no mail for six months, and we had no prospect of sending any out in the foreseeable future. Incoming mail from home usually came with each airdrop, a month or two apart, but we had no way of answering it. Our best hope was a chance call by a passing surface vessel, ice conditions permitting.

Our real communication with the outside world was the shortwave radio, and we had a strong receiver in the barracks. We listened regularly to Radio Berlin, which featured the dulcet voice of Berlin Midge, whose honey-dripping commentary could arouse passion in a cigarstore Indian, let alone spark the ardor of all the heroes of the Base Ice Cap Detachment. I don't recall ever hearing the infamous Axis Sally–maybe we weren't tuned in on her wavelength–but Midge suited us just fine. We also listened to Radio London, featuring another female voice, though not of Midge's class; the unfamiliar British accent sounded more prim than sexy to our unsophisticated American ears, unattuned to the crisp sensuality of the female British voice.

Radio Schenectady was the real source of all our solid news. Schenectady had a powerful radio transmitter that always came in loud and clear. Several times daily it broadcast a test signal cast indelibly for some reason into my memory, like my army serial number: "Magnetism is a property of the atom. We affirm that iron, nickel, gadolinium, gaseous oxygen, and in fact all substances are magnetic because they have magnetism in their atoms." Then Schenectady went on with the news. Schenectady broadcast in several languages, and Johan Johansen understood and listened to them all. The rest of us preferred Midge and were just a little irritated by Joe's insistence on hearing out everything repeated in English, German, Norwegian, Danish, and French, though we all were gripped by the news of the titanic struggle then culminating in Europe. With the landings in Normandy on D-day, June 6, 1944, the ultimate outcome no longer was in doubt.

To us, however, the most electrifying news came during a seventy-mile-per-hour blizzard on Christmas day in 1943, when the great German battle cruiser *Scharnhorst* eluded British patrols and slipped from hiding in a Norwegian fjord. A battle cruiser was a cross between a cruiser and a battleship–bigger than a cruiser and with the guns of a battleship, but not as heavily armor-plated as a battleship and hence more maneuverable and faster in the water. This vessel, its sister ship *Gneisenau,* the battleship *Tirpitz,* and the superbattleship *Bismarck* all had previously wreaked havoc with merchant convoys in the North Atlantic, and news of its escape aroused consternation on both sides of the ocean. All East Greenland outposts were ordered on full alert, including radio silence and nighttime blackouts all day long. Resolutely, we gripped our carbines; we really were at war. Up at the weather shack, Homer "By God" Loar, whose hearing surpassed anyone else's in camp, heard submarines charging their (goddamn) batteries down in the fjord, and he half-coherently relayed the word down to camp, but we suspected his audial acuity was merely responding to ice pans grinding rhythmically in the ground swells near the shore.

A little reflection disclosed our desperate plight: here was one of the most feared vessels on Earth, lurking in the vastness of the North Atlantic Ocean, headed no doubt for southeast Greenland for one last shot at the most lucrative possible target of opportunity to glorify forever the Fuhrer and the Third Reich. Could our station be that target? Here were we, a snowbound outpost buried behind a hill facing the Ice Cap, invisible from the ocean, beleaguered by a blizzard, with seventy miles of solid pack ice between ourselves and open water, and so well hidden that friendly aircraft in radio contact had trouble finding us with our lights on. What a target! But even if we were plainly visible to the battle cruiser's guns, we reasoned, wouldn't a determined Nazi skipper pass us over reluctantly for an easier and possibly even more rewarding target like a convoy of fat cargo ships bound for Murmansk? Or would he carefully maneuver through the ice to bombard Atterbury Dome in one last desperate try for the iron cross? Logic aside, we could not question orders, and we obediently celebrated Christmas in the dark. Meanwhile, up at Ikateq, obedient airfield guards unlimbered frozen weapons that were too stiff to fire. Then the proud *Scharnhorst* was spotted by a squadron of Allied warships, cornered, and ignominiously sunk, and our test of strength was past. Half elated and half disappointed, we went back to the business of watching the weather and shoveling snow.

The *Scharnhorst*, in fact, never even remotely approached Greenland in its brief foray, despite our fantasies about a possible engagement. Its closest approach was at least seven hundred miles from the nearest point of Greenland and more than twice that distance from Comanche Bay. It steamed out of Alta Fjord in northern Norway late in the afternoon of Christmas day (early morning, our time), intent on mauling an Archangel-bound convoy halfway between Norway and Svalbard (Spitzbergen). Instead it encountered a British-led escort fleet of eighteen destroyers and four cruisers led by the battleship *York*. Though the *Scharnhorst* tried to break off the action, it was tracked down by radar and took four torpedos plus many hits from the heavy Allied guns. Before the day was out it sank with a loss of 1,934 lives.

22
Gearing Up for the Far North

By today's standards our trail gear was primitive, but for its time it was the best available. Eider down was used in the best sleeping bags but most of the better quality fillings were goose down, and we had some very good, heavy-duty trail sacks filled with wool. We slept in sacks in the barracks as well as on the trail and for fourteen months never saw a bed with sheets and blankets. I used a rolled-up parka for a pillow. Down parkas hadn't yet arrived on the scene. Quilted parkas didn't exist either; we learned about them from the Chinese during Harry Truman's "police action" in Korea. Threads like polyester hadn't yet been invented. Nylon was brand new and was just starting to make its way into the clothing market. Most of its production was allocated to parachutes, but large quantities went to the nylon stockings requisitioned by air force pilots for distribution to their female clients overseas. We did have two big bolts of red nylon cloth that we cut into marker flags for trail use on the Ice Cap.

For comfort and warmth, then as now, layered clothing was the key. Some special gear touted as top-of-the-line was largely ignored by most us in favor of more conventional cold-weather duds. Each man had an amply proportioned "zoot suit," purportedly adequate for sleeping outdoors in weather below zero, but no one ever tried it. It had a two-piece outer windproof shell, pants and anorak, with draw strings like clothesline rope for easy tying while wearing mittens. The shell was worn over two loose-fitting double liners, inner and outer pants and tops, made for "alpaca" (actually a synthetic fabric that resembled deep-pile carpeting). The outer liner was somewhat bristly, but the inner one was soft and comfortable. Nobody ever wore the full zoot suit indoors or out except to pose for a portrait, but the underlayers made satisfactory lounge clothes in the chilly environment of the barracks. The tops had cowls like a monk's hood, and Bill Cadigan wore his indoors much of the time, looking like a mendicant friar in an Irish monastery. Doc Johnson wore his a lot too, and so did Max Morris, but I preferred a turtleneck sweater.

After the war, zoot suit liners appeared in army surplus stores, decorated with brightly colored piping sewn along the seams to give them a touch of chic, and they became fashionable *après-ski* wear among the trendy younger ski set. Military gear at the end of the war was surplused en masse by the War Assets Administration at ridiculously low prices, and the surplus stores made obscene profits on its resale. The customer, of course, did well too. Only the taxpayer suffered. Surplus down sleeping bags were sold in Sioux Falls, South Dakota, for five dollars each, and even in those times, that was cheap, but the seller got them in bulk quantity from the WAA for much less. In the snow belt from Lake Tahoe to Boston, the market was flooded with surplus skis, boots, and parkas, all dirt cheap.

Foot gear for the zoot suit was a pair of bulky suede-and-canvas mukluks intended for wear over wool socks and gunnysack liners. The mukluks, however, lacked ankle and arch support, lacked traction on hard snow (your feet would go out from under you with the least misstep), and weren't waterproof in wet snow. They couldn't be worn with skis or snowshoes but probably would have been OK for motor tobogganing. Our standard foot gear for all-the-time wear was the leather-topped, rubber-footed, Canadian shoe pac, still popular among duck hunters and the outdoorsy set and still sold in sporting-goods stores throughout the snow belt. These boots haven't changed significantly in fifty years, although new lowcut versions are now in demand in wintertime suburbia. We wore our pacs over two pairs of wool socks (light and heavy) plus felt innersoles. I substituted cotton GI socks for the light wool ones most of the time, except on the Ice Cap, and never got cold feet.

Captain Innes-Taylor, whose wisdom was far reaching, had thrown in a lot of extra items, some from L. L. Bean and some from Abercrombie and Fitch, including elkhide moccasins, Swiss alpenstocks, and hand-forged crampons. Barry Borden got a pair of Swiss-made downhill skis. Innes-Taylor ordered non-GI cold-weather clothing as might be worn in the north woods, such as red, blue, and gray checkered Woolrich and Pendleton shirts. With a mixture of bravura and pride, we were the only outfit in the U.S. Army authorized to wear them, and they caused quite a stir around the air bases at Bluie West-1 and Bluie East-2. "Whose army are you guys with?" asked a laid-back lieutenant at Ikateq, with a twinkle in his eye. He must have been the chaplain. We also wore water-repellent, wind-resistant duck-cloth pants lined with wool flannel. Those items were GI. The whole ensemble was worn over heavy fleece underwear and beneath a double whipcord fur-trimmed parka, and thus clad, I don't recall ever being cold. For a hat I usually wore a knit wool GI helmet liner under the hood of my parka. Some men wore sheepskin flight helmets; I gave mine to a smiling native child. We also had big wolverine-trimmed fur mittens that everyone brought home as souvenirs of the war, though we seldom wore them in Greenland. They were intended for trail use, but instead we usually wore wool-lined, canvas-backed leather ski mittens that were adequate for summertime on the Ice Cap and were much more practical than the fur mitts.

For skiing, I had archaic, square-toed, laced, leather boots that were eminently suitable for crosscountry and downhill skiing. Virtually the same boots were standard equipment in most pre-war ski resorts of the late 1930s and early 1940s. Nowadays, wearing the bone-crushing plastic ski boots of today, I sometimes long for those happy days. We also had some less satisfactory ski-mountaineering boots with cleated rubber soles too thick and too stiff for the available ski bindings. They were forerunners, perhaps, of the costly but ungainly climbing boots students were wearing in the 1970s on college campuses and around Aspen. Some of us tried them around the camp but not on the trail. Ski poles also were a bit ungainly by today's standards, made mostly of bamboo (or of laminated, glued bamboo) or of thin steel tubing, with rattan-and-leather rings. They were shorter than today's ski poles—about waist high and adapted to the deep crouch affected by skiers in those days.

Our wool socks were top quality and must have been worth a lot of money. Each man had ten, repeat ten, pairs. The secret of warm, healthy feet was keeping the socks clean and dry. Similar rules applied to underwear, but some of the hands figured they could beat the system by rationing their clothes through the year and thereby never having to wash any. After about a month's wear, they'd stash the dirties into a barracks bag and break out a replacement. When the supply of clean new clothes inevitably ran out, the idea was to empty the bag on the floor and pick out what appeared to be the least soiled, then rotate the most recently worn duds into the bag. This strategy would work for eternity. Rather amusing, but in extreme weather on the trail it could mean severe frostbite, and around the barracks it could mean alienating your roommates. In the narrow confines of the weather shack it wasn't amusing at all. The socks of one unnamed weatherman from Georgia had the smell of death, and while he slept, Max Morris and I unceremoniously burned them behind the building.

Early in the spring of 1943, when we picked up our Arctic gear down in Boston, we were surprised to receive complete nor'easter rainsuits–the Captains Courageous type, affected by the fisherman of Gloucester. Appalled, I explained that we were going to an undisclosed destination in the polar regions where we would encounter only blizzards. Rain? Yes, Greenland gets rain in the summertime, and southeast Greenland gets a lot of it. You can expect rain at sea level from mid-June to mid-August. Heavy downpours, sometimes lasting for days, drop from gloomy stratus overcasts, often under driving northeast gales. On the wet eastern slope of the Ice Cap, you can expect snow and blizzards all year around, at least at altitudes above about fifteen hundred feet, though rain on the eastern slope isn't unheard of in late July or early August as high as three or four thousand feet. But if a storm starts out as rain above about fifteen hundred feet, it usually soon turns to snow.

We also were surprised but delighted to receive heavy felt Nelson Eddy campaign hats–the Smoky Bear type–with the blue-and-gold piping of the Army Air Corps. I still have mine after half a century. At the time we were puzzled as to why we were issued campaign hats, but later learned that the wide brims were ideal props for mosquito netting, which was sorely needed around the weather station for about two weeks near the first of August, when countless mossy pools warmed by the Arctic sun nurtured swarms of frantic mosquitoes.

Being a light sleeper, I found rest increasingly elusive in the bustle and congestion of the weather shack under the constant daylight of the approaching summer. By early June, the ferocious storms of winter had passed, and with Barry Borden's blessings, I hauled up a trail tent from the warehouse and set it in the snow a few yards from the shack, where I had a nice view of the fjord.

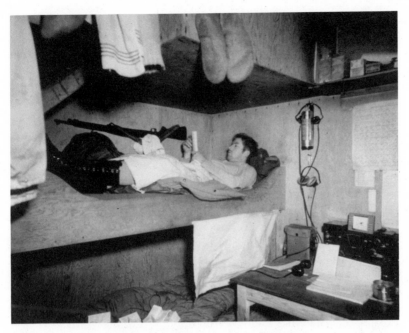

Fig. 22–1. Howard Sullivan sacked out at the weather station. The bottom bunk was reserved for daytime sleeping for the weatherman getting off night shift. At lower right is the work desk.

Borden understood–he was a private sort of person himself. When I got off shift at midnight I crawled into my tent, read a book or old magazine for half an hour or so in the light of the sky, then pulled my sack up over my head and dropped off to sleep. The snow by now was melting fast, and in due time I found my tent perched on an insulated snowy platform (insulated by the tent itself) surrounded by muskeg.

Our two-man nylon trail tent was the best then available though far inferior to the excellent mountain tents on today's market. It was shaped like an A-frame, similar to a boy-scout pup tent, but with a sewn-in floor and thin bamboo wands slipped into sleeves at the corners for support. It was grommeted down with nylon ropes front to back, side to side, and corner to corner, with aluminum pins for anchorage into the snow. We had two models, winter and summer, both designed for rigorous duty in the Arctic. My summer tent at Atterbury Dome was fitted with mosquito netting and was treated with water repellent, hence lacked the great ripping strength of the winter tent, but it stood up well even so in a stiff wind. I had no trouble with forty-five or fifty miles per hour. On the Ice Cap, just for assurance, we dug out tent platforms a couple of feet down into the snow surface, then piled snow blocks around the windward side to lessen the onslaught. We had only one blowdown, and that was after a hard, battering piteraq ripped out the supporting bamboo wands. Our shouts could hardly be heard above the roar and flapping of the fabric.

Our tent was sleeve vented for fresh air at the gable opposite the entry. Otherwise, the tent was nearly airtight when the entry was shut, and because we burned gasoline for fuel, good ventilation was a needed precaution against asphyxiation. The entry was a tubelike extension just big enough to crawl through but also big enough for you to whisk the snow off your clothes and shoes before crawling the rest of the way into the living area. Every trail party carried a whiskbroom for just that purpose. Once inside, you could pucker the entry shut with a pull of a drawstring—which was why our tent, in a quartermaster's vulgarism, was dubbed "Tent, mountain, winter, 2-man, nylon, with asshole-type entry."

Our dogsleds were called Nansen sleds after the eminent Norwegian explorer, scientist, and statesman who had designed them many years before. They came unassembled in precut hardwood, and we laced them together with rawhide. The lacing gave greater flexibility over a rough snow surface than would have been possible with a more rigid, bolted metal frame. Sleds need to bend, and flexibility forestalls breakage. Johan Johansen made his own fan-hitch dog harnesses. Tony Colombo's tandem-hitch harnesses were government issue. For dead-reckoning navigation we towed a bicycle wheel rigged with a simple odometer that read to tenths of a mile.

Rations at base camp were gourmet compared to what we ate on the trail. We traveled light, especially by dog team, and our bill of fare reflected our concern for low weight and high energy yield. Dog food was our main cargo, so our own food and payload couldn't be very heavy. We ate mostly canned link sausages, sea biscuits, coffee, and "pemmican," which was a rather nourishing concoction of raisins, rice, coconut oil, and other unspecified ingredients. (The original pemmican of the American Indians was a mixture of suet and wild berries, sometimes with a pinch of pulverized dried meat.) I usually stocked up on the hard, bland, GI chocolate D bars, made from an insipid blend of bittersweet chocolate and ground cereal. I thought they were quite palatable and enjoyed munching them on the trail, but Joe refused to try. We carried a few cans of stew from the C ration, and we drank a lot of refreshing lemonade made from a packaged powder and snowmelt. (Unlike the nourishing but not-tasty K ration, hermetically sealed in waxed cardboard and intended for emergency use, the C ration contained a selection of canned goods comparable to those stocked in a modern grocery store.) Our only source of external cooking heat was the primus stove.

✳

23

The Whiteout and Other Arcane Arctic Phenomena

Nearly everyone has heard about the Arctic or polar whiteout, but few people really know what it is or can imagine what it truly is like, and even fewer people have experienced it. It comes in several forms, and its causes are varied, but its main effect on a person is disorientation and loss of visual perspective, and at times even a feeling of vertigo. Weird side effects include hallucinations, or at least strange illusory images. Whiteouts can be caused by heavy snowfall, blizzards, fog, and milky overcasts–by anything that scatters the incoming light, reflects it back and forth from ground to sky, and eliminates all shadows. The horizon disappears and the ground merges with the sky. If you cast a shadow or can see the ground, you don't have a whiteout. The ground, therefore, must be covered with snow. If rocks, buildings, or other objects intrude, the effect is dispelled, so most of our whiteouts were confined to the Ice Cap.

Snowfall, ground blizzards, and fogs all can cause whiteouts by restricting visibility, in extreme cases to virtually zero, and eliminating your perception of the ground underfoot. We had Greenland fogs that reduced visibility to twenty or thirty feet–on occasion for several days–and blizzards that reduced it to ten. Under nighttime darkness a severe blizzard might cut it to five or six feet. A flashlight beam carries just a few feet. Driving snow heightens the confusing effect by stinging your face and blocking your vision. The buffeting wind upsets your balance and may force you to your hands and knees, all in a featureless white vacuum.

Johan Johansen and I were once caught on the ice cap in a whiteout caused by ice fog. Most fogs are made from trillions of microscopic droplets of water, droplets that may be supercooled to temperatures of only twenty to thirty degrees Fahrenheit but remain liquid nonetheless. Microscopic water droplets resist freezing. Ice fog, though, is made of tiny ice crystals suspended in the air by their own near weightlessness. They in effect are cirrus clouds down on the ground, and they form only at appropriately low temperatures. Because they consist of solid crystals rather than liquid droplets, ice fogs have unique optical properties unlike other fogs. Cirrostratus overcasts–the thin, veil clouds high enough and cold enough to consist of ice crystals–cause the solar and lunar halos and the sun dogs on the arms of the halo that you occasionally see at any latitude and often see in the Arctic. Ice fogs are close kin. Our ice fog moved in on a very light breeze. The ice simply sublimated out of the moist air, chilled by the frigidity of the Ice Cap. It formed a ground fog perhaps twenty feet deep–not deep enough or dense enough to completely halt the penetration of sunlight, but enough to drastically reduce visibility and cause a total whiteout. The ground underfoot and the horizon just disappeared. Each tiny crystal individually refracted and scattered the light and in aggregate they caused unusual optical effects. Standing objects such as bamboo trail wands, ski poles, dogs, and people were backlighted by ethereal, halo-like auras, fading into the fog and looking a bit like St. Elmo's fire, but a phenomenon I haven't seen described in the literature. Eyebrows, whiskers, parka-hood fringes, and dog fur were quickly flocked with frost. The fog itself had a pearly luminosity that conveyed a sense of unreality. We weren't alarmed and had no reason to be, but we decided that further travel would be fruitless and it was time to make camp.

Possibly the strangest whiteout of all is caused by a milky overcast, the old buttermilk sky of Hoagy Carmichael. To some purists, this is the only true whiteout. Seasoned Antarctic travelers call it "white day." Buttermilk skies are usually made from thin altostratus (high stratus) overcasts–thick enough, though, to prevent the sun from casting a shadow. Altostratus is mainly a liquid-water-droplet cloud. The light scattered through the overcast removes all contrast from the snow-covered landscape, and if the sun is visible at all, it is but a pale white disc. Tracks and hummocks, even crevasses, all disappear from view. Horizontal visibility, though, can be unlimited, so that mountains forty miles away appear as gray charcoal drawings on a flat gray backdrop: gray on gray. Up on the Ice Cap, all reference points are lost in the dull light, the lack of perspective tricks the mind, and your sense of distance falters.

With our team of dogs, Joe and I were headed west, and we were puzzled by an unfamiliar nunatak far ahead. We were following a rutted snowmobile track that I couldn't see but could feel underfoot by keeping one ski in the rut. I was skiing ahead of the dogs to urge them on. Then suddenly the "nunatak" drew alongside and turned into a crumpled black paper cover from a film pack, dropped earlier along the trail by camp photographer Doc Johnson. When we first sighted our "nunatak" it was really just a hundred feet or so away. A bit farther along the trail, seat-of-the-pants navigation indicated that we were nearing the weather party camped thirty-five miles inland, and we strained our eyes anxiously for a first glimpse. Headed west, we didn't want to overshoot our objective, because our westerly bearing would eventually take us into a dangerously crevassed area reaching tens of miles into the Ice Cap from the head of Kjoge Bay. Mind you, we could see Anikitsok fifty or sixty miles to our left, but we couldn't see the ground we were standing on.

Traveling now on a dead-reckoned compass bearing, we finally sighted a tent not more than a quarter-mile ahead, and the dogs quickened their pace. They were as anxious to reach camp as we were. Joe spotted Don Galbreath circling the tent, as if to take a leak, and I confirmed his observation, but imagine our surprise when the tent turned into a bent-over trail flag not a hundred yards away. Galbreath simply vanished without explanation, but what really surprised us was that the dogs were fooled too. They clearly thought we were coming into camp, and they sped on at a fast trot anticipating a meal and rest.

Other effects of the polar whiteout are equally puzzling and no less disconcerting. The high surface of the Ice Cap is like a frozen sea, and on a bright sunny day the illusion is complete. Under the intensely dark blue sky, the Cap itself is as blue as the bounding main, and although the horizon is flat as a billiard table, the brilliant surface itself rolls along in detail like a Grant Wood Iowa landscape, or like a whole train of frozen ground swells. These swells might be fifty to a hundred feet high and a quarter-mile across from top to top. Toward the crest of the Ice Cap each one is a little higher than the one behind it, and the dogs strain hard on the uphill sides but coast along easily on the downslopes. In greater detail, the entire surface is broken into choppy frozen waves–*sastrugi*–a few inches to a foot or two high and three feet to several yards long. Generally, they are about a foot and a half wide.

Sastrugi is a Siberian word for the rough surface texture of a snowfield, drifted into washboardlike ridges and eroded by the wind—comparable in some ways to the sand dunes of a desert or the choppy waves of a wind-lashed sea. If the weather is cold, dry, and windy, the sastrugi may be hard as pavement and rough as sandpaper. Usually they have a blunt or overhanging leading edge, like a breaker on a beach, but facing toward the wind, and a long tail tapering downwind. Similar forms sculptured out of rock by the desert winds of Egypt are called yardangs. It struck me as interesting that two such utterly different sets of climatic conditions could lead to similar landforms; aside from their contours, the one thing they had in common was the wind that shaped them.

Sastrugi can make travel by dog team arduous and by snowmobile hazardous. Tracked vehicles may tip over, throw their tracks, or break a spring (though the oversnow vehicles of today are obviously sturdier and more stable than the antiques of World War II). In a whiteout invisible sastrugi can flip a dogsled or dump an unwary skier on belly or backside. I've stepped unwittingly off the end of one and fallen flat on my face. Few men of our group hadn't done the same.

Another weird illusory effect of the whiteout is the sensation of skiing along the bottom of a narrow ravine, or on the top of a narrow ridge, when you know perfectly well that the ground is flat. Though at a loss to explain its reason, I experienced it many times on the Ice Cap. Possibly it relates to refraction of the dim light passing through the chilled air; one such effect, well known elsewhere, is a kind of mirage called looming.

High veils of cirrostratus clouds sometimes cause whiteouts, too, though they seldom are thick enough to eliminate ground shadows completely, because they never fully obscure the sun. But they do cause brilliant solar and lunar halos, false suns, and sun dogs. These phenomena seem to be more common in the Arctic than in more temperate regions, where cirrostratus clouds are less common. Along the Front Range Corridor of Colorado, where I now live, cirrostratus and its optical effects are very rare. On the other hand, Greenland seldom sees the billowy, cotton-puff cumulus clouds of the Front Range or of other more temperate realms. We saw them occasionally far out to sea, but we never saw them over the land or the Ice Cap.

Cirrostratus was a reliable storm precursor in southeast Greenland. Its presence generally gave two or three days' notice that a storm was in the offing. The pattern was almost classic. Spectacular cometlike mare's tails or fishhook clouds first streamed across the sky. These gradually merged into a luminous veil of cirrostratus, which then thickened and lowered into altostratus, then into dark gray nimbostratus. Here the whiteout took over as the snowflakes began to fall and the wind began to rise. At this point the whiteout was full blown, and anyone on the trail could expect to experience the effects just described.

Optical illusions, though, are not restricted to times of whiteouts. Because the chilled air over the Ice Cap is coldest just above the surface of the ice, where thermal radiation is the most intense, the density of the air is much greater near the surface than aloft. Light rays accordingly are refracted or bent as they pass through the near-surface layer of air. (Any change in the density of a translucent medium refracts the passage of light.) The bent light path gives visibility to objects that actually are below the horizon; it causes the coastal mountains to loom above the curved marginal slope of the Ice Cap. This effect is just the opposite of the familiar heat mirage that travelers see on highways in summertime when light bent down from the sky looks like pools of water on the heated pavement or when weary travelers think they see a lake in the desert.

Some investigators suspect that the Vikings of Iceland first spotted the coastal mountains of Greenland from far out to sea, beyond the range of normal visibility, during a looming mirage. The effect would be intensified by the chilling of warm air over the cold waters of the East Greenland Current (though that condition probably would also cause fog). More likely, the air between the two islands was chilled by a heavy icepack. In any event, the highest mountains in Greenland are just opposite Iceland, across the Denmark Strait, and their visibility would be reinforced by looming.

Up on the Ice Cap, the refraction is most effective when the air is still: any wind stirring up the surface layer destroys the mirage. Strong clear-weather windstorms, though, have their own bag of refractive tricks. These effects are seen mostly in summer, when the air is not full of driving snow. The intense gustiness causes fast-changing refractions as the turbulent air, perhaps thousands of feet thick, breaks into countless thin layers of rapidly varying density. The gustiness also causes rapid pressure changes, especially in small buildings. Inside the weather

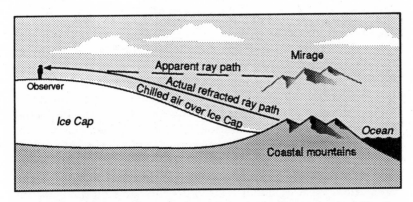

Fig. 23-1. Explanation for the looming mirage. Atmospheric refraction in the chilled, near-surface air enables an observer on the Ice Cap to see coastal mountains that actually are below the horizon.

station at Atterbury Dome, the stylus at such times made an inky smear on the barograph drum, and outside the station, the far side of the fjord became a wavy blur, vibrating in and out of focus as one stared in disbelief, braced against the wind and hammered by the gusts. "Min Gud!" cried Johan Johansen. "By the yumpin' Yesus!"

As the clear-air gale started to wane and die out, we sometimes saw arrays of whirlwinds near the margin of the Ice Cap, some of them hundreds of feet high like the big dust devils of the Desert Southwest. Ours of course were filled with snow, and we could watch their approach from Atterbury Dome. When they got close to the station, we'd dash for cover just as they jarred the building with seventy-mile-per-hour gusts. The barograph would go crazy, and we'd give thanks to the steel cables guyed across the roof.

The Snowquake

Another improbable but distressing phenomenon, the snow-quake, is occasionally reported by glacier travelers. Though far from being an illusion, and especially frightening during a whiteout, it is not at all dangerous. I first heard about it from Wade and finally experienced it up on the Ice Cap. Without warning, the snow suddenly gives way beneath your feet, like a trap door, accompanied by a barely audible whoof. Just a few square feet may fall, or perhaps an acre, and although it seldom drops more than a few inches, the effect is always the same: instant terror, as the heart leaps to the throat. Well up on the Ice Cap there is little danger of crevasses, except within the drainage lines of the big outlet glaciers, which we studiously avoided, but the thought of crevasses lingers in the back of the mind anyway, and it flashes into consciousness in the instant of the quake, along with a great rush of adrenaline. Grown men at such times have been known to lose control of bodily functions.

Snowquakes are caused by the same conditions that foster avalanches, but on flat ground instead of steep mountain slopes. Newly fallen snow has fairly high cohesion, whether in Greenland, Antarctica, Vermont, Norway, Utah, or Colorado. As the snow accumulates, all the little random six-pointed flakes tend to interlock in a stable configuration that stands high on a fencepost, clings to a telephone wire, or creeps down the hood of a car. But when a heavy snowstorm is followed by prolonged bitter cold, the flakes reconstitute themselves into an unstable, noncohesive form through a process called metamorphosis. The ice molecules rearrange themselves into round, sugarlike grains, greatly diminishing grain-to-grain contact and reducing the number, but enlarging the size, of the intergrain pore spaces. Fewer grain contacts mean lower strength. Hydrologists call it depth hoar, and on a steep mountainside where it destabilizes the snow pack, it breeds deadly avalanches. On flat ground it causes snowquakes.

Meanwhile, water molecules are also moving upward from the depths of the snow toward the surface, in the direction of lower vapor pressure, where the shifting molecules add to the thickening crust but deplete and further weaken the depth hoar underneath. All it takes now is the weight of a dauntless but unwary hero and dog team—the crust collapses, and down comes London Bridge. I've experienced only two snowquakes, but two were quite enough.

24
Rocky Craig

Rocky Craig was the most conspicuous landmark east of camp. It rose above Apuseq Glacier as a massive gray hulk, and it stood like a dark sentinel just off our route to the Ice Cap station. Even now few people have had the good fortune to ponder its lonely beauty, but in 1943 when Barry Borden and I saw it for the first time, we were sure we had to climb it, and we nagged Wade until he agreed to let us try. Known to the Greenlanders simply as Nunataq, Rocky Craig was bounded by Apuseq on three sides. The fourth side was a chiseled sea cliff dropping away to the ocean (*nunataq*–"belongs to the land"–refers to any rocky landmass projecting through a glacier. As a common noun, and as anglicized, it usually is spelled with a "k" instead of a "q.") On the inland side of Rocky Craig, Apuseq pushed up against the peak in a long, sloping snowfield, then split into two tongues of ice that flowed down to the sea on either side of the peak, both heavy with crevasses. From out to sea Rocky Craig loomed like a stone parapet shouldered with ice, halfway between our own Igtip Kangertiva on the west and Qardlit Ikerat ("bay shaped like trousers") on the east. Qardlit Ikerat headed below another navigational landmark, an unblemished white pyramid that the army called Snowy Slope.

During the fall and winter of 1943 there was ample time to study Rocky Craig's cliffy profile from Atterbury Dome and to evaluate possible approaches across the glacier. Wade, however, wasn't enthusiastic about our compulsion to make the crossing. The crevasses formed a maze of crescentic fractures nested one behind another across the full width of the glacier and entrained toward the ocean. Many of these cracks were twenty or thirty feet wide and several thousand feet long. We could only guess at their depth. Except at the mouth of the glacier, where some of

Fig. 24–1. Rocky Craig across Apuseq Glacier, as seen from Atterbury Dome, August, 1944. Apuseq here is about five miles across. Rocky Craig is 1,680 feet high.

them stayed open all year around, they were bridged over with snow most of the time. They usually opened up in July or August and started to bridge over again in September when overhanging cornices of drifted snow gradually bridged them shut. Each cornice cantilevered a bit farther across each crevasse with each passing storm. Even in fair weather a certain amount of drifting snow blew down the slope of the glacier, carried along by a steady breeze off the Ice Cap. This was the gravity wind or katabatic wind mentioned earlier–a sheet of cold, heavy air flowing downhill like a flood of water.

Although the crevasses were thus bridged over well before the end of winter, their locations on the glacier were marked by telltale, troughlike sags. In late summer, when the snow was generally too wet to drift, the cracks reappeared. Bear in mind that the ice was constantly moving and that the crevasses resulted from tensional fracturing as the glacier crept slowly toward the sea.

Down near the sea, the snow melted completely off the glacier in summer, and the whole surface was fractured blue ice. Here, the crevasses were widest, here they reappeared first in summer, and here they bridged over again last in the fall. How deep were they? On theoretical grounds, they probably didn't exceed two hundred feet–about equal to the height of a fifteen-story build-ing–owing to the plasticity of the ice at depth. The ice is brittle at the surface of a glacier and to a depth of several tens of feet, but at greater depth the confining pressure of the overlying ice column makes the ice increasingly plastic and gradually squeezes all the fractures shut. A crevasse thus tends to be wedge-shaped, tapering downward to a mere crack at the bot-tom, but often narrower at the rim than just below, or even closed, because of the cornicing effect of the drifting snow. The bottom may be partly filled with snow from collapsing bridges.

When Wade finally gave Barry and me the nod in June of 1944, the crevasses had been bridged over for several months. By then the bridges were at their thickest and strongest, we judged, but by the same token, the crevasses were concealed and hard to detect. You could see the sags they made in the surface of the snow, but you could never be quite sure of their safety. We did know, though, that they diminished gradually in number and size up glacier, so we skirted most of them by heading somewhat north of a direct line to the peak. We were aiming at the snowy ramp on the peak's north shoulder, where we could reach nearly to the summit without taking off our skis. We slipped tentatively across each sag, testing each one ahead with a ski pole–a mini-mal safety precaution carrying few assurances, and not exactly standard for glacier crossings. Looking back on that procedure now, after all these years, I recoil in horror. We both knew better.

Between base camp and Rocky Craig, Apuseq was about five miles wide. We reached the far side in two easy hours and took another hour to climb the peak, but we paused often to enjoy the view. The first visibly bridged crevasse was about a mile out of camp, and it seemed as wide as a Los Angeles freeway. We crossed several more, then traversed up the snowfield to the summit in a series of easy switchbacks. We scrambled the last few yards up a scree slope, and the view from the top exceeded all expectations. Sixteen hundred and eighty six feet below, gen-tle swells from the North Atlantic rose softly against the rocks. Out from the shore lead, floating ice reached to the horizon, and scattered bergs rode silently above the shifting pack. To all ap-pearances the bergs were motionless, but they were drifting slowly southward with the East Greenland Current.

Far to the southwest, far beyond the dark mounds of Atterbury Dome and Husryggen, the Ice Cap sloped down to the ocean past Holms Nunatak, Hvitsadlen, Anikitsok, and Kap Løvenhørn, dazzling in the midday sun. Whole mountains were overwhelmed by ice, and the steep outer margin of the cap was contorted by great open crevasses plainly visible thirty miles away. By comparison, those in Apuseq seemed like cracks in a sidewalk. Our eyes scanned the skyline around to the north, following the crest of the Ice Cap all the way to the broad shoulder where Apuseq itself pulled away from Snowy Slope. Then farther northeast, the Ice Cap again reached the shore, spilling into the ocean in a dozen outlet glaciers buttressed by scores of dark nunataks. Rocky islands offshore brooded under a bank of blue-gray stratus clouds that hid what we had hoped would be a distant view of Sermilik Fjord and Angmagssalik Island. Sermilik ("belongs to the glaciers") was the longest fjord in our part of Greenland, and its many outlet glaciers were real berg makers. Angmagssalik was noted for its craggy coastline. Denied that view, we turned again to the east where Apuseq met the ocean in awesome silence directly below our feet. Parted by Rocky Craig, Apuseq's twin outlets were rent by uncounted blue crevasses that gave an impression of immense force in suspended animation. Our view was almost aerial: we looked straight down at the glaciers' broken front. Then we fashioned a cairn of rough stones to proclaim our visit and wondered if anyone had stood there before us or if Erik the Red had viewed this silent scene from his longboats a thousand years before. The rocks, I noted, differed little from those at Atterbury Dome. They were layered gneiss, full of biotite, sloping gently northward beneath the glacier. I took a few pictures, we skipped down the scree slope, buckled on our skis, and glided swiftly down the incline to the glacier. Then we retraced our track through the crevasses, less cautiously than outbound, and headed back toward camp where Wade stood watch with his transit.

Visiting Rocky Craig was an exhilarating experience and I cherish its memory, but in the wisdom of hindsight and the passage of the years, I now view it as a foolhardy adventure fraught with deadly peril. Wade should have rejected our entreaty. In the brashness of youth, we shrugged off the hidden dangers, complacent in the sureness of our own invincibility. If in memory I exaggerate the risk of those sags in the snow, I still wouldn't trade the experience, but I wouldn't repeat the trip on the same terms for a million dollars.

25
Greenlanders Out of the Mists

Early one morning as we were hassling one another over breakfast, we were astonished to see through the mess hall window a
small, dark, slender figure of a man suddenly materialize out of
the fog–a real Eskimo in this unpopulated part of Greenland.
"Eskimo" is a name disdained by Greenlanders, who call themselves *Kalatdlit,* variously spelled. Our stretch of Greenland's
east coast was uninhabited except for ourselves, largely because
of its hostile climate and lack of equable living space, and none
of us had previously met a Greenlander. Although nobody else
lived in our area during World War II, some six hundred people
lived in the mountainous but more sheltered Angmagssalik district 150 miles or so to the northeast. In southern and western
Greenland, native villages were numerous, but by agreement between the army and the Danish authorities, they were off limits
to the military, and few GIs every met or saw a native.

Our Greenlander was apprehensive, but warm smiles and
handshakes soon put him at ease. He spoke no English or Danish, and we certainly spoke no Greenlandic, but through his easy
sign language we learned that he was camped across the fjord,
where he had seen our antennae poles, and his entire family of
fourteen souls of three, or perhaps four, generations was down
at the beachhead. He indicated that they had come by boat from
a settlement about sixty miles north called Isertoq–"place of the
muddy water"–pointing out their travel route in detail on our
wall map. Muddy water usually means a place where a glacier
is dumping a lot of rock flour into a stream, lake, or fjord. We
were impressed by his knowledge of geography and his ability
to read maps, though we shouldn't have been, because Greenlanders have long been known for their clear memories and en-
cyclopedic understanding of their native land. Their lives depend

Fig. 25-1.   Three young Greenland women and the family matriarch.
Except for their kamiks–boots–their summer dress is 1930s western.

on it. He wondered why we lived in so inhospitable place as Igtip
Kangertiva. His western-style clothing was old and threadbare,
but he wore handsome, hand-sewn sealskin kamiks, boots.
(*Kamik* is a West Greenland word. These people called a boot
atertagaq.) His family, he indicated, would like to barter with us
for much-needed warm clothes. He wrapped his arms across his
chest and made gestures of shivering. Captain Wade said no, we
couldn't trade government property, even though we had a whole
warehouse full of it.

Everyone in camp hurried down to the beachhead to meet the
family. Aside from the fact that these people were real native
Greenlanders, we hadn't had any new faces in our midst since a
ski plane had landed briefly several months before. I slipped on
my skis and took off, arriving moments later at the fjord, far
ahead of all the footsloggers. Few of our people had had any ski
training aside from a little crosscountry; most didn't even know
the rudimentary snowplow turn, and they weren't inclined to
risk life and limb, as they saw it, in the run down from camp. At

the beachhead station I was confronted by a whole gang of wide-eyed Greenlanders led by an elderly matriarch, who immediately lined everyone up like an infantry squad according age or status. I then went down the line shaking hands with each person, from seniors to juniors, as each one in turn solemnly bowed. There were three other men, three women–one nursing a baby–three girls, a toddler in a skirt, and three small boys, all with beautiful smiles and flashing white teeth. All, that is, except the two oldest women, whose choppers were worn to the gum-line from a lifetime of chewing sealskin to keep the rawhide soft and pliable.

Next, after an awkward pause, I offered a round of cigarettes, having heard that the native people liked to smoke. In fact, they considered tobacco a great luxury. Starting with the matriarch, who accepted graciously, I again went down the line, and when I got to the small children, the old lady smiled broadly and indicated that they, too, should share. Reluctantly, I complied. When all had smoked their cigs down too short to hold, they spat on the butts, and tucked them behind their gums like chaws of tobaccy.

By now the gang from camp had begun to arrive, and the meeting took a more festive turn, with lots of jokes and laughter. Some of the guys made raucous remarks that fortunately were not understood by our visitors, who laughed politely anyway. We broke out a five-gallon can of hard candy from a stash at the beachhead station and filled the anoraks of all the happy kids. We also rounded up some surplus outerware, mostly old jackets and sweaters, after the Greenlanders again hugged themselves with further gestures of cold and shivering, and Captain Wade relented. One grinning little boy marched out of the warehouse with a dirty wool sock on the end of a long stick, and everyone had a good laugh. We gave all the kids sheepskin flight-crew helmets, and they wore them with pride and delight. The men combed the ground around the station, glancing our way for approval as they scrounged old boards, lengths of wire, rusty nails, tin cans, and other discarded items from the treasure trove.

They proudly showed us their gear, pointing out each item and describing its function in sign language. They solemnly repeated each name over and over as we tried in vain to pronounce it. Each man had his own kayak and hunting harpoon, *savikataq,* exactly like those I had read about as a schoolboy. Each kayak had a small white sail designed as a blind for concealing the

Fig. 25–2. Arctic madonna and child. The baby is traditionally garbed in sealskin anorack, trousers, and kamiks.

hunter as he stalked his quarry in the ice floes. The harpoon had a detachable head of ivory or bone, though some were metal, fastened by a rawhide thong to an air bladder, *usikatak*, designed to stay afloat, place a drag on the harpooned seal, and prevent the kill from sinking. The double-bladed kayak paddle, *pautit*, was made of driftwood–probably wood that had floated across the Arctic Ocean from Siberia–artfully edged by a thin band of bone fashioned to protect the paddle from abrading ice.

The kayak had a very shallow draft, a narrow beam, and a cockpit covered with sealskin that could be drawn tightly closed around a man's waist to shed any water that washed over the desk. It was a fragile little work boat, but it had proved its utility in a thousand years of use. I was impressed by its grace, beauty, and craftsmanship, having once put together a kayak myself, back in the thirties, from a mail-order kit. (Mine had aluminum ribs, hardwood longerons, and doped-canvas skin, a far cry from the sleek fiberglass whitewater kayaks on the market today, but even these are blatant imitations of the originals.) With unabashed showmanship, the men slipped into their kayaks on shore, then waddled ducklike on their hands across the rocks to

Fig. 25-3. A proud hunter shows off his kayak and gear. The prize is two eider ducks–*ugpaterqorteq*.

the water. Once afloat, they threw and retrieved their harpoons, frolicking and laughing like little boys.

Ulo, woman's knife

All the women and children traveled in a single, large skin boat called an *umiak*, together with all their personal effects, food, cooking and camping gear, two baskets of duck eggs, two small dead seals, and several small, dirty, snarly sled dogs. The umiak had two sets of oars, *iput* (for rowing by four women) and a tiller or paddle for steering from the stern. We exchanged some clothing for a seal carcass–for dog food–a big bearded seal floating alongside the umiak, but by prior agreement the Green-

Fig. 25-4. *Umiak,* "the women's boat." All the women and children traveled together in this skin boat.

landers kept the hide, which one woman deftly removed as we watched, entranced. Bending over from the waist, she used an odd knife blade called an *ulo,* shaped like a half-moon, which she sharpened by rubbing two blades together. The thick skin of the bearded seal was destined to cover another umiak, or possibly be tailored into the feet of kamiks, the uppers being make of bearskin.

Today, sad to say, the kayak and umiak have largely disappeared from East Greenland, along with the arts of their construction and use, replaced by the outboard motorboat, which surely is a safer and more convenient mode of travel, if less elegant and picturesque. I was privileged to have seen them in their time, but I would be reluctant to cross the open water these people routinely traveled, even in a motorboat.

One Greenlander showed off his ancient firearms, a rusty shotgun as I recall, and a rifle, and he proudly displayed his quarry, some eider ducks, *ugpaterqorteq.* When we noticed the kids sucking duck eggs through holes poked in the shells, we were quickly offered a basketful, and we just as quickly accepted, not having eaten fresh eggs for nearly a year. But our appetites waned at breakfast time when we discovered that all the eggs contained embryonic ducklings, some with horny beaks and pin feathers.

Ugpaterqorteq, the elder duck

In the back of the warehouse we had a bolt of luminous red nylon cloth for use as flagging to mark trails on the Ice Cap. In exchange for the eggs, we gave each woman about ten yards, which they accepted with joy and enthusiasm. Expert seamstresses, they reappeared the next day in artfully tailored, high-fashion, slinky red gowns.

Back on the beach, when two of our guys quarreled loudly over some forgotten triviality, the Greenlanders seemed bewildered by our outbursts of temper, and they showed alarmed concern. Their severe and hazardous lifestyle, it seemed, had only heightened their fellowship, close family ties, and cheerful good humor. With Wade's approval, we invited the whole family to dinner at the beachhead station, and what our menu lacked in haute cuisine, it made up in festive warmth. Everyone wolfed down the C rations, canned meat-and-vegetable stew, canned pilchards, and Cookie's chocolate pudding, but the Greenlanders graciously and laughingly declined the Vienna sausages, and to this day I wonder what they thought those were. We washed down the dinner with a pot of coffee, and when all stomachs were filled, the women washed the dishes, the men lit up their pipes, and the kids romped outside barefoot in the snow. The women scraped up and saved all the uneaten food. They also washed out the empty tin cans and carted them off to the umiak, a windfall to this desperately poor little family.

After what the Greenlanders apparently considered an appropriate lapse of time, but really just two days, the women and children piled into the umiak and the men slipped into their kayaks. Four widely smiling *nuliakeq*–women–leaned heavily on two sets of oars as the little flotilla slipped slowly into the pack

Fig. 25-5. Angmagssalik Fjord near Gustav Holm's campsite where he first met the people of East Greenland.

ice. An unforgettable sight, the men hurling their harpoons in playful abandon and the kids waving their arms in a gesture of warm farewell. We waved and they waved until the ice closed around behind them and they were gone. Meeting these people was a joyous experience at a time of stress and tedium, leaving us with memories to last a lifetime.

The East Greenlanders, or more specifically the Angmagssaliks, were unknown to most of the world until a chance meeting in 1884 with Danish explorer Gustav Holm, who lingered nine months in their villages to study their customs and ethnology. He later published a scholarly treatise describing all aspects of their lives, a monumental work in cultural anthropology. Their emergence from stone-age isolation preceded their visit to us that summer at Comanche Bay by only sixty years. Perhaps the matriarch had been alive at that early time. Until Uncle Sam arrived on the scene, her lifestyle had little changed.

Just how and when her ancestors made their way to East Greenland is something of an anthropologic mystery, but language studies indicate closer ties to the polar people of northwest Greenland than to their more populous southwestern cousins. The languages of the southwest and east coasts are quite dissimilar, isolated linguistically for many generations by the frigid barrier of the Ice Cap, the pack ice, and the storms of Cape Farewell. The East Greenlanders, thus, appear to have traveled north then east past Peary Land, the most northerly land on Earth, then south along the rugged East Greenland coast, a migration that must have seen the slow advance of many generations of people. Artifacts and former dwelling places have been found in many places along the northeast coast, a vast empty region of towering cliffs and abyssal fjords locked in by heavy, permanent sea ice, but less hostile in most respects than the stormy region they live in now. The winter in northeast Greenland, as Johan Johansen had told me, is longer, darker, and colder than at Comanche Bay or Ångmagssalik, but storms are fewer and less intense, and summers are longer, warmer, and drier.

Legends and stories passed on to Gustav Holm and subsequent investigators indicate that the East Greenlanders knew about their west coast cousins and in fact made occasional trips south around Cape Farewell to trade with the people of the Nanortalik—"home of the bear"—area in the southernmost settled part of the land. How this commerce escaped the diligent attention of the nineteenth-century Danish administrators is rather mystifying, particularly in view of the fact that Nanortalik was the staging area for the Holm expedition and for other attempts to penetrate the southeast coast by earlier explorers.

26
Ski Touring Putulik

Off-duty hours at the weather station allowed time for exploring the entire peninsula of Atterbury Dome–Putulik, as the Greenlanders called it–and the Dome was a convenient takeoff place. Over the months I crossed and recrossed its wide summit and circumnavigated its desolate periphery from the front of Apuseq Glacier to the shore of Comanche Bay–what geologists call "birddogging." Every turn yielded exciting new discoveries. In some ways Putulik is more like an island than a peninsula. Bounded by water on three sides, it faces Apuseq on the fourth, a crevasse-laced arm of the Ice Cap and every bit as formidable a barrier as the ocean itself. I wondered if Putulik might in fact be an island buttressed by glacial ice. If the subglacial floor of Apuseq is below sea level, and chances seem good that it is, the ice-covered floor would be engulfed by seawater if the ice were to melt back just three or four miles. If you could look back over recent geologic time, moreover, you would see that all the outlet glaciers of the Ice Cap in southeast Greenland have shrunk. They were once much larger than now. All the offshore islands were once bound tightly to the mainland by an expanded Ice Cap, just as Putulik is today. Nearly all these islands yield evidence of their past glacial cover, chiefly in the form of glacial polish and scratches on the exposed bedrock surfaces and of scattered glacial boulders left behind by the vanished ice. Over the short haul, the Ice Cap now seems to be about in equilibrium, but over the long haul, the margin of the Cap has been retreating, and its retreat has exposed new headlands and islands in its wake.

Note on map 4–1 the precarious tie of another small landmass, Sipulik, just east of Putulik. Almost surely an island, Sipulik is joined to Apuseq by a narrow neck of calving ice only half a mile wide, and its separation from Apuseq seems imminent. It could

Fig. 26–1. Apuseq Glacier, looking northeast toward Rocky Craig. The ice cliff to left of center is about two hundred feet high. Part of the lateral moraine is in the foreground.

happen in our lifetime–perhaps even in the next few years, unless climatic change makes the ice expand. In the half-century since my visit, the separation may already have taken place. Even Rocky Craig may be an island buttressed by ice. We can only speculate, but a few geophysical probes with seismographs or radar out on Apuseq would quickly settle the matter.

Most of Putulik's coastline is ledgy, and in a few places it drops away in sheer, dark cliffs that permitted good viewing from above of the many seals and sea birds down below. Right down by the water in most places an ice foot fifteen to twenty feet high formed a barrier to passage from land to water and vice versa, where the shore-fast ice broke away at the waterline, but it gave me a sense of security from any unseen perils of the deep–from *nanoq* the polar bear, for example, stealing ashore on my scent. I always hoped to spot a walrus or a whale but never succeeded.

I managed to reconnoiter just about all the rocks on Putulik and longed to map them in geologic detail, but Greenland Base Command had other ideas. Such subversion was discouraged, especially if you had any thoughts of carrying the information out of Greenland. Soldiers were not supposed to commit anything to paper, least of all a map, although Don Galbreath and

Bill Cadigan kept clandestine diaries and managed to sneak them out of Greenland when they returned home. The army's attitude was that if any written matter fell into enemy hands it might jeopardize the war effort, even a geologic map of Comanche Bay. The army did encourage hobbies, such as rock collecting, and I shipped home fifty pounds of assorted specimens for only five dollars, courtesy of Uncle Sam.

The best time for solitary touring was about the middle of June, when the weather was fair, the air warm, the sun high in the sky, and the snow cover still wide enough to make every part of the peninsula accessible on skis. Atop Atterbury Dome I discovered some dark igneous dikes stretching across country like prehistoric roadways. Dikes are straight-walled injections of lava, cooled and solidified in place as they rise up toward the Earth's surface from magma storage chambers deep below. I later learned that these injections are part of a huge "swarm" of dikes. They extend hundreds of miles along the East Greenland coast, increasing in size and number toward the great fjord Kangerdlugssuaq, 250 miles northeast of Angmagssalik. The same swarm reaches south at least forty miles from Atterbury Dome to Umivik.

All these dikes are related to an ancient volcanic terrane long since eroded down to its roots, a terrane that included parts of Scotland, Ireland, and Greenland fifty million years ago, before the three land masses were rent apart by continental drift. This was the Tertiary Period, when both the geography and the climate of Greenland were very different from today. West Greenland was forested with oaks, poplars, sycamores, tulip trees, ginkgos, conifers (including metaseqouia), and many more species—even ferns. These trees would be comfortable today in the U.S. South or the Gulf Coast states. Crocodiles thrived in northern Canada, and the tiny fossil horse, *Eohippus,* grazed the western basins of North America. Bizarre creatures now extinct skulked in the background. All along coastal East Greenland, igneous dikes were being injected upward from the depths of hell itself, much like the great fire fountains of Kilauea Volcano today on the Island of Hawaii, and their outpourings build a high lava plateau covering thousands of square miles.

Volcanism died out in Greenland millions of years ago, but activity persists in Iceland on the Mid-Atlantic Ridge between Scotland and Greenland, where a massive edifice of volcanic rocks is still growing with each eruption and where earthquakes, hot springs, and gaping ground cracks provide additional evidence of the seething cauldron below. Iceland today remains one of the most intensely active volcanic centers on Earth.

I also discovered two pipe-shaped deposits of asbestos, one of which contained exceptionally long, silky fibers that surely would have had real value, were they not so remote and inaccessible. After the war I considered trying to promote and peddle the deposits in the commercial marketplace, but abandoned the idea when the link became known between asbestos and cancer. The same deposits contained soapstone, or steatite, a soft mineral which is very easily carved, and at idle times in the barracks I worked little pieces into humanoid visages, which I unthinkingly left behind when we closed up camp. Now I wish I had kept them. Soapstone may be rather common in our part of Greenland, because many early artifacts made from it were collected by the Graah expedition in the nineteenth century. An island southeast of Putulik is called Aqitseq, which means "soapstone," and the early Greenlanders may have stopped off there for raw material to make cups, bowls, and amulets, and perhaps votive figurines. I wished I could have explored there for a few hours or days.

One summer day while touring high above Comanche Bay I happened onto a sun-warmed meltwater pool in a hollowed granite outcrop overlooking the fjord, and the blood vessels pounded at my temples. Except for rare unpleasant sponge-offs in the chilled air of the barracks, where you could see your breath at any time, I hadn't had a bath for more than ten months, and though not overly fastidious, I was thunderstruck by the possibility. No one at Comanche Bay had been wet all over since Sandbag fell into the fjord, and only someone who had gone unbathed as long as that could fully appreciate my euphoria. I quickly unbuckled my skis, slipped off my clothes, eased into the tepid water, and slowly lay submerged in full view of the distant blue Ice Cap and a fjordful of floating bergs. Where else on earth could this happen! Finally, when my skin began to wrinkle, I reluctantly climbed out, dressed, and grudgingly skied back to the weather station and my unwashed colleagues.

On another sunny day just after the summer solstice, the air temperature at base camp reached a sizzling sixty-five degrees Fahrenheit. This unlikely heat wave triggered a primal urge to partake of a ritual snowbath, like the Vikings of old. A year earlier down in Maine at an Arctic-training camp on Mount Katahdin, at a place called Chimney Pond, I had been deeply impressed by Willy Knutsen, a Norwegian friend who snowbathed every morning. Captain Willy would first plunge into icy Roaring Brook before rolling in the snow, and he seemed purified by the experience.

Willy was a handsome Norseman in the heroic Viking mold – tall, lean and muscular, bronzed skin, blond hair, soft-spoken, and an expert skier. Before accepting a commission in the U.S. Army, he had smuggled shot-down British airmen out of occupied Norway in a small seagoing launch. Off duty around the big air base at Presque Isle, he was pursued by relentless coteries of females turned on by his lilting accent and modest continental demeanor. Willy subsequently commanded a remote air/rescue station near Goose Bay, Labrador, and on my return from Greenland in November, 1944, I enjoyed Scotch whisky and caribou steak at his festive table.

Back at Comanche Bay, emulating Willy, I emerged from the barracks clad only in a bath towel before the startled eyes of Don Galbreath and Homer Loar, themselves stripped to the waist and sunbathing on the roof. But with my first step outdoors into the snow the wisdom of the experiment grew doubtful: I should have kept my shoes on. Five steps more, and in one motion, I was down, rolled over once, up on my feet, and back in the barracks, the entire exercise lasting about fifteen seconds. Fully convinced of the health-fostering properties of the experiment I concluded, nevertheless, that the same end could be served as well by proper diet and regular exercise, and I never so indulged again. No one else at Comanche Bay even tried it once.

As quickly as the snows of winter began to disappear in the warmth of the summer sun, patches of green exploded in the cracks and hollows of the rocks – not the luxurious herbiage of southwest Greenland, settled almost a thousand years before by Erik the Red, but real greenery nonetheless. Incidentally, the popular mythology about Erik's prowess as a real estate con artist – about how he coined the name Greenland to attract unsuspecting settlers – is patently false. This myth is widely entrenched, even recorded in the sagas, but as anyone who has been there knows, the district around Eriksfjord is as green in summer as Ireland, and the name given by Erik could hardly be more appropriate. The Greenland colonies, moreover, could scarcely have survived four hundred years on a Viking scam, and the deep fjords of southern Greenland look more like the Vikings' ancestral homeland of Norway than the stony grasslands of Iceland.

Comanche Bay, of course, was something else. Wade thought it was more like Antarctica than any other part of Greenland, but even here we had a profusion of miniature Arctic plants for the few weeks of summer, and you had to admire their hardihood. They opened tiny, delicate flowers of exquisite beauty. The most prevalent was the *mamartoq* or crowberry *Empetrum nigrum,* a low-growing member of the heath family, rarely taller than a few inches, with shiny evergreen leaves, white bellflowers, and sweet black berries much favored by the local ravens, who had little else to eat before the arrival of the U.S. Army. Up at Angmagssalik, the crowberry was also savored by the Greenlanders, who ate it with seal blubber. Another interested party was Sgt. Donald S. Galbreath.

Don Galbreath had majored in botany at Oregon State University before being drafted into the army. After the war he went back for a master's degree in wildlife management and was hired by the state of Washington. Don was entranced by the sparse Arctic flora of the Comanche Bay district, and he set out to collect and catalogue all extant species. This was no insignificant chore, even in an area as barren as Atterbury Dome, but he returned from a long traverse with an impressive collection, which he proudly spread out on the mess hall table to separate, press, and dry for further study. He stepped from the room for the briefest moment, perhaps to check a reference in the NCO Club, but when he returned, his collection was gone. Tony Colombo, assessing the situation in a masterstroke of culinary timing, smothered Don's specimens in oil and vinegar and devoured the whole lot−a gastronomic coup after so many months on a greens-free diet of warehouse food and C rations. Don's fuse was short, and he was ready to kill, but Colombo lacked malice and pleaded contrition, complimented Don on his choice of vegetables, and hoped he would soon harvest more.

Don was a forgiving soul. He collected another set of specimens, seventy-eight in all, deflected Colombo's further gustatory advances, and donated his collection to the herbarium at Oregon State University. The commonest green plant around Comanche

Bay was the sedge or wiregrass, which favored the marshy edges of ponds. Even the Arctic hare isn't partial to sedge, but other more palatable plant species besides the crowberry included angelica, *quaralik;* bilberry, *tungujortoq;* rosewort (a kind of sedum), *nunarssuk;* and various seaweeds savored by the Greenlanders.

Late in June of 1944, after the ice breakup in Comanche Bay, I was skiing high on the fjord side of Atterbury Dome when I was astonished to see a large gray naval vessel cruise slowly into the fjord. It proved to be the famous coast guard cutter *Northland* making a courtesy call, and it wasn't as big as it first appeared, but it was the largest man-made object we had seen in a long time, and its crew exceeded ours several times over. Down at camp all free hands headed for the beachhead to welcome the shore party.

The day being warm, barechested Captain Wade had shed his shirt and dropped his dirty longjohns down over his skipants. As he extended his hand in greeting to the skipper of the *Northland,* he said, "Hello, my name is Wade." The skipper shuddered. Like the navy, the coast guard observed strict rules of dress and was much more precise about military bearing, discipline, and decorum—what the GIs called "chicken shit"—than the Army Air Corps and especially the Base Ice Cap Detachment. Expecting a bit more formality and a smart military salute, the skipper was less than ecstatic about Wade's breach of propriety, and his disapproval was thinly veiled by his correct demeanor. But he discreetly said nothing about the matter and instead invited all hands aboard the *Northland* for lunch. The invitations did not include baths.

Only Homer Loar, by God, was correctly attired. Homer appeared at the Beachhead Station impeccably clad in his dress ODs, inexplicable behavior at Comanche Bay. No one had previously worn ODs there in anyone's memory. The coast guard, of course, took him to be our executive officer, as no one wore any insignia of rank, least of all corporal's stripes, and they invited him to tour the ship before lunch in the officers' mess.

Whether or not Homer encouraged this deception remains unclear, but he was quickly in too deep to back off, so with outward calm he went along, inwardly fearful that someone would spill the beans and land him in the brig, disgraced and court-martialed for impersonating an officer. No one let on, and he was

Fig. 26–2. Coast guard cutter *Northland* pays a courtesy call to Comanche Bay, summer of 1944. Beachhead station is in the foreground.

addressed respectfully as Lieutenant Loar for the rest of the day by everyone. In our complicity, perhaps, we shared his guilt. The *Northland*'s crew was very cordial and hospitable, though they seemed to view us with mixed curiosity, pity, and contempt. Little did they understand the fierce pride and *élan* of the Base Ice Cap Detachment. Used to the aseptic sterility of their vessel, the few crewmen who hiked up to our camp were appalled and revolted by the squalor, and they politely declined our return invitation to dinner, excusing themselves for the press of duty.

At mess aboard ship, the entree was fried chicken, and we ate far better than we had for more than a year. We were segregated by rank into officers, first-three-graders, and lower-grad noncoms. I ate with the last-named group, who informed me that the officers got all the white meat, the first-three-graders got the thighs, and we could expect nothing but the wings and assholes. My best recollection, however, is that we ate very well, and I envied the coastguardsmen both for the quality of their chow and their great good fortune in visiting the many outposts and backwaters of Greenland. They were actually being paid for what they did, but being a landlubber, a skier, and a free spirit, I wouldn't have traded places with any of them.

27
The Head of the Fjord

Among other items on our wish list, Barry Borden and I placed a high priority on visiting the head of the fjord—the head of Igtip Kangertiva. There, sandwiched between the glaciers, was an ice-free expanse of bare rock that cried out for exploration, a land-mass as large as Atterbury Dome but more diversified and containing many hidden valleys, rivulets, and even small lakes. The head of the fjord itself was modified on the west by a lakelike embayment a mile long, separated from the main fjord by a rocky prong and fed by the meltwater of a small glacier tongue that terminated in a snowy cornice hundreds of feet above the shore. A narrow strait connected the bay and the fjord, and the tide raced in and out through the opening in its twice-daily turn-around. Reasonably well sheltered from the piteraq by walls of polished gneiss on three sides, the bay was only minimally open to the fjord. This place, I thought, would make a great summer-time campsite, though in winter it might be vulnerable to·ava-lanches. I studied the whole scene from afar, and viewing it through the theodolite only heightened my desire to see it up close. Our chance came on a fair day in August, 1944, after Wade (now Major Wade) gave his consent.

The chief obstacle in our path from base camp to the head of the fjord was the four-mile-wide west arm of Apuseq Glacier. Apuseq flowed down from the Ice Cap in a broad lobe that broke off at sea on several fronts, including Comanche Bay. Near Comanche Bay its west arm piled up in a jumble of contorted ridges and swales of rough blue ice. Each ridge had buckled under the pressure of thousands of tons of flowing ice, and each was bro-ken by countless large crevasses. These were mostly long, arcu-ate fractures transverse to the direction of ice flowage, about parallel to the line of our intended crossing, but in the more

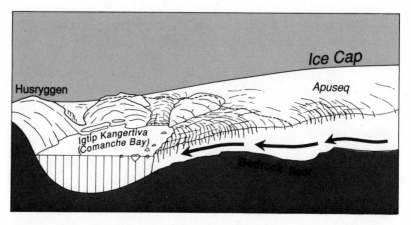

Fig. 27–1. Sketch section through Apuseq Glacier and the head of the fjord, not to scale, looking north. Arrows show the flowage pattern of the glacier over its irregular floor. The resultant crevasses open and close as the near-surface ice is alternately tensioned and compressed. Dashed line is our traverse of August, 1944.

tumultuous areas the crevasses ran in all directions in a chaos of yawning blue cracks and shattered seracs. Seracs are random pinnacles of ice that rear above the general level of the glacier.

Luckily for us, crevasses were fewer and narrower in the intervening swales than in the ridges. As a glacier creeps slowly along, its surface is buckled into swales and ridges–possibly abetted by some irregularity in its bed or by crowding of the ice by convergent flowage. Because ridge tops are under tension, the ice fractures like a bar of taffy candy when you bend it too fast. But in the swales of Apuseq, where the ice was under compression, most of the crevasses that had formed in the ridges upstream closed again as they moved downstream. The pattern is like a rapid in a mountain torrent where the waves break into splashy froth over a large boulder or pile up in a bend, then pool out in the still water below. We sagely plotted our route through the swales.

Barry and I left camp on heavy corn snow or firn. We coated the bottoms of our skis with sticky black pine tar, to improve gliding on the wet firn, and it worked beautifully, but we were soon off the firn and onto porous bare ice, rough and abrasive, and it scraped off the tar as though it were soft butter. The ice was layered in distinctive blue bands standing on edge in a way that produced a peculiar foliate texture much like the layering of a metamorphic rock. The layers were depositional sheets, formed thousands of years ago when snow fallen on the Ice Cap in storm after storm was compressed into ice, then was tilted up on edge by flowage down the glacier. In that respect the ice was like the deformed strata of a mountain range, where each layer of rock was one depositional unit bent and buckled by the uplift of the mountains. (Glacier ice in a broad sense *is* a metamorphic rock. Any naturally formed crystalline aggregate that makes up a sizable portion of the Earth's crust is regarded as rock, by definition, and if it has been significantly recrystallized by deformation, it is a metamorphic rock.) Conspicuous sheets of clear blue ice cutting across all other bands were products of internal shear deep within the glacier.

Barry and I were joined on our junket by Lt. Herbert G. Dorsey, Jr., who had recently arrived at Comanche Bay from Washington, D.C., having left the U.S. Weather Bureau for active duty in the army. Herb Dorsey was a research meteorologist, a graduate of M. I. T who had once wintered on Mount Washington in New Hampshire, where the winter wind occasionally blew nearly as hard as at Atterbury Dome. (Tornadoes not included, Mount Washington claims the world's highest recorded wind gust–220 miles per hour, measured back in the 1930s.) Dorsey had also been with a weather expedition to the stormy Antarctic Peninsula, then called Palmer Land, due south of Cape Horn at the southern tip of South America. Windwise, Palmer Land and southeast Greenland were close rivals for the world's worst weather, although Wade said he had never seen winds like ours in Antarctica. Dorsey was a friend and colleague of Richard Foster Flint, eminent glacial geologist at Yale. Flint, too, was then serving in the army, as CO of the Arctic, Desert, and Tropic Information Center, a sort of special-climate intelligence force. Wade served there briefly after his stint in Greenland. Right after the war, coincidentally, I assisted Professor Flint on a reconnaissance project to map glacial deposits in South Dakota for the U.S. Geological Survey. Flint had been in northeast Greenland in the middle 1930s with an expedition headed by Louise A. Boyd for the American Geographical Society, so we had a certain amount of common ground on which to compare notes, and perhaps that was why I was hired. Flint and Dorsey meanwhile had collaborated on meteorological articles for technical journals, speculating about the nourishment and growth of past continental ice sheets. With all those credentials, Dorsey came to Comanche Bay as a polar consultant and ramrod to jack up the Base Ice Cap Detachment and get us moving on the right foot, or so we understood at the time. Besides being an eminent meteorologist, Herb Dorsey was an accomplished and daring skier.

About a mile onto Apuseq Glacier, making our way gingerly through the crevasses, we headed for a broad swale. Each of us carried an ice ax, and I carried a coil of rope, but we had no real need for either. Ice axes were used chiefly for opening dog-food cans around camp. On bare ice such as this, where every crevasse is plainly visible, you can be selective about crossing over. Snow-covered ice is more deceptive and consequently much more dangerous. A suggestion from Barry that we rope up drew only derision from Herb. "Besides," asked Herb rhetorically, "wouldn't you rather fall in a crevasse in Greenland than be run over by a truck in New York?" Barry didn't reply. Moments later, Herb slipped on the ice, his skis went out from under him, and he fell flat on his backside between two gaping crevasses not five feet apart. Feigning utmost consternation, and with a knowing side glance from Barry, I swallowed a silent chuckle, but we still didn't rope up. Freezing to death in a crevasse in Greenland might be a better way to go than being flattened by a truck in Manhattan, but I had no wish for either. Though we didn't rope up, we did ski cautiously—there is something arresting about the inky-blue interior of a yawning crevasse.

We paused at times to take stock, double back around false leads, and admire the awesome grandeur of the glacier. For lunch and a thermos of coffee, we headed for a large nunatak on the far side of Apuseq, separating it from the smaller glaciers at the head of the fjord. Surprisingly, we were assailed by swarms of hungry mosquitoes as soon as we got off the ice, despite a lack of standing water and a near dearth of vegetation. Hardly a likely habitat, but in the absence of warm-blooded prey, mosquitoes seek out the juices of plants, and crowberries did grow even there from cracks in the rocks. But at the scent of human flesh, which probably was rather strong in our case, the mosquitoes rose in buzzing clouds. Summer is short in southeast Greenland, and the mosquitoes were trying to make the most of it. After flailing our arms and batting the air through a hasty lunch, we hurried to the high, upwind side of the nunatak just outside the bordering moraine where, besides avoiding the mosquitoes, we could make better time across the snow on skis than across the rocks on foot.

I was surprised by the small size of the moraine–about seventy feet high and not very broad–considering the vast expanse of ice behind it. A moraine is the terminal deposit of a glacier, where the ice meets the land and drops its load of basal and englacial debris. I mused over its bouldery constituents, the great jumble of angular blocks of granite and dark gray gneiss. Some blocks were the size of a two-car garage. How far had they traveled before emerging at the ice margin, and how long did it take? All these boulders had been quarried by the moving glacier from the rock floor of the Ice Cap, then carried along within the ice as if on a conveyor belt for untold miles to the ice margin. Here at my feet lay silent clues to the nature of rock formations hundreds of miles away beneath thousands of feet of ice.

Despite much study, little is known about the movement of ice beneath polar ice caps. The motion is a bit like the outward spreading of molasses on a cold platter, but ice is a crystalline solid, not a viscous liquid, and its motion therefore is more complex. It involves pressure gradients, shearing and recrystallizing within the ice-crystal lattice, grain-to-grain slippage on films of intergranular water (melted under pressure), and gliding of the ice on its bedrock floor. The colder the glacier, the less understood its motion.

Complex calculations for the motion of some parts of the Greenland Ice Cap, plugging in factors such as slope profile, ice thickness, and drainage area, have concluded that the ice in some places moves as much as 390 feet per year–more than a foot per day–fifty-five miles from the glacier margin. Most of the Ice Cap probably is much more stagnant than that, and the basal ice moves even more slowly than ice at the surface. Surface ice rides piggyback on the ice beneath it, so its motion is the sum of all ice movements underneath. At the World War II air crash site northeast of Comanche Bay, the ice reportedly had moved about a mile in the fifty years since the crash, or about a hundred feet per year. Near the center of the cap, the motion must be even less, almost zero. Glaciologists studying ice cores drilled near the center of the cap in recent years have found that the deep ice is many thousands of years old and is virtually stagnant. As it slowly approaches the coast, however, it gradually accelerates, especially around the heads of big outlet glaciers where it funnels in from several directions.

The ice moves fast at the head of Kjoge Bay. The actual velocity of the big glaciers there is unknown, and measuring it would be a formidable task, but as the ice pours into the bay from the west, north, and east, its velocity increases dramatically, and the prodigious outpourings of icebergs bear rumbling witness to the fact. Back at base camp, when the air was still, we could hear reverberations like the sound of distant thunder as the ice broke free and calved into the bay. Heading deep in the Ice Cap, the big glaciers formed distinctive, fast-flowing "ice streams" bounded by less active ice and clearly defined by trains of open crevasses.

Over in West Greenland, the motions of a few big outlet glaciers have been measured accurately by standard surveying methods, and the velocities have been astonishing. The apparent champion, as once measured by William S. Carlson, is the famous Jacobshavn Glacier, which averages about 125 feet per day, day in and day out, year after year–probably the fastest continuously flowing glacier in the world. Rink Glacier and Upernivik Glacier in the same part of Greenland are leading contenders in the same velocity range. Both these glaciers are on the central west coast. Those in Kjoge Bay may be contenders also, if their output of bergs is any indication. By way of comparison, few glaciers in the Alps of France or Switzerland move 125 feet in a whole year.

Herb, Barry, and I traversed over to the small outlet glacier at the head of Comanche Bay. This handsome body of ice had little obvious forward motion, although abundant crevasses near its steep headwall indicated appreciable flowage. There the glacier poured from the Ice Cap in a precipitous icefall, then flattened out into a broad bowl. We skied across just below the icefall, threading our way through a pattern of short but very wide crevasses. Down below the bowl, perhaps a thousand feet below the icefall, the glacier tapered to a narrow tongue that terminated at the fjord in a smooth-faced ice cliff. We paused for a few photographs and wondered if Wade could see us through his transit. We noticed in passing a massive lateral moraine smeared against the side of the aforementioned nunatak high above the ice. It gave some idea of the extent of shrinkage of this particular glacier since its last expansion many years before.

Fig. 27–2. Crevasse near the border of the Ice Cap, near the head of Comanche Bay.

We were now directly above the head of the fjord on the margin of the cap, and from our lofty vantage point we could see seventy miles straight out to sea. Under a sparkling sky, Comanche Bay was deep blue and nearly free of ice, but the North Atlantic was packed solid as far as the eye could see, and this in the middle of August. Close in against the shore of Kjoge Bay, a lead of open water maybe half a mile wide was kept free of ice by the rise and fall of the tide and the steady offshore breeze from the Ice Cap. The Greenlanders in their skin boats used such shore leads to travel from place to place up and down the coastline.

Most of the ice out to sea, the field ice known to the Greenlanders as *sikorssuit,* had drifted a thousand miles south from the polar basin, born in the frigid Arctic Ocean and carried along by the East Greenland Current. This was salt-water ice and it had a distinctly salty taste, unlike the fresh-water berg ice that originated as snow on the Ice Cap. Texturally the berg ice was different too; it held countless tiny bubbles of compressed air entrapped as the snow slowly compacted into ice under the pressure of its own weight. The transformation from snow takes place at varied depths, depending on the ambient or average temperature of the glacier. At our locality the changeover may have taken place at around a hundred feet. At that depth, the air spaces in the ice cease to interconnect, and the density of the mass increases to about six-tenths that of water. New-fallen snow averages about one-tenth the density of water and, as noted earlier, deep glacier ice may be as dense as nine-tenths.

We tracked on across the glacier to a cliffy outcrop of dark-colored rock hanging over the far west side. From its color and glittering feldspar, I guessed it was an uncommon igneous rock called anorthosite (but common in Wyoming, Minnesota, and the Adirondacks). I regretted having no time to study these rocks more closely, but our immediate objective was a second small glacier at the northwest corner of the fjord, and time was pressing on. From this vantage point we would see up close the great calving bergs at the head of Kjoge Bay, but first we were to cross about a mile of rocky ground. Here were many small meltwater pools warmed by the August sun. We chanced on a pretty little alpine tarn, deep blue under the summer sky and free of ice. Countless such lakes dot the ice-free borderlands of Greenland.

The glacier at the corner of the fjord was long, narrow, covered with snow, and free of visible crevasses. It headed into the Ice Cap, like most glaciers in our part of Greenland, but it drew little apparent sustenance from the Ice Cap itself. Rather, it was nourished by heavy direct snowfall and by a huge quantity of snow blown off the rocks by blizzards. Its surface was flat and featureless, but it terminated near the fjord in a snowy snout that dropped away steeply for hundreds of feet. From there, we exulted briefly at the savage grandeur of Kjoge Bay and its glaciers, then we turned back under gathering clouds. We retraced our steps as Wade watched from afar, more relieved than we when we plodded into camp, tired but charged with the knowledge that we had walked and skied where no one had before.

Once again I pondered the small size of the moraines bordering the Greenland Ice Cap. They were much smaller, for example, than the huge moraines of the American Midwest deposited by comparable-sized ice sheets that once covered much of the North American continent. In repeated advances and retreats across the country, these ice sheets picked up and redeposited unmeasurable quantities of weathered rock and soil over the landscapes of North and South Dakota, Minnesota, Wisconsin, Montana, Nebraska, Iowa, Illinois, Indiana, Michigan, Ohio, New York, all of New England, and parts of Pennsylvania, Kansas, and Washington. During all that time, Greenland was continuously buried by ice, and its Ice Cap effectively scoured its own bed down to firm, fresh rock. At times of large-scale glacial expansion, when the Ice Cap was even bigger than now, the ice dumped all available rock material directly into what is now the sea, beyond its present shores. If the big moraines of the Greenland Ice Cap exist at all, therefore, look for them below present sea level. Much debris, of course, was rafted far out to sea in icebergs, then was scattered over the bottom of the North Atlantic as the bergs wasted away in more temperate waters.

During glacial expansions, sea level fell far below its present height, because of the vast amount of water stored in the Ice Age glaciers. The shorelines, consequently, retreated scores of miles seaward from their prior positions, and land bridges appeared between previously isolated islands and continents, such as Sumatra, Java, and Asia; New Guinea and Australia; and Alaska and Siberia. The great Ice Age mammalian faunas utilized these bridges to enter new habitats and fill empty ecologic niches.

Greenland alone still contains about 620,000 cubic miles of water locked up as ice—a rough estimate, but well more than half a million cubic miles. If all this ice were to melt at once, all the sea ports of the world would be flooded by nearly twenty feet of rising water. Fortunately, the Ice Cap is now in a state of near equilibrium, with indications of a slight positive balance—it is storing a bit more ice annually that it is losing by melting and calving. (But if the greenhouse effect we hear about comes into play, all bets are off.)

The small moraines we visited at the head of the bay are products of a climatic deterioration and mild reexpansion of the glaciers during the last few hundred years—the period known as the Little Ice Age. During that time, glaciers in the Alps poured out of their mountain bastions and threatened the Alpine villages, halted only by the intervention of the clergy. Greenland's climate worsened, and the Norse colonists disappeared, their fate still unknown. Though their disappearance is shrouded in the dusty pages of time, most research suggests that their demise stemmed from three main causes. First, they suffered growing privations when trade with their European partners was broken off near the end of the fourteenth century. Norway, which ruled the Greenland colonies, was in the midst of debilitating political turmoil, the effects of which were compounded by severe weather and, in 1349, by an outbreak of the black plague. Norway had no time or energy for its New World colonies. Second, the colonies themselves were smitten by the worsening climate. And third, the enfeebled colonial survivors were massacred early in the fifteenth century by hostile natives ("trolls" in the words of the colonists), ending four hundred years of European settlement. Though racial mixing between colonists and Greenlanders may have happened toward the end, during the climatic downturn, as some historians have suggested, native legends of the final slaughter have been passed by word of mouth down through the years (described, evaluated, and recorded in detail by William Thalbitzer).

The onset of the Little Ice Age thus was an important factor in the late medieval history of southern Greenland. A worldwide reexpansion of the ice began near the end of the Middle Ages and ended about 1850. Since then the glaciers of the world have generally been shrinking, though some of them today are expanding once more—in Norway, for example. Many investigators in fact believe we are now living in an interglacial period, and they speculate that the continental ice sheets will return to North America and Europe within the next few thousand years. What a sight it will be as they engulf Manhattan, Detroit, Chicago, and Minneapolis.

Strangely, small glaciers in the high mountains of East Greenland—small compared to the Ice Cap—have built higher, more massive moraines than the Ice Cap itself. These moraines have been fed by avalanches of snow and rock plummeting down the craggy walls of the great peaks and ridges high above the ice. The mountain glaciers are well supplied with frost-riven rock, but the Ice Cap has only its well-scoured bed to draw from, where easily loosened rock has long since been carried away. Many outlet glaciers of the Ice Cap carry almost no debris.

28
The Big Push

Early in the spring of 1944, as the days grew longer and the weather brightened after months of wearisome storms, Wade pushed plans for renewed trail operations, with the view of fulfilling our mandate to build and occupy weather/rescue stations on the Ice Cap. These operations had been suspended the previous fall on orders of Greenland Base Command, to secure and assure the safety of our coastal installations. With the lengthening daylight, we were ready to try again by the middle of March, but more bad weather and mechanical problems with the T-15 snowmobiles brought us back to reality and square one. Other than the weather, our most vexing problem was the continued failure of the differentials–failure aggravated by the deep, loose snow. The T-15 worked best on a hard, smooth surface, which seldom existed on the Ice Cap, winter or summer, though the summer surface clearly was the better for travel. As a corollary, the machine was prone to throw its tracks in the same kind of snow that broke down the differentials. The T-15 was a temperamental machine that hadn't been field tested under true operational conditions before arriving at Comanche Bay, and we suffered the effects of it. Thrown tracks nearly always happened in deep, loose snow, and that meant we first had to dig out the bogged-down snowmobile to get at the undercarriage, then decouple and wrestle the tracks back into place, a chore that might require several hours. Big Bob Johnson was the key man in most such ventures, aided by his cohort Maurice Bisson and anyone else who might be on hand. Most of us just stood around the offered gratuitous advice. I usually tried to be on official business somewhere else, either at the weather station or off with Joe and the dogs.

Weatherwise, April was abominable–one round of blizzards

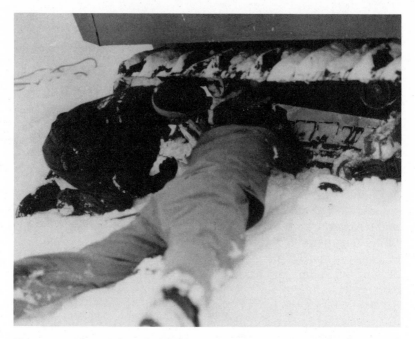

Fig. 28–1. Struggling with the thrown track of a T-15 snowmobile.

followed another. We were forced to sit tight again until May, and it occurred to Bob Grahl and me that the Ice Cap Detachment's only contribution to the war effort was the hourly weather report out of Atterbury Dome. Other people surely harbored the same thought. At base camp we did the chores, dug out coal, shoveled snow, played acey-deucy, and waited out the blizzards. Wade grew increasingly restive. Minor bickering and antagonisms surfaced in some quarters, and some people stopped speaking to one another—a behavioral pattern repeated endlessly in Arctic expeditions since time immemorial. The only physical tiff I know of happened when a man had a tooth knocked out for advising Colombo how to handle his dog team. This I learned secondhand much later, having been at the weather station at the time of the incident. The fact that we had so little bickering through the months was a tribute of sorts to the generally high spirits of our laid-back group and perhaps to the selection process that had brought us all together. Nowadays it's called cabin fever, but Wade didn't seem to understand despite his extensive prior polar experience. An honorable man, his chief interest as a college professor and scientist, he said in a meeting in the mess hall, was "things," not people, and his frankly detached attitude did little to improve matters. As a geologist myself, I could empathize with Wade's feelings, but as a corporal bucking for sergeant, I allied myself more closely with those in camp who griped about ratings "promised" but not materializing–few things help morale more than an occasional promotion. Attaboys are fine, but they lack the punch of increased pay. The weatherman felt they were being treated unfairly vis-à-vis the radiomen, and the radiomen felt the opposite, though they came into the expedition at grades a step or two higher. We were locked into a table of organization that specified a fixed grade structure in proportion to the number of men in the organization and their specific duties. What those numbers and duties were with respect to a twenty-one-man Ice Cap operation was never made clear, although at the outset we had been given assurances of lofty increases. Few of us, I suspect, were underpaid for what we were actually doing, which was mostly lying in our sacks, looking at the ceiling, and listening to the wind. I dreamed up another irrelevant limerick and posted it surreptitiously on the bulletin board, though everyone knew its source. Even if it did little to ease tensions, it drew a chuckle or two:

Young polar bear

Quoth young bruin with a gleam in his eye,
To convention I cannot comply.
Seal meat may have merit,
But I really can't bear it.
I've a taste for banana cream pie.

At the end of April the weather again improved, and optimism soared. Fair weather in southeast Greenland is the equal of any in the world. Wade ordered Colombo and Johansen out on the trail to reconnoiter surface conditions and evaluate the possibility of a snowmobile convoy, so with two teams of feisty dogs, they pushed out about nine miles before making camp at dusk under a light snowfall and a fresh east wind. During the night, the snowfall intensified and the breeze became a gale. Colombo and Johansen were camped on Apuseq, hardly even up on the flank of the Ice Cap, and when the weather soured, it held them tent-bound for six days through one of the worst blizzards of the year. Colombo and Johansen had no radio, and without radio contact we were concerned about their safety, though we had confidence in their ability to cope. Six feet of snow fell overnight at Atterbury Dome for the second time that winter before the storm climaxed on May 6 with winds exceeding a hundred miles per hour and temperatures falling to six below zero Fahrenheit. Don Galbreath's diary mentions winds averaging forty-one miles per hour for five days straight. We hadn't had such a storm since January. Finally, during a lull, Tony and Joe struggled back to base camp. Running downhill, tails to the wind on a wind-packed surface (the wind now out of the north), the dogs made good time. Besides, they always ran best toward home. By tacit agreement with Wade, Tony never set foot on the trail again, and his dogs were never hitched up again as a team. Joe just shrugged and headed for the barracks, after a detour to the lower warehouse to stash his gear and check out the compasses.

Meanwhile, back in February, Wade announced that Tex Fincher and I would set up a temporary weather station 150 miles southwest of Comanche Bay on the crest of the Ice Cap. That point was near the center of the south dome and close to the flight line of aircraft en route to Europe via Bluie West-1 and Iceland. The plan was to strike out from the Ice Cap station, not yet built, and head south well inland toward our objective. We would thus avoid topographic irregularities and the bad crevasses of the border zone. It would be a difficult objective to attain, and our transportation would be a T-15, but we could count on maximum support (which meant chiefly airdrops) from the army and navy. Tex had considerable mechanical skills, besides being an accomplished radio operator and maintenance man, and everyone had confidence in his tenacity, ability, and warm good nature. Route finding would hinge on my navigational skills as a geologist. Together, we thought, we would make a powerful team, and we were anxious to get started.

Though we were unaware of the reason at the time—even Wade didn't know—the army urgently wanted weather information off the Ice Cap to support the forthcoming D-Day landings in Normandy. The landings were top secret, and none of us had even heard of Normandy in that context. More complete weather data were needed to serve the projected heavy air traffic to Europe as well as to bolster the North Atlantic weather-forecasting network for tactical reasons. Tex and I were enthused about our prospects, though our task was soon thwarted by the upcoming foul weather of March and April. In the spring of 1944, overland travel of any sort wasn't physically possible in the blizzards of southeast Greenland. I doubt that it is today.

Another glitch turned into a memorable experience. I was having toothaches from a filling lost three months earlier while eating homemade vinegar candy (which was a sort of taffy and very tasty; made from a recipe in *Fanny Farmer's Cookbook*). Biting down hard on vinegar candy could lock your jaws just as surely as a touch of tetanus. When the sharp edge of the broken tooth scratched my tongue, I buffed it down with a fingernail file. Doc Johnson deftly prepared temporary fillings one after another from his pharmaceutical stash, and they worked fine for a while, but the toothaches gradually intensified, and it became obvious that I couldn't expend much time and effort on the Ice Cap in that condition. Finally, after an exchange of radiograms, a Noorden Norseman ski plane dispatched from BW-1 landed on Apuseq and whisked me up to Ikateq (BE-2) to a waiting dentist who promptly extracted the offending molar. Wade had laid out and flagged a temporary landing strip on the glacier, and from then on it was known as the Comanche Bay Air Base. The guys at BE-2 had heard of the Ice Cap Detachment and viewed us with a certain awe, so with their compliments we received a box of cigars, and I served as their courier. Then after a quick snack at the Ikateq mess hall, I boarded the waiting Norseman and returned to Comanche Bay.

Earlier that morning, when the Norseman first landed at Apuseq to fly me to the dentist, a doctor climbed out of the plane. When I scrambled aboard, he stayed behind to interview all hands, and after quick checkups of everyone in camp he decided that detailed physical exams were called for all around. His recommendation led to the visit of Dr. Huie Smith. He also asked how everyone felt about another winter with the Ice Cap Detachment, and all agreed they wouldn't mind if they could get out for a short R and R. When I returned from Ikateq, he climbed back

Fig. 28–2.   Noorden Norseman ski plane readying for takeoff from
Comanche Bay to fly author to dentist at Bluie East-2.

aboard, and that was the last we ever heard of him, but months
later all of us were hospitalized for observation in BW-1.

The flight to Ikateq made the months of toothaches almost
worth the trip. A cheery copilot handed me an aeronautical
chart, and I followed our route mile by mile, amazed that I was
getting paid for it, and agog at the myriad peaks, fjords, bays, and
glaciers. Where the Ice Cap terminated on land its moraines
were plainly visible from the air, even though the melt season
hadn't yet started; the wind must have kept the ridge tops clear
of snow. We followed the coastline, never going very far inland
nor very far out. The service ceiling of a Norseman was nothing
like that of today's jets. We flew at about two thousand feet, and
at an airspeed of only 125 mph we could scrutinize all kinds of
landscape details unseen by today's high-altitude air travelers.
Our flight was escorted by a C-47 cargo plane whose crew enjoyed the trip as much as we did. Flying a bit faster than we
could, they made many side excursions in and out of the
branching fjords, and I was just a bit envious. They pulled alongside us repeatedly to snap photographs–few things making better pictures than a rugged mountain backdrop with an aircraft
in the foreground.

For the first sixty miles or so our flight was over country much
like our own Kjoge Bugt district and, in fact, was a part of the

same Hvitserk or Midjokull mentioned in the sagas. Hvitserk was the Vikings' first Greenland landfall, where the Ice Cap came down to the shore in a broad irregular front and where the only landmasses were isolated headlands, nunataks, and near-shore islands surrounded by in floating ice. One large bay below us, Ikerssuak, was particularly crowded with icebergs and was comparable in size and all respects to Kjoge Bugt itself, even as to the large outlet glaciers pouring into it from all sides. (Ikers-suak means "large bay"; modern maps label it Ikertivaq, which means the same thing.) Then we approached Angmagssalik Is-land, and the whole scene changed. The wide expanse of the Ice Cap gave way abruptly to a vast archipelago of rugged alpine peaks interlaced with frozen fjords.

One especially imposing landmark was Kap Tycho Brahe, a dark sentinel at the mouth of Sermilik Fjord, named for the fourteenth-century Danish astronomer. Facing the ocean with a sea cliff more than three thousand feet high, it reminded me of Cape Farewell. Sermilik bounds the Angmagssalik archipelago on the west, separating the islands on the east from the Ice Cap and its tributary glaciers on the west. The largest fjord in our part of Greenland, fully as wide as Comanche Bay is long, Ser-milik is seven to eight miles across and sixty miles long, and is ramified by several large branches and many small inlets. It is flanked on the west by the white wall of the Cap, and it heads north into a wilderness of granite pinnacles nearly buried by massive glaciers and snowfields. The unnavigable inner reaches of Sermilik are always crowded with bergs. From the Norseman I could easily make out the shaggy details. Legend says its shores once harbored caribou, but I wondered where they found room to stand and what they ate. In fact, some rather broad land-masses abut the shore, and grasses in summertime are locally deep and lush. If the Greenlanders believed caribou once thrived there, they probably did, although the Greenlanders also be-lieved that cannibal giants lived there too—the *Timersit*, who fre-quented the Ice Cap west of the fjord and forayed down to the archipelago for an occasional meal. Their supposed existence cast some doubt on the Greenlanders' credibility. The Timersit were invisible to ordinary people but could generally be seen by shamans or *angakoq*, according to H. Ostermann (1938), who documented the beliefs of the East Greenlanders in olden times.

Then we rounded the corner of Angmagssalik Island and

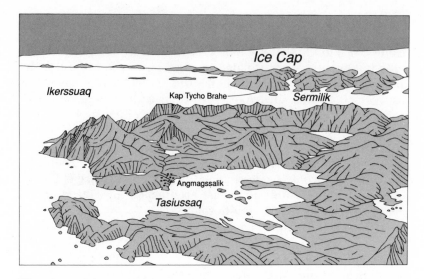

Fig. 28–3. Angmagssalik Island, looking south toward Ikerssuaq.
The village of Angmagssalik is on the south shore of the bay called
Tasiussaq.

headed toward BE-2 as I tried to look out on both sides of the
plane at once. Below us was the village of Angmagssalik,
shielded by mountains heavy with snow on the shore of a pretty,
protected bay called Kong Oscars Havn by the Danes and Tasiussaq by the Greenlanders–"the bay that looks like a lake." Its outlet to the ocean was a narrow strait not far from the mouth of
Angmagssalik Fjord, a fjord second in size only to Sermilik itself.
Fifty miles up Angmagssalik Fjord, the landing strip at BE-2 was
covered with ice, and it seemed that we were going to go off the
end of it before our skis came to a stop. You can't brake skis the
way you can wheels. The strip terminated at a deep ravine, and
I wondered how many planes had ended up there. Mountains
surrounding the base were incredibly steep, and I also wondered
why the whole base hadn't been taken out by avalanches. The
GIs told me with a chuckle that the control tower had in fact
been destroyed twice.

Back at camp, later in May and early in June, a few more
assaults were tried on the Ice Cap. Each ended with partial success as loads of equipment were cached along the trail, each a
bit farther out than the last. My trip southwest with Tex Fincher

was postponed indefinitely. The Ice Cap station had priority. Joe and I made a few forays with the dogs, struggling against the wind and shifting drifts and radioing back snow conditions to base camp. One day we made just three and a half miles. Temperatures ranged from below the teens to the high twenties, and once we reported rain, but it soon turned to snow.

Our radio was a "portable" job called an SPF, a transmitting and receiving set with a voice range of perhaps two to three hundred miles and a key for sending Morse code that carried considerably farther. For convenience we preferred to use voice, although Wade demanded that everyone learn the code, for safety's sake, before being allowed on the Cap. The SPF took up a large part of our cargo space. It was powered by a generator hooked up to a power source like an exercise bicycle, complete with pedals and handlebars and twice as hard to pump. (Joe did the pumping as I transmitted and received—who could understand an old Norwegian broadcasting in broken English, or would want to?) All this weight reduced our payload on the sledge. For an antenna, we stretched about a hundred feet of wire between two skis planted in the snow at right angles to a line-of-sight direction to base camp, and our transmissions came in loud and clear.

We transmitted on a predetermined schedule lasting only a few minutes, but we spent a lot more time setting up and taking down the apparatus, including unloading and reloading the sledge. Our call letters, from the dog team, appropriately, were WVHD—William Victor Howe Dog—and some of our transmissions carried quite far, because Greenland Base Command castigated us a time or two for unnecessary breaches of wartime security. But despite GBC's protestations, we all felt that regular communications with base camp were an essential safety precaution.

On June 12 a big convoy of eight men and seven T-15s, each pulling a heavily laden sledge, optimistically left base camp but was halted shortly by poor surface conditions. A week later the convoy resumed, traveling by night to take advantage of the better nighttime surface. Even fairly high on the Ice Cap the surface tended to soften under the midday summer sun, but the snow hardened as soon as the sun dropped low on the horizon. At that time of year we had twenty-four hours of daylight, so visibility for travel was good any time except in bad weather. Our convoy

Fig. 28–4. Supply convoy on trail on the Ice Cap, July, 1944.

lost one differential at twenty-seven miles, dropped off its cache at fifty-four miles, and returned to base.

A second convoy set out on July 5. This trip cost three differentials and two abandoned machines. Wade decided then that the Ice Cap station would have to be built at the fifty-four-mile cache, which was not nearly as far out as originally planned, but we had to face the realities of our timetable and capability. The fifty-four-mile site was at an altitude of about 5,650 feet. Arriving on site, the convoy dropped off its load and headed back to base, leaving Bill Cadigan, Tex Fincher, and Don Galbreath behind to report Ice Cap weather. They kept a T-15 for emergency use. Herb Dorsey was left behind also, in command, as an act of courtesy on the part of Wade, but as soon as the convoy was out of sight Herb decided to move on, despite Wade's decision to stay put, and ordered his crew back on the trail. "We're heading inland," he said, and the T-15 broke down twenty-four miles later. Herb wanted to make weather observations closer to the crest of the Ice Cap, he argued, and under ideal conditions that would have made sense, but when Wade learned of it, he was catatonic. Meanwhile, when Joe and I then arrived at the vacated station site, amazed to find no one there, we radioed base camp for instructions. Go on to Herb's camp, we were told, and take along some motor oil from the fifty-four mile cache for the T-15, then stand by for further instructions. Tex by this time had repaired the snowmobile, but its crankcase was dry.

Joe and I approached Herb's camp with a team of very tired dogs, having pushed the twenty-four miles beyond our intended destination, but just as camp came into view, perhaps half a mile away, we saw a tiny figure skitter around behind the tents and head inland. This time it was no mirage. We knew it was Herb, who had again decided on his own to make a quick dash to the crest of the Cap to establish elevations and geographic fixes. He carried a surveyor's transit and a bundle of trail flags, but no tent or sleeping bag. He knew he had to leave before our arrival, in case we had orders to the contrary. We radioed back again for further instructions and were tersely ordered to "bring back Dorsey" and return all hands to the Ice Cap station. Tex typed us an official copy. Even on the trail, the radio operator carried a typewriter to back up messages for the record. Granted permission to rest the dogs first, we sacked out for a few hours, then headed off once more, easily following Herb's faint ski tracks in the hard snow. His trail was arrow-straight and well-marked with bamboo wands, and here and there were discarded candy wrappers. Though a mere corporal in the army, I was beginning to feel like a Northwest Mountie.

With Herb's headstart, it took us twelve hours on the trail to overtake him, even though he was within our view for the last few miles. As we topped each low rise, we'd see him topping the one ahead. Surely, we judged, he saw us too. Finally, when light snow began to fall, Joe said we'd have to stop before the next hill unless we overtook him sooner—the dogs could go no farther. I nodded assent. Then suddenly there was Herb on his knees in the snow just a few yards ahead. With a small entrenching shovel he was digging a snow hole for shelter, and he looked up disinterestedly. "Well, how's it going," he asked more in salutation than in question, and when we replied that we had orders to bring him back, he asked if we had something in writing. We nodded affirmative, and when he saw our radiogram he cooperated willingly. "I expect I'll be court-martialed," he added, "but I couldn't let this opportunity pass by." Joe and I understood. We were out ninety-eight miles by then, at an altitude of 7,800 feet, and had talked of dashing on across the top ourselves. Yet Wade's irritation was understandable also; Herb's caper, he feared, would disrupt the whole expedition. We stopped for the night, then turned back.

Meanwhile, a third convoy set out on July 16, "hindered," in Wade's words, "by the failure of two differentials." Greenland Base Command was now airdropping differentials almost routinely, and Lardass Johnson was busier than the floor manager of Filene's basement. On July 18, 1944, despite these odds, the Ice Cap station was erected and ready for occupancy, the culmination of a year of cold sweat and fears by BICD and two years of planning, goading, and cajoling by the army air force. Wade savored this moment of glory, and the air force rewarded him with a gold leaf—a majority. Borden made captain.

In the euphoria of Wade's promotion, all was forgiven at the Ice Cap station, and we were advised by radiogram to "open the barbed wire." All of us were quite hilarious, the first detachment of troops ever stoned on the Greenland Ice Cap. (Being "stoned" in those innocent times simply meant imbibing a little too much booze.) Joe silently poured a glass of gin, drank it down slowly, then rose and stalked back to his tent, only slightly glassy-eyed.

Our Ice Cap station, the first such permanent-type structure eve built on any ice cap, according to Wade, was a prefabricated building made of hollow-cored, insulated, weather-treated plywood panels, all bolted together on site. Its outside dimensions were about thirty feet long, twelve feet wide, and ten feet high. The panels were about six inches thick, and once laid out, were quickly assembled with no more than a couple of wrenches and a hammer. The entry was a heavy-duty affair exactly like a door to a walk-in frozen-food locker. The station's weatherworthiness had already been tested back at base camp by the identical structure erected there for a radio station after the big fire. We added a small, separate generator and coal-storage shack outside, covered with heavy tarpaulin cloth. So, at last, we were ready to transmit all kinds of surface weather information from the Ice Cap all year around, including air pressure, temperature, winds, humidity, cloud conditions, and precipitation. Though we had no capacity up there to make hydrogen or hence to run balloons, we soon were transmitting weather reports every six hours to all our allies around the world. The balloons would have to wait.

Figs. 28–5 and 28-6.   Above: The Ice Cap station at midnight. Below: Interior of the Ice Cap station.

The Letdown

As things turned out, however, we never did get the chance to send up balloons from the new station. At the very moment of success, the purpose and value of all our efforts on the Ice Cap became moot. New, long-range aircraft were now bypassing the Ice Cap route to Europe, and the upturn of the war assured an Allied victory. Ice Cap operations were canceled, and we were ordered off the Cap by August 1. With all our time, toil, and equipment invested, we thought the army surely would reconsider and allow long-term occupancy. The station, after all, was designed and built for year-round use, and its climatological research value would be enormous, but despite Wade's heartfelt pleadings the army was adamant. The station accordingly was carefully closed down, fully equipped with food and all supplies needed for ongoing operations and ready to start up again at a moment's notice. We still harbored expectations that the army would relent. Galbreath and Cadigan even added extra lengths of stovepipe and bolted a twenty-five-foot-long pole to the roof to help pinpoint the structure after its inevitable burial beneath the snow come winter. The pole, we guessed, would remain exposed for at least a year, but the army held firm, and we never returned. I was particularly incensed at leaving behind an unopened case of Hershey bars.

Joe and I were first to leave. With a brisk wind at our backs, I rigged up a sail of lightweight canvas and bamboo trail poles–a square-rigger. Then we said our goodbyes, broke the sled runners loose, and took off like a scared rabbit. The dogs were on their feet instantly, and they just trotted alongside with slack traces and big grins on their faces as we made an astonishing twenty-five miles in three hours. We though we could reach base camp in one day, but then the wind began to back around to the east and spoiled the fun. We even tacked on one runner for a while, but my design was not suited for crosswinds.

Since it was about time to make camp anyway, we lowered the sail and laid over until morning. "Shall we open the compass, Hønsen?" Joe suggested as we crawled into our sacks. "No, let's wait," I pleaded, and luckily we did, because we awoke early to a driving snowstorm out of the east, and we struggled along all day on a compass bearing, straining for each mile, watching for the next trail flag. Any appreciable departure from our correct course in this part of the marginal zone would jeopardize our safety in badly crevassed areas on either side of the trail. We made camp near Max Demorest's old Ice Cap station, and though the station was deeply buried by snow and nothing remained of it to be seen, I thought about Demorest and his sad fate a lot that night before drifting off to sleep.

Next morning the weather had cleared. About six miles out we met deep slush directly athwart our path—almost a shallow lake—but the undeterred dogs quickened their pace as they sensed our approach to camp, and with Rocky Craig and Atterbury Dome as guide posts, we glided uneventfully toward home. Soon the dogs were in a dead run, heading in on the rotting remains of a long-expired seal just outside the camp perimeter. Now beyond even Joe's control, all dogs plunged into the spoiling flesh, burying their heads and shoulders in a frenzy of bloody indulgence, gorging themselves in gluttonous surfeit. They had earned their pleasure so we waited patiently, then finally pulled them off, untangled their besmeared traces, dragged them to their pipe chains, and headed for the mess hall. We had been on the Cap for the last time.

29

Bob Bartlett and the
E. M. Morrissey

After we abandoned the Ice Cap station, the only reason for keeping our camp going boiled down to servicing and running the weather station at Atterbury Dome, and that wasn't a job for nineteen men. By the first week of August it was clear that we were going to be phased out and would be up for reassignment. For the first time in our thirteen-month struggle with the weather at Comanche Bay we had more leisure than we knew what to do with, and I spent a lot of time ski touring. Getting around on skis was easier than on foot, even in August. I made one-day forays all over the peninsula—*qeqertaussag*—munching on K rations and D chocolate bars, looking at rocks, and marveling anew at the wonders of the Arctic summer. Down near the south point of land—*kujatleq*—I discovered another asbestos deposit, though from outward appearances it wasn't as fine a deposit as the one I had found earlier.

On August 19 a small trawler dropped anchor in the fjord. It was the *Polarbjorn* carrying Johan Johansen's Norwegian trapper friends and orders for his return to BW-1. Joe needed no urging. Leaving his dogs in our care, he quickly packed his few belongings and was down at the beachhead, and with him aboard, the Norwegians raised anchor on the twenty-second after celebrating their reunion with two days of drunken revelry. On duty at the weather station, I didn't even see him off. By the end of August thin coatings of ice reappeared on the fjord on still nights. On September 5 our replacements for the weather station were brought in by PBY and were soon exhilarated by their first clear-weather piteraq blowing seventy miles per hour out of the north. Though it was a mere foreboding of what soon would follow, they seemed enthused about the prospects, and I wondered months later how they fared.

Erqernianagssaq, the ptarmigan

One of the new guys spotted a ptarmigan on the roof of the instrument shelter and grabbed a rifle to blast it down, but he was quickly deterred by our spontaneous rage. We had been feeding a small flock at the station all winter, and they had become quite tame. In fact, most ptarmigan in this part of the world had little fear of people and could easily be approached within a few feet if you made no quick or threatening moves. Eventually, as winter drew on, our replacements would feel the same kinship we shared with the sparse wildlife of the area, including the ptarmigan and our resident ravens.

On September 8 a trim two-masted schooner dropped anchor off the beachhead station, and word flashed through camp that it was the *Effie M. Morrissey* commanded by Captain Robert A. Bartlett, heroic figure of monumental exploits. Newfoundlander Bob Bartlett was the famous Arctic skipper who in 1909 had piloted Robert E. Peary's controversial expedition to the North Pole. (Far out on the polar ice Bartlett inexplicably was ordered back to camp just before the final dash to the pole. In that Bartlett was a highly skilled navigator, could his talents have proven embarrassing to the assault party? Could the party in fact have never reached the Pole? People will forever have doubts.) Bartlett subsequently commanded the ill-fated ship *Karluk,* which was crushed by ice in 1912 in the Chukchi Sea northwest of Alaska while on charter by explorer Vilhjalmur Stefansson. Stefansson, who had gone ashore on his own in the Canadian Arctic and was not aboard, said little about the incident in recounting his own adventures. Bartlett led the passengers and crew across the ice to makeshift shelter on Wrangell Island north of Siberia in the Chukchi Sea. Then he set out on an epic six-hundred-mile sledge journey to Nome to seek help, leading to the rescue a year later of the starving, scurvy-racked survivors, who, awaiting his return, had suffered unspeakable hardships through the long winter night.

Now, thirty-two years later, Bartlett had contracted with the

Fig. 29–1. The *Effie M. Morrissey* at anchor in Comanche Bay, September, 1944. The beachhead station is in the background at right.

U.S. Army to ferry part of our crew up to Ikateq, and I was one of the designees. I was going aboard ship with the great Bob Bartlett. Bartlett, however, was not a social animal—at least not with American GIs, whom he viewed with quiet scorn, according to one biographer. The GIs, he said, were spoiled malcontents, although how the writer knew is unclear, because Bartlett was dourly uncommunicative. An old man by the time I boarded his vessel, he had little more than a year to live. On board ship he stayed to himself, taking his meals alone in his captain's quarters, even though his own more personable younger brother, who was his first mate, ate with the passengers and crew.

The *Morrissey* was a well-tested veteran of Arctic waters, a sleek, stunning ship 110 feet long with a fifteen-foot beam and an icebreaker prow, reportedly fitted out by Bartlett for Arctic travel soon after he acquired the vessel many years before. The galley and quarters were below deck. The head was a small outhouse cantilevered out over the water from the starboard gunwale, and to flush it you just doused it with a bucket of salt water hoisted up over the side with a long rope tied to the rail. In really rough weather the bucket wasn't needed. The "Noofie" crewmen who ran the ship were small of stature, and to stand up in the head you had to hunch low like a coal miner. The radio operator on board was a tall, thin, amiable young American sergeant who walked with a decided slouch.

Almost as soon as we raised anchor and waved a bittersweet farewell to the beachhead station, I climbed the rigging for a better view. As we cruised quietly down the fjord toward the open sea, a short but memorable chapter in all our lives was drawing rapidly to a close and we eagerly yet reluctantly accepted its passing. Someday, we all said, we surely would return, but deep down we all knew that we would probably not. Comanche Bay was not your average scheduled port-of-call. We were seeing Comanche Bay for the last time, and its rocky ramparts yielded all too quickly to the ice floes outside. Fourteen months of total isolation in a remote wilderness outpost thousands of miles from one's home surroundings and utterly different from anything in one's prior experience is a long time in the life of a young man, easily equal to five years of an old man's life. The psychology of isolation is hard to understand and even harder to express in words. Our lives and our reason for existence during those months had been totally enmeshed in the Greenland Ice Cap and this tiny tract of land beside a small bay on the empty southeast coast. A shortwave radio was a tenuous tie to an outside world that existed only in memory and imagination. Reality for us was snow and ice in an unworldly beautiful land, incredibly bad weather, twenty-one men, thirty-five dogs, and unspeakably monotonous rations. Now, that reality itself was vanishing.

From the rigging I looked down forty feet to the deck and saw the whole ship below me slip gracefully through the ice. Atterbury Dome was to port, dropping fast behind. Growlers fore and aft rubbed the ship's planking, their mostly submerged bulk like turquoise in the water. I looked back at chiseled Anikitsok sinking slowly beneath the curvature of the Earth. The Ice Cap shrank to a thin white line behind a bank of gray sea fog. On deck, Bob Bartlett stomped his feet against the cold and beat his arms around his chest as he bellowed commands to his helmsman. The wheel of the *Morrissey* was at the stern, directly over the rudder, and the helmsman steered blindly but deftly from behind while Bartlett watched the ice from the foredeck in front of the bridge.

We were now beyond sight of land, coursing due northeast. As we neared the thinning margin of the pack ice, the swells rose larger and larger beneath the ship, inversely proportional in size to the closeness and density of the pack. In the rising seas, no longer dampened by the ice, the ship's masts began to swing like inverted pendulums, and discretion told me to get the hell down on deck. Clouds darkened the sky and the blue water turned gray.

Bartlett's weathered old face was framed by shaggy white ringlets hanging from his temples and over his ears below his balding pate. With Bob Grahl and Max Morris, I took a position near the bowsprit where we could watch the passing scene and gaze in awe at the countenance of the great Captain Bartlett not ten feet away. Don Galbreath huddled out of the wind close against the bridge, braced against the roll and pitch of the vessel, his jaw set and his face a parchment gray, his weary eyes underlined by green triangles. Don was tough, but he never would have made a good sailor.

From our vantage point at the bow, Bob, Max, and I looked out at two long, straight lines of frothy bubbles about five hundred yards apart right across our course and reaching the limit of sight on both sides. In fact, we sailed right across them. Periscope wakes! But the mate scoffed indulgently at our wild-eyed naivete–they were just spindrift, blown up by the wind (and settled on the water in two perfectly straight lines). Nothing more was said, but our own logic told us we were right: the submarine's skipper just didn't want to expose his position for a second-rate target like an aged schooner that wasn't worth a shot from the deck gun, let alone a torpedo. Or perhaps they were in fact the wakes of torpedos. Shortly thereafter, a patrol plane scrambled out of BE-2 and flew low over the *Morrissey,* almost buzzing us. Then it banked out to sea, and there the incident ended. Had the mate radioed in to the antisubmarine patrol? We never knew. By September, 1944, the North Atlantic, of course, had been swept rather clean of Nazi U-boats.

Darkness was falling when the sharp skyline of Angmagssalik Island came into view. We dropped anchor in a sheltered cove near a native settlement that I took to be the village of Angmagssalik but later concluded was Kap Dan on the lesser island of

Fig. 29–2. Apusiajik Glacier north of Kap Dan.

Kulusuk, "shaped like a bird's back." We were headed for Angmagssalik Fjord, the large water body that separates Kulusuk
from Angmagssalik Island and that harbored BE-2 farther north
at Ikateq. (Angmagssalik means "where the caplin are," these
being sardinelike herring much prized by the Greenlanders for
food. Ikateq means "the shallow water.") When we went below,
the cove was crowded with majestic icebergs, riding ghostly at
anchor in the black waters of the night. I went to sleep thinking
of the next day's cruise up Angmagssalik Fjord. I had seen its
rugged walls twice before but in a different season and from a
different perspective–once up and once back, at rim level in the
Norseman ski plane on my visit to the dentist. Everything then
had been white, and the fjord frozen hard. Now we would see
the bare rock walls fully exposed, before their harsh lines were
softened by the lasting snows of winter. My geologic eye preferred the bare rock.

Angmagssalik Fjord was new to the rest of the passengers and
to the crew also, I judged, because Bartlett kept consulting his
charts. With its many tributaries the fjord forms a tangle of intersecting waterways crowded by towering islands and half-awash
skerries; shipboard navigation had to be precise. From Kap Dan
to Ikateq is thirty-five miles of scenic splendor. Unlike Comanche
Bay, where the subdued walls were scoured smooth by an over-
riding Ice Cap, Angmagssalik Fjord was fashioned by a network
of giant valley glaciers grinding laterally as well as downward,
sapping their walls and floors, crowding close to one another,
each glacier rasping its bed with the very rock debris eroded
therefrom. Many glaciers in fact had crowded in so close that
only narrow arêtes remained between them, knife-edged ridges
surmounted by stunning horns and pinnacles, gendarmes and

217

minarets. As the glaciers slowly disappeared, sea water a thousand feet deep backed up the drowned-out valleys, making them a maze of blue abyssal fjords.

Even now, dozens of small glaciers hang from the walls of Angmagssalik Fjord and its many branching arms. A few large ice tongues reach clear to tidewater, and sprawling icefields cap the highlands back from the water. In summer, grasses and banks of wildflowers crowd the few footholds along the shores, but cliffs and rocky ledges elsewhere plunge to the water. The skyline is chiseled endlessly. Glistening pillars of granite tower above the water–whole ranges of Grand Tetons. Ramparts of contorted gneiss pitch off at crazy angles, gneiss tortured by deepseated upheavals 2.8 billion years ago and brought to Earth's surface by eons of erosion–marvelous places for aspiring young rock climbers to gain a first ascent, perhaps, and lasting fame.

We weren't privy to all those marvels from the deck of the *Morrissey* that day, however. As morning broke, a drizzly overcast hid everything but the lowermost walls of the fjord, and we faced intermittent rain and drizzle all the way to Ikateq. Two-thirds of the way there the fjord divided three ways, and Bartlett slowed to get his bearings. Suddenly a delegation of kayakers appeared alongside, laughing, joking, waving, and paddling valiantly to stay abreast. Hanging over the rail, we cheered and urged them on, and they responded with added drive, but they slowly lost ground, dropped behind, and disappeared in the mists. Where had they come from? How had they spotted our ship? Just a moment of visual contact and they were gone forever.

Now we were on the last leg and in just two hours were docking at a metropolis of six hundred men, Bluie East-2. A larger vessel was tied up alongside, and a man with the voice of authority high up on deck yelled down to a dogface on the pier below: "Catch my barracks bag!" As it plummeted over the side, the hapless GI was bowled over by the impact. Clutching the man's bag, he toppled backward off the pier, ten feet into the icy fjord, with a resounding splash. The man on deck was outraged–all his belongings were soaked–and his curses filled the air. After fourteen months of isolation, we indeed were back in the army. Then we debarked, piling into a big truck that delivered us to the transient barracks and heading en masse to a scalding-hot shower–our first since the summer of 1943. Civilization had its amenities, and the army wasn't all bad.

Ikateq (BE-2) and Comanche Bay are only about 150 miles apart, but few places in Greenland could be less alike. In Comanche Bay's harsh setting of wind, ice, and snow, the prevalent dimension was horizontal, and vistas were tens of miles across. Ikateq, in contrast, was hemmed in by vertical mountains towering right over camp—from the window of the transient barracks you craned your neck to see their tops—and the farthest visible point was only four miles away.

There was plenty of ice. Small glaciers poured down the mountains in all quadrants, and bergs filled the water. Right across the sound—Ikateq was open at both ends—a truly lovely glacier descended the heights in a smooth lobe graced by dark morainal bands, but the big scene was dominated by rock. Craggy granite peaks brooded over the short dirt runway. Piercing the sky, they rose elegantly from the water's edge in smooth catenary curves, their lower slopes heavy with grass. But in winter they bred avalanches that twice wiped out the control tower and menaced the camp itself.

Sheltered in its mountain redoubt, Ikateq was the banana belt of southeast Greenland, because it escaped the furious onslaughts of places more exposed. Its high latitude and the long shadows of its mountain ramparts shortened the winter days and lowered the thermometer twenty to thirty degrees below the norms at Comanche Bay, but the climatic influence of the Ice Cap was moderated by fifty miles of intervening mountains that also tempered the anger of the North Atlantic storms. Which is colder—perfectly still air at forty below zero, or one hundred knots of wind at five above? Check out the chill factor and note the small difference, but the "warmer" wind is infinitely more dangerous. Ikateq Sound froze over early in the fall and stayed frozen all winter, and its air was bitterly crisp. But the wind of Comanche Bay not only sapped the heat from the human body; its attendant ground blizzard blanked out visibility, and its powerful surge hurled loose objects through the air like random guided missiles. Comanche Bay was open nearly all the time, kept free of ice by the relentless winds off the Ice Cap, but even though the open water itself moderated the temperature, Comanche Bay was far less hospitable than its colder but less windy neighbor.

Ikateq Sound merges northeast with a large fjord called Sermiligaq, "the fjord with glaciers at its head." Sermiligaq (not to be confused with Sermilik) is four to six miles across and about twenty-five miles long. Two mountainous Islands guard its mouth–Erik den Rodes and Leifs Øer, named a hundred years ago by explorer Gustav Holm for the settler of Greenland and his celebrated son. Sermiligaq heads in a splendid wilderness of giant peaks and interconnected valley glaciers, a region drained wholly by flowing ice. Duly impressed by its alpine grandeur, European explorers dubbed the region Schweizerland, and the name still stands. Mount Forel is the highest summit at 11,024 feet, named to honor the memory of a Swiss alpinist. Dozens of lesser peaks have Danish, French, or Greenlandic names, but scores are still unnamed. Most of the myriad glaciers lack names too, though the names of a few of the bigger ones suggest the origins of their European discoverers, the legends of Norse mythology, or the bland descriptions of the Greenlanders: names such as Glacier de France, Midgardgletscher, Helheimgletscher, and Apuserajik. Best known–but far from being the largest–is Knud Rasmussen Glacier, which meets Sermiligaq at the very head of the fjord in an ice front a mile and a half wide.

Though minutes by air from Ikateq and a short trip by boat, Sermiligaq was seen by few GIs. Ikateq, itself, should have been a marvelous place to escape the boredom and confinement of an Arctic duty post. A mile-long tarn just north of camp teemed with Arctic char. Lemmings, hares, foxes, and ptarmigan skulked the deep grass along its banks. (Its outlet through camp was closed to all but the camp commander, who was an ardent fly fisherman.) Picturesque icebergs clogged Ikateq Sound; easy strolling along the shore opened fresh new vistas at every turn; rocky tundras invited nature study, but all these exciting places were posted by the army. Off limits–too hazardous. Soldiers were restricted to the immediate camp area. Besides, Ping-Pong and pool tables, in the army's view, affordable ample recreation in the day room. What more could a soldier want?

We stayed at BE-2 about two weeks, gravitating between the mess hall and the pool tables in the day room. We strove earnestly to be first in line at chow and first back at the day room, before the regulars finished eating. (No one was sorry to see us ship out.) On one trip through the chow line I noted a slight, dark-complexioned man clad in GI dress, but wearing kamiks. He looked around with a toothy grin, and I smiled back. He was just a cheery Greenlander trying out the cuisine, and a deadpan cook filled his tray without a change of pace or a hint of recogni-

Fig. 29-5. Knud Rasmussen Glacier at the head of Sermiligaq.

tion. I made a few calls at the weather station to exchange gossip with the men on duty and catch up on meteorological events. (Also, one of the weathermen had devised his own recipe for mojo.) A hurricane from the Caribbean, I learned, was running out its course in Denmark Strait between Greenland and Iceland, not far from Ikateq, though the air at the base was calm. Then I stopped off at the camp library to browse through its collections and found a little book about the *Morrissey*, which I avidly consumed. One GI who frequented the bookshelves and talked intelligently proved to be illiterate, though he covered his shortcoming well. When I saw him last, he was intently studying a book held upside down, as the librarian nodded knowingly with a sideward glance.

The *Belle Isle*

On the evening of our last day in camp, we boarded the S.S. *Belle Isle* to be assigned quarters for our return to Bluie West-1. The *Belle Isle* was a big, eight-thousand-ton merchant ship refurbished to carry passengers. Ships that size seldom cruised Greenland waters, and it looked like the *Queen Mary*. The enlisted bunkroom was astern, under the ship's fantail where all

Fig. 29-4. Icebergs in Angmagssalik Fjord, viewed west toward the mountains of Angmagssalik Island.

the motions of the vessel were duly magnified. The officers' wardroom was amidships, where the motions were minimal. Canvas bunks for the GIs were stacked four high, though most of them were empty, as the ship was traveling light with few troops aboard. There was little cargo either, so the ship sat high in the water and bobbed like a cork.

Immediately on boarding we were ordered to strip for a "short-arm inspection"–army lingo for an abasing physical exam intended, ostensibly, to forestall the spread of "social diseases" or "V.D." Since no one at Ikateq had even seen anyone of the feminine gender for many months, we concluded that the army's sole purpose was to harass, humble, and humiliate the enlisted personnel. The army could best manipulate its men, we reasoned, by destroying their personal dignity. Officers, of course, being immune to V.D., were exempt. Short arms were also required of GIs every payday, before they drew their wages, in duty stations worldwide, except in isolated duty like the BICD, where no one was paid until returned to regular service. The examining physician evinced little pleasure in his work. With pinched face and furrowed brow, he surely was only carrying out army regulations.

Even though the water in Ikateq Sound was glassy as a mirror when the *Belle Isle* pulled away from the dock that evening, many ashen-faced soldiers retreated to their bunks and didn't reappear until we reached BW-1. The open sea was a different matter: the big ground swells arose as soon as we crossed the mouth of Angmagssalik Fjord, and nearly everyone on board came down with *mal de mer,* including the skipper and most of the crew. As the stern pitched and rolled, the propeller rose clear out of the water on top of each swell, racing the gear shaft and shaking the ship into convulsions. Then the cupboard doors sprang open in the galley, pots and pans avalanched across the room, and I learned the meaning of "a loose cannon." In the head, when the overtaxed plumbing overflowed, walking grew precarious on decks awash with barf. With each pitch and roll, the toilets erupted like geysers.

Bob Grahl and I climbed up topside just behind the bridge for fresh air, faces to the wind, where we could maintain a horizon, watch the stars, and stare across the roaring seas toward the coastline glistening in the moonlight. All the black swells were frothed with ghostly whitecaps. The mate, a kindly Norwegian, pointed out the flukes of a whale, and we settled down in our parkas against the warmth of the stack for a most enjoyable interlude.

Early on the third day, the crew ran short of able-bodied kitchen help and a call was put out for volunteers. As servicemen on a merchant ship, we weren't required to pull KP, but I naively obliged and was led below to a ladder that went clear down to the bilges, where the sides of the vessel came together over the keel. Here were crates of potatoes moldering in the gloom, many of them visibly rotting, and the smell of fungus permeated the dank, heavy air. With the compliments of the cook, I was graciously handed a paring knife by an apologetic seaman who quickly retreated up the ladder. Then my fingers went through the first potato I tried to pick up. Few people, I judged, had peeled rotting potatoes in the bilges of an empty ship tossing in the tumultuous seas of East Greenland, and I chalked the whole incident up to experience. Little wonder that the galley had run short of help.

On the fourth day out the *Belle Isle* was due to reach the shelter of Eriksfjord, and everyone aboard eagerly anticipated the calming of the waters. Eriksfjord reaches sixty miles inland, clear to BW-1 and smooth sailing all the way. However, the Greenlandic name of the fjord, Tunugdliarfik ("the turnaround place"), proved to be prophetic, because we arrived at its mouth after nightfall, and the skipper was disinclined to negotiate its outer skerries in a gale after dark. Good thinking. Instead, he turned the ship back out to sea and steamed in circles until daybreak, riding the bounding main while his hollow-eyed passengers clung to the edges of their bunks.

Inside the fjord at first light, spirits and water conditions improved notably. Everyone was topside hanging over the rails, but this time to gawk at the scenery. As at Angmagssalik Fjord, I had passed here twice before, once by air at 180 miles per hour and once by ship asleep below deck. Now I savored every moment at a leisurely ten knots. The fjord was calm, the sky was blue, the air was crisp, and the sun was warm. Reddish brown crags topped off the heights of the fjord walls, and snowfields and small glaciers hung from sheltered recesses in the walls. Grass carpeted the lower slopes, still green even this late in the fall.

The grass in southwest Greenland makes for good pasturage, so herding is the chief occupation. The *Belle Isle* overtook a Greenlander headed upfjord in a weathered motorboat, towing seven dories loaded to the waterline with sheep. Our bow wave set the boats to rocking, and when an alarmed sheep jumped overboard, the Greenlander simply took his convoy around in a wide circle and with one arm hoisted the waterlogged animal back aboard. Then he looked up at the *Belle Isle*, grinned broadly, and waved us on. We cheered and returned the greeting. Musing over the incident, I wondered how an American sheepman might react to like circumstances; in my mind I saw a red-faced herder shaking his fist in rage and bellowing obscenities.

Tunugdliarfik doesn't generally contain a lot of ice. Only one tidewater glacier dumps bergs there—Qoroq Sermia, "the valley glacier"—and though large, it wasn't highly active. Qoroq Sermia is at the head of a deep arm ten miles long that joins the main fjord six miles below Narsarssuak. Qoroq, though, sometimes fills the arm with bergs after an occasional debacle of calving, and tidal currents scatter them up and down the fjord. (Now in the 1990s, half a century later, tourist leaflets describe Qoroq as a highly active source of bergs. Times and glaciers seldom remain the same.) Some of Tunugdliarfik's ice comes from the adjacent Bredefjord ("broad fjord," known in Greenlandic as Ikers-

suaq, "the big fjord") by way of Narssaq Sund, which links the
two fjords together about halfway up from their mouths. Bredefjord gets its bergs from prodigious outpourings directly off the
Ice Cap, and the whole upper end of the fjord is always too
crowded with ice to permit navigation.

At Narssaq Sund we cruised close by the town of Narssaq, "the
plain," instantly distinguished by its uncommon odor: besides
being a woolgrowers' paradise, it has a large fish-processing
facility, and the olfactory combination is awesome. Narssaq,
population about two thousand, clings to the south end of a
mountainous peninsula in the center of a region celebrated in
the geologic literature for its rare-mineral occurrences and unusual structures. Geologists call it the Gardar district of southwest Greenland, named for the Old Norse bishopric of Gardar at
a narrow isthmus on the east side of the fjord. The stone ruins
of Gardar are easily reached from Tunugdliarfik after a two-mile
trek across scenic grasslands. During the war the whole area
was off limits to GIs, however, and most soldiers never visited a
Norse ruin and never met or even saw a Greenlander. The re-
striction was not entirely of the army's doing; the Danish authorities were hardly anxious to see fraternization between the army
and the native populace, and they probably were right. The natives, if not the GIs, were better off.

Southwest Greenland—broadly speaking, the Julianehaab district—is climatically the most temperate and demographically the
most populous part of Greenland. Except for the bergs and glaciers, it recalls the northwest Scottish Highlands, though its inner
reaches are far more rugged. Erik the Red's choice was well
made: as Greenland goes, this area is hospitable. The deeply indented coastline shelters the countryside from both the storms
off the ocean and the icy blasts off the Ice Cap. Windstorms
rarely exceed seventy miles per hour. Thickets of Arctic willow
stand taller than shoulder-high in sunny ravines, and white
birches in some secluded valleys reportedly reach twenty-five
feet high. Up at Comanche Bay, on the other hand, birches don't
grow at all, and the tallest willows are barely ankle high. They
creep along the ground like prostrate vines.

Soon we were easing into the army dock at BW-1, debarking,
and after a short wait, piling into a canvas-topped army truck for
delivery to the transient barracks, which would be our home

while we sweated our return to the States. First, though, we were ordered to the local army hospital for a few days of clinical observation to quench rumors that all members of the Ice Cap Detachment had gone mad during the winter. Our psychiatric exam consisted chiefly of three questions: (1) Would you like to be a soldier, (2) do you like girls, and (3) do you like boys? These were written questions, and our answers were never returned, so we never learned if we had passed or failed. Possibly our reactions were observed through one-way glass. Bob Grahl, though, figured I had flipped. Bob was shaken by the shrill scream of an army nurse just outside our room in the infirmary, and he assumed I had grabbed her from behind as I was mopping the floor in the hall. After all, nurses were a novelty to us; we hadn't seen one since leaving Presque Isle. There had been no nurses in Greenland when we headed for Comanche Bay fifteen months before, so on returning to BW-1 and the unexpected sight of women, any normal soldier could hardly help being aroused. But all I had done was set my scrub bucket down near the door, momentarily, and the unsuspecting nurse had planted her foot in it as she strode out of the room. I didn't begrudge her a scream, but I was quite blameless.

At any rate, we must have sailed through the psychiatric exam, because we were soon back in the mainstream of army life. We were ordered down to the squadron orderly room for work detail, still wearing our red and blue checkered Woolrich shirts. There a belligerent young shavetail recently arrived in Greenland threatened us with the stockade. We had again been issued buckets and floor mops and, in his view, lacked the proper attitude toward our work assignment. Hearing of this, Major Wade arranged work details of his own, and I spent the rest of my stay plotting and drafting maps, compiling weather statistics, and doing chores appropriate to the final report for the expedition. I made maps from aerial photographs, using a mirrored plotter called a sketchmaster, now considered quaint and primitive gadgetry by all working cartographers. Down at the blueprint shop, where I went to run off a roll of sepias, an agitated captain asked suspiciously, and with just a hint of hostility, what I was doing there. The success of the entire war effort, it seemed, hung in the balance at Bluie West-1 and all permanent party, as Henry David Thoreau would have said, "led lives of quiet desperation." Once, when a GI at the local weather station didn't respond quickly enough to a question, the weather officer reportedly demanded that he speak, and the soldier replied with a loud "Woof, woof!" All these hot tempers could have been cooled by a short tour of duty on the Ice Cap.

As winter set in again, there were few chances for off-duty excursions into the countryside. Sixteen months earlier in the bloom of late summer, we had covered much of the area around BW-1 on foot, but now the ground was getting white, the days were growing short, and the thermometer was hovering near minus forty. I hiked over the hill toward Qoroq Sermia, hoping for a mountaintop view of the glacier, but it was farther than I thought and I was soon turned back by the shortness of the day. A small tarn high on the mountain abounded with Arctic char, and I wondered how they got there, as the outlet to the fjord was a long ribbon of cascades. Fertilized fish eggs supposedly have been carried from one place to another stuck to the feet of aquatic birds, but that possibility seemed unlikely in Greenland. Probably the cascades were less formidable than they looked from above, and the fish simply made their way upstream to spawn.

One thing that had improved markedly since we had left Comanche Bay was out diet. The morning chow line at BW-1 stretched far down the street in total darkness, but in the brightly lit kitchen a conscientious cook served fresh eggs and bacon prepared to order, all we could eat; Bob Johnson ate a dozen in one sitting. Just inside the open mess hall door, the dinner plates (no more metal trays) were stacked in solemn grandeur like Grecian columns but were all frozen together. Though the kitchen was as hot as a coal-fired power plant, the adjacent dining room was more like a walk-in refrigerator. Each soldier in turn pried his plate loose from the stack, and despite the good intentions of the cook, fresh eggs sunnyside up on the griddle were a frozen slab of rubber on your plate by the time you found an empty place at the table. They still beat a powdered-egg omelet, and no one complained.

We were now promised home leave for Christmas, but when Thanksgiving came and passed we began to have doubts. On Thanksgiving day, ten B-17s were scheduled to arrive from Presque Isle, and the transient mess hall accordingly prepared meals for ninety men. But when bad weather forced the planes to lay over at Goose Bay, the few soldiers who showed up for dinner ate well. The mess sergeant pleaded for all hands to eat more turkey, in fact more of everything, and we cooperated, gourmands all. I thought back to sterner times at Igtip Kangertiva when our Thanksgiving entree was a choice of Vienna sausages or canned bully beef.

At BW-1 it wasn't hard to understand why some GIs loathed life in the far north. The reason was simply boredom. Too many places were off limits. There was no place to go, nothing to do except drudgery, and the weather wasn't like Miami Beach. One day the PX got a shipment of low-cut dress shoes—oxfords—and although there was no earthly reason to buy oxfords in Greenland, let alone wear them, a line of soldiers two blocks long formed outside the PX door in minus-thirty-eight-degree weather when the word got out. There was little else to spend money on. PX cigarettes cost five cents a pack, beer was furnished in the rations—one bottle per day—and liquor simply didn't exist, although transient flight crews sometimes had a bottle or two available at fifty dollars each. (In today's money, that would be about 500 dollars.)

The local Greenlanders soon learned about the excess currency at BW-1, learned of its intrinsic value, and found ways to funnel some of it off. Most GIs were eager to get souvenirs of any kind to take back from their tours of Arctic duty, and the PX officer acquired a carload of native-made sealskin mittens, booties, purses, hats, and jackets to fill the need. These items were expertly sewn pieces, actually works of art, and the entire stock was quickly sold out. Many soldiers bought them for wives and sweethearts back home. Hardly anyone realized, however, that once indoors near the warmth of a human body or an overheated stove, each work of art would yield up the odor of what it had been tanned in, namely human urine. The Greenlanders had been tanning skins in urine for centuries, but traffic with the army lasted only days.

One weatherman, though, who had been at an outpost up north at the west coast village of Egedesminde, showed me a carton full of ivory carvings that he had traded for cigarettes—exquisite figurines, seals, walruses, and polar bears, probably two dozen in all. These were beautifully done pieces, carved before the postwar surge in demand for native art and hence not made to satisfy an artificially created market. Perhaps too eagerly, I offered a king's ransom for a single piece and drew just a derisive sneer. What value, he asked, had money, "where the only things for sale were low-cut shoes and doodaws soaked in piss?"

30
The Last Days

With winter running into December and full blown, we spent as much time as possible sacked out in the transient barracks. Most of us had already seen enough snow to last a lifetime. One evening I was approached by a Lt. Donald A. Shaw, whose name I recognized at once because he had commanded a small weather outpost at Cape Adelaer, about halfway between Cape Farewell and Comanche Bay, and was a highly regarded polar expert and trail man. Lieutenant Shaw had received a direct commission from sergeant to lieutenant in the field and therefore was a sort of folk hero to the lower echelon. Administratively under Wade's command, he reconnoitered the marginal areas of the Ice Cap by dog team west of Adelaer to evaluate snow and possible aircraft landing conditions, and in so doing made significant contributions to a knowledge of the regional geography, including the discovery of a large, previously unmapped fjord.

Lieutenant Shaw showed me a hand specimen of a brass-colored metallic ore he said he had gotten from a Greenlander, and he wondered if I could identify it. It was chalcopyrite, I replied, an important ore of copper, $CuFeS_2$, often associated with lead and zinc, and occasionally with precious metals. Lieutenant Shaw didn't say where the Greenlander got it, but since that time, chalcopyrite has been reported and even mined at several places in West Greenland and at one or two places on the east coast also. Mineral exploration, development, and mining in Greenland, of course, are hampered by isolation, severe weather, and difficult field conditions, and to open a mine, Lieutenant Shaw needed good ore and lots of it.

Years later Shaw was still in the army—a colonel—still in Greenland, and still a trail man. He continued to explore high up on the Ice Cap in the central part of the island, still checking snow and ice conditions and possible landing sites. At that time the air force was making a big push toward a better understanding of all aspects of the Ice Cap, including its meteorologic, climatologic, physical, chemical, and three-dimensional makeup. Greenland was still strategically located with respect to the whole Northern Hemisphere, and an enormous amount of new data was forthcoming, but I heard nothing more of Colonel Shaw's copper deposit.

On December 10, 1944, we got our shipping orders, and our tour of duty was over. Just hours before our departure, as a sort of goodwill gesture, Greenland Base Command ordered a shakedown inspection, pawed through all our gear, and confiscated everything that looked usable, including things we had been issued down in Boston eighteen months before. The army had a perfect right to do this, but it seemed a bit tacky. Then we stuffed what remained into our duffel bags and climbed aboard a bulbous Curtis C-46 transport plane, known affectionately as the "flying cigar" or derisively as the "flying coffin." From Greenland's icy mountains to India's coral strand, in the words of Reginald Heber, most flying cigars went to the China-Burma-India theater as lend-lease for Chiang Kai-shek. Mao Tse-tung probably got them after the revolution, but the few used along the Arctic air routes never fell into his hands.

The flying cigar was oversized and underpowered, and its airspeed only slightly exceeded that of a Goodyear blimp. Our plane labored down the runway, lifted off, and bade farewell to Greenland's icy mountains. Then it droned along for about six hours at 140 miles per hour to reach Goose Bay 860 miles distant. Seat belts were unheard of in those days, but passengers were cautioned by the crew chief to remain seated (on wall benches) during takeoffs and landings. The benches folded up against the wall when not in use, but for most of our trip across the Labrador Sea we sacked out on top of the cargo piled in the middle of the cabin.

Our landfall was made in the darkness of the winter night, but through the righthand windows of the plane we could see the rugged, snow- and tree-covered mountains of coastal Labrador. Trees! The air base at Goose Bay was lit as brightly as a big city, and we landed smoothly on its snow-covered runway. Goose seemed a lot bigger than it had when we'd been outbound a year and a half before. Our perspective of course had changed, after

Comanche Bay, but there were in fact many more buildings on base than there had been on our previous visit–hangars, warehouses, shops, motor pools, and storage lots. The northern route had become the main flyway east, as the war had shifted from the Mediterranean region to northern Europe, and the changes were reflected in the size and activity at Goose.

After such a long day's night, we checked in at the billeting office, chowed down, and headed for the sack. The transient barracks was a big, hall-like place, and before falling off to sleep I listened half awake to a couple of GIs arguing loudly about the North Atlantic Ocean–whether it was frozen solid all the way to the bottom. Then I drifted off and as everything went black, I became aware of being shaken. It was Willie Knutsen, my Norwegian friend from Maine. Captain Willie was now base rescue officer at Goose, and he suggested that Bob Grahl and I join his crew for cognac and caribou steaks at the rescue shack. He wanted to know all about the Ice Cap. Willie drove a powerful and maneuverable oversnow vehicle that would have been useful on the Cap, a half-track affair with skis up front and tracks behind that seemed much more effective then our T-15.

The rescue shack was six miles from beautiful downtown Goose on the edge of a clearing in the woods where the snow was about six feet deep and the thermometer hovered somewhere in the minus twenties. At the shack we were greeted by two more buddies from down-Maine days, both ex-cooks but now rescuemen and five-stripe tech sergeants. Bob and I were still three-stripers–buckass sergeants, in army lingo. We hadn't fared as well promotionwise, despite the promises of our recruiters in Maine, but neither of us would have traded our Ice Cap experience for any number of stripes at Goose Bay. Being ex-cooks, Willie's men were chefs extraordinaire, and they prepared as fine a meal at Willie's table in the wilderness as we had ever eaten, though our evaluation may have been colored by so many months of C rations, Viennas, and powdered eggs. But midway through our repast the phone rang urgently: Mayday from control tower! A plane crash at the end of the runway. Get down ASAP, repeat ASAP.

Willie's response was reflexive. With hardly a farewell handshake, he and his men were off, leaving Bob and me afoot in the black of the Arctic night with a morning plane to catch. We shrugged, finished our steaks, bundled into our parkas, and headed back toward the air base, guided providentially through the darkness by the ceiling light at the base weather station. A powerful vertical beam, spotting the base of the clouds and measuring their height by triangulation, wasn't a beacon to the promised land, but it led us back to the base on time, and the hike down that squeaky, crunchy, snowy road lit by the stars in the still of the night was in fact a pleasurable experience.

That was the last time I saw gallant Willie Knutsen and perhaps was a fitting finale to seventeen months' service in the Arctic. The flight to Presque Isle was uneventful, and by the drone of the engines I pondered the short months of memories that were enough to last a lifetime. Had the whole episode been a frivolous waste, Elliot Roosevelt's pipe dream, or was it the nail that saved the shoe that saved the horse ... that won the war? How did our contribution compare with that of Willie Knutsen? Of a tank crew or a rifle battalion? By today's standards, our achievement was minimal. A single cargo helicopter, or a ski-rigged C-140 cargo plane, could now do in a few hours what our whole Ice Cap Detachment did in fourteen arduous months, and do it better. But what is the measure of true achievement–the output of a metal machine or the striving of a person's heart and soul?

31
Epilogue

The Arctic has a magnetism that few visitors ever fully understand or overcome, especially long-time visitors. It eases its grip grudgingly, and it draws people back. But as the years moved by after World War II, the odds slowly multiplied against my ever returning north, despite the attraction. Greenland was off the transportation routes, and visits were not encouraged by the local authorities. The great island was too remote and too inaccessible for a person of average means to see the way clear to getting there.

Then in 1977 at a Scandinavian travel show in Denver, Icelandic Airlines (Icelandair) advertised selected excursions to Iceland that featured a side trip to southeast Greenland. Greenland was finally awakening to the enormous potential of its natural scenic grandeur and to the idea of revenue enhancement through the tourist trade, and Icelandair was helping it along. Ever since the time of military service, I had believed that the unique beauty of the island and the unspoiled charm of its native culture, once discovered, would inevitably lure those venturesome, particular travelers grown jaded by the great capitals of Europe. Now Icelandic was offering short scenic one-day round trips from Reykjavik—Iceland's scrubbed-clean capital—to Kulusuk, with the possibility of individually arranged stays of several days across the fjord at Angmagssalik.

All this became possible when the U.S. Air Force installed a radar station at Kulusuk as a part of the North American Defense Early Warning System (DEW line) and built an airstrip at Kap Dan to service it. Suddenly the possibility of returning to southeast Greenland became a reality, and my wife and I leaped at the chance. "You've been talking about Greenland since the day we married," Ellen said, "and now I can see it for myself." We flew to Kennedy from Denver, boarded Icelandair for Reykjavik, where we spent a couple of days at the Loftleider Hotel, then enplaned for Greenland in a high-wing, two-engine Fokker Friendship crowded with wide-eyed tourists from northern Europe. We were the only Americans on board. The Fokker was owned by Loftleider Airlines, a subsidiary of Icelandair. Its high wing gave everyone a good view from the windows. Just after takeoff we flew low over the big snow-capped cone of Snaefells Volcano, Jules Verne's legendary entry place to the center of the Earth and Iceland's answer to Japan's Mount Fuji. Then we headed west along the sixty-fifth parallel, left Iceland behind, and entered the gray skies of Denmark Strait. From the air we were retracing the route of Erik the Red and his Viking followers a thousand years before.

The flight to Kulusuk takes about two hours by Fokker, about 470 miles, but Loftleider had a surprise in store. As we neared Kulusuk, and looked down on the thickening pack of floating ice, the flight attendant proudly announced "a scenic side trip before setting down." I had chosen a righthand window in the airplane where, I figured, we'd have a better view of the approach to Greenland, but now the pilot put the plane into a steep right turn and placed coastal Greenland to our left. I scrambled to the other side of the aisle.

We passed close over a cluster of dark, jagged rocks that rose hundreds of feet sheer out of the ocean, supposedly the Gunnbjarnar Skerries. We turned left and right, threading up and down the maze of fjords, skimming low over fleets of icebergs, banked sharply inside the fjord walls, and buzzed the ridge lines. We pivoted over Erik den Rodes Island, then headed up Sermiligaq Fjord toward the crevassed front of Knud Rasmussen Glacier at the entryway to Schweizerland, where a hundred icy peaks pierce the sky. As seen from the air, coastal Sweitzerland is dominated just slightly by the splendid white horn of Ingolfs Fjeld rising above the host, named for the first settler of Iceland and towering over a pretty fjord with the tongue-twisting name of Kangerdlugssuatsiaq, "the rather large fjord," shown on some maps as Kangerdtitivatsiat, equally tongue-twisting.

We turned south to Ikateq, and my heart leaped to my throat as we passed twice over the old airstrip. The flight attendant announced that this had been an American air base during World War II, and I announced, ahem, that I had served there. Visibly

Fig. 31-1. Kangerdlugssuatsiaq ("the rather large fjord") and its alpine backdrop northeast of Angmagssalik.

astonished, she replied that I was the first American to her knowledge who had ever returned, and my stature rose a notch or two in the minds of the other passengers. Then the pilot headed down Angmagssalik Fjord toward Kulusuk, detoured briefly over the villages of Kungmiut ("the river people"), Angmagssalik, and Kap Dan, and alighted softly on the runway. I stepped just as softly from the door and walked several feet off the ground to the little airport terminal where we waited in the cold, damp air for the helicopter that would ferry us the fifteen miles across the fjord to Angmagssalik. It was just thirty-three years since I had been on the ground in East Greenland, thirty-three years since I had peeled potatoes out at sea below deck on the *Belle Isle,* and the present seemed less real than the past.

The most astonishing thing about Kulusuk, and all the other villages, was the pavement. The former dirt trails were now paved with asphalt. Greenland is a possession of Denmark, but after World War II it gained autonomous self-rule and full representation in the Danish parliament. Greenlanders now share citizenship equally, wanted or not, with the Danes and as such also share equally the privileges and amenities thus entailed, including paved streets. On the socialistic theory that equals must be treated equally in all respects, moreover, local stores were stocked with an incredible array of Danish goods and foodstuffs including, sad to say, soda pop and candy bars, which have done little to improve the dental hygiene of the populace but have greatly increased the business of the local dentist.

In 1977 the dentist for the District of East Greenland was a dedicated Danish émigré, Dr. Aksel Rom, and he deplored the dental caries spreading through the villages like an epidemic— caused, he said, by candy and soda pop. In 1944 there probably wasn't a tooth cavity in all of East Greenland, American army bases excepted; the native diet was high in fat and protein and low in carbohydrate, and it simply included no agents of tooth decay. But in 1977 Dr. Rom was obliged to make periodic calls by helicopter to all the outlying villages of the district, and he marveled that he was paid for doing so. (I too would have flown the route happily without pay.)

At Kulusuk Ellen and I piled into a big cargo helicopter for the flight to Angmagssalik, crowded in beside miscellaneous crates and cartons. The helicopter service was owned and operated by two resident Swedes who said they had taken out Greenlandic residence to protect their earnings from the confiscatory Swedish income tax, though they returned to Sweden occasionally to renew acquaintances with their wives and children in the mother country. Europeans employed in Greenland received large pay differentials over what they would make in Europe, as an inducement for their coming, and considering the attendant hardships, the Swedes wanted to keep some of it for themselves.

Travel by helicopter in Greenland is the way to go in the latter part of the twentieth century. The big plexiglass windows yield great viewing of the stunning scene racing by below and of the distant peaks shrouded in mist and heavy with ice. Besides, fixed-wing aircraft are hindered by a lack of runways, and float planes are hindered by floating ice. I was reminded of a story making the rounds in Presque Isle Army Air Base in 1943. A bill of lading for the delivery of some goods to Greenland specified shipment by rail, but when the supply officer was informed that Greenland had no railroads, he just shrugged and said, "Send it by truck." Even now, supplies and people in Greenland have only two travel options, water and air—mostly water, because of the scarcity of airstrips. Although very little floe ice (salt-water ice) remains in Angmagssalik Fjord by late summer in most years, countless bergs and growlers of all sizes and descriptions still persist. The bergs are replenished continually by fresh calvings off the big glaciers, and with the ebb and flow of the tides the bergs tend to concentrate in the back bays and arms of the fjord. As our chopper skimmed low over the indented shoreline of Kulusuk Island we saw water so crowded with bergs and growlers that travel by boat would tax the skills of the best local navigator. We stopped briefly at the village of Kap Dan to take on cargo, and I momentarily glimpsed a misty ghost of the *Morrissey* anchored offshore; then we made the big leap across Angmagsalik Fjord.

Kap Dan is home for about three hundred Greenlanders who make their living by fishing and sealing and by carving in bone and ivory for tourists and art dealers. Most of the ivory comes from whale teeth, which I once heard are shipped in chiefly from Alaska. Kap Dan and Kungmiut claim the greatest carvers in Greenland, artists who do exquisite figurines and miniatures of bears and seals, but who specialize in the *tupilak* (plural *tupilait*).

Tupilait are fanciful little hobgoblins stemming from the mythology of East Greenland and possessed of supernatural attributes. In older times the makers empowered their creations with a capacity to cast deadly spells and wreak fearful vengeance, mostly on individuals who had somehow maligned the maker. In those days, as reported by explorer Gustav Holm, tupilait were made from driftwood, bone, and fur in varied combinations. Nowadays ivory is much preferred over wood or bone by collectors who are willing to pay well for high-quality native art. In view of U.S. legislation protecting marine mammals, however, legal ivory is becoming scarce, so more and more tupilait are being carved from caribou antlers. Antlers provide an acceptable renewable resource, suitable for very pleasing artwork.

Tupilait are partly anthropomorphic and partly animal–hideous humanoids with heads, arms, and legs of bears, dogs, or seals. The more frightful the creation, the greater its power. Rare females can be recognized by top-knotted hairdos (which were worn by adult women of Greenland until the first part of the twentieth century). Some ingenious creations resemble men from one viewpoint, and seals, bears, or dogs from another. The carver instills a certain capricious charm into each exquisite if grotesque piece, governed by random variations in the shape of each individual bone, antler, or tooth and by the moods and inclinations of the carver. In recent years the art has spread to West Greenland, in response to demand, but the tradition and the art itself originated in the villages of Angmagssalik Fjord.

We were joined in our visit to East Greenland by a Swedish woman named Lisbeth Halvardson who was a teacher in special education and spoke fluent English. Speaking Swedish, Lisbeth

Fig. 31-2. A tupilak from Kungmiut.

could converse smoothly with Danes speaking Danish, or with Greenlanders speaking Danish. Then she would translate for us into English. Ellen, who speaks fair Swedish herself, did the same, but a bit more haltingly. Swedes insist that Danes talk as if they have a mouth full of potatoes, and the Danes cheerfully agree—they drop most of their d's, gargle their r's, and slur over whole words. The words don't sound much like they look in print. A Danish friend once told me that I might learn to speak Danish, or read it, but not both. Most of the local Danes also spoke English, but none of the Greenlanders did. On the other hand, quite a few Greenlanders spoke Danish, but few Danes spoke Greenlandic.

The Greenlandic language, which is a variation of the Inuit tongue common to all the people of the Arctic Basin and the Canadian archipelago, is a difficult language for Caucasians to master. *Inuit,* meaning "people," is the plural form of the noun *inuk.* (Southwest Greenlanders call themselves *Kalatdlit,* singular *Kalaleq.*) *Kalatdlit Nunat* is the "land of the people," what we call Greenland. The Greenlandic term *qavak,* which denotes stupidity, is the root word in *qavdlunaq*—European or southerner. The *kabloona* of northern Canada shares the same Inuit root. Complex Inuit word constructions are made from simple words by adding tongue-twisting affixes fore and aft. The town name Angmagssalik, for example, is a Danish rendering of the Greenlandic word meaning "where the angmagssat (caplin or sardines) are." The Greenlanders themselves call the town Tasiussaq, meaning "bay that looks like a lake," the inlet having a

239

Fig. 31-3. The view from Hotel Angmagssalik, looking northeast across Tasiussaq (the bay) toward Mount Qerneratai, "the dark one".

narrow entry that gives it the appearance of a lake. The word for lake is *taseq*. Thus the affix *ussaq* makes a salt-water bay from a fresh-water lake. *Tasiussarsik* is a smaller bay. A small lake or pond is called *taseraq*, and villagers who live on the shore are *tasermiut*. Tasiussaq is also the map name of the bay itself, though the Danes call it Kong Oscars Havn, so named by the explorer Nordenskiold in 1883. One further complication: the dialect of East Greenland differs so much from that of West Greenland that the two linguistic groups can't communicate in their own tongues except through interpreters. East Greenlanders have a softer dialect that slurs or drops the sounds of many letters pronounced in the west. For example, g before m, s, or d is silent, and some map makers have taken to spelling such sounds phonetically on maps: Ammassalik, Kummiut, Timmiarmiut. Such spellings unfortunately will eventually hide the words' etymological roots. Detailed information of Greenlandic vocabularies and dialects appears in reports by Rink (1887), Schultz-Lorentzen (1927), and Osterman (1938), listed here under Further Reading.

At Angmagssalik we checked in at the village's only tourist

accommodation, the Hotel Angmagssalik, a small, rather tidy place run by Kelly Nicolaisen, a Dane, and his wife Erika, a Greenlander. Though the accommodations were not lavish, the view made up for them. Sitting high on a hill overlooking the village, the bay, and the mountains beyond, the hotel had a million-dollar view that varied hour by hour as the sun slowly circled the summer sky and long, blue shadows crept across the hillsides.

Kelly was a tireless and a talented hotel manager. To meet the rising demand of visitations, he at the time of our visit was completing an annex that would more than double his accommodations, and in his spare time he commanded a small cutter, the *Timmik*, which he used for ferrying guests to and from Kulusuk and for chartering scenic excursions up and down the fjords. In winter he offered overnight dogsled trips on the frozen fjords to the outlying villages. Meanwhile, Erika prepared Danish and native dishes from her kitchen, including pot roast of seal (which resembled beef in taste and texture), seal-blubber soup (delicious), and poached salmon (extra delicious), served with a selection of fine wines. The drinking of wines and liquors in East Greenland is closely regulated by the local authorities, for in some parts of Greenland, alcoholism has become a difficult social problem.

Kelly was much interested to learn of my wartime experiences in Greenland so many years before, and word of my supposed exploits spread rapidly through the Danish community. How had life been at Pikiudtleq (Comanche Bay area), how was the hunting, and what of the downed aircraft on the Ice Cap? All sorts of questions. I circled on a map the location of the P-38s and the B-17s.

I arranged for a one-day trip to Ikateq to revisit the ruins of the air base at BE-2. Kelly said his cutter couldn't make the round trip in one day but a friend, Robart Christiansen, had a speedier vessel that could, and we negotiated a deal. Robart was a construction contractor who sailed for pleasure and he knew the fjords well. His vessel, however, proved to be a fiberglass outboard motorboat—we had negotiated a trip fifty miles up Angmagssalik Fjord in an outboard motorboat across choppy embayments and through impossible-looking ice floes! But we went ahead anyway, and after an early morning departure, we were soon pulling ashore here and there to stretch our legs, visit the

Fig. 31-4. The angular peaks of Angmagssalik Fjord at Kungmiut.

local natives, and enjoy a few refreshments. For lunch and coffee we stopped off at Kungmiut, mainly a fishing village but also a prime center of native carving. Back on the fjord, we slowed down to photograph icebergs. Robart confided that he had once driven race cars in Denmark, and for recreation he sometimes waterskied in Kong Oscars Havn when there wasn't too much ice. Ellen was duly impressed but thought a more conservative approach to life might have been more reassuring in the pack ice of Angmagssalik Fjord.

At Ikateq old memories welled up as we walked around the moldering campsite. The dock was surprisingly intact, but no buildings remained—just the bleached white ruins of their wooden footings and the rusted skeleton of the machine shop. In a more temperate climate even these would be gone. I tried to recall the camp layout, the location of the transient barracks, the dispensary, the pool room, and the mess hall. Even the street plan was just a vague outline. Everything worth salvaging had long since been removed, including three buildings hauled bodily to Angmagssalik, where one now serves as the local post office.

About a dozen totally rusted army trucks stood forlornly buried to their axles in the dried mud and sand, their engines hauled away by happy scavengers. The engines would be useful anywhere in Greenland but not the trucks themselves. A big rusted boiler stood like a stark monument at the site of the former mess hall, and hundreds of red, rusted oil drums littered the ground

Fig. 31-5.   A glacial horn looms silently over the old army dock at BE-2.

between the old runway and the fjord. Though incongruous in that starkly beautiful setting–some drums were almost hidden in the lush grass–these relics of the past somehow seemed to belong there. A pair of ptarmigan alighted on a drum not fifteen feet away to check out our presence. BE-2's gravel runway was spongy soft from thirty-four years of frost heaving, but it looked as though a few hours of work by a heavy equipment operator could have made it serviceable.

Directly across Ikateq Sound, which is about a mile wide at that point, the lovely glacier opposite the old air base had shrunk noticeably since 1944, and I was just a bit disappointed in its appearance. Though is was unnamed, we called it Ikateq Sermia–Ikateq Glacier. Its once elegant outline was now deeply furrowed by ablation, so much so that is medial moraines stood high above the intervening ice as irregular, formless ridges. A branch of the glacier had been severed from the main trunk by wastage since 1944 and now terminated in a ragged icefall poised

243

Fig. 31-6. Rusting oil drums littering the ground at BE-2.

at the lip of its hanging valley. Smaller glaciers up and down the sound had also pulled back noticeably from their former terminal moraines. These moraines, shaped like great stony horseshoes, accumulated during the Little Ice Age that began in the Middle Ages, oversaw the demise of the Viking colonies in the fifteenth century, and ended in the middle of the nineteenth. A similar record of ice expansion and retreat is preserved in alpine regions throughout the Northern Hemisphere.

I picked up an old porcelain insulator for a memento and trod reluctantly back to the boat, where Ellen, Lisbeth, and Robart waited patiently aboard. I asked Robart if we might continue up the sound to Sermiligaq to catch a glimpse of Knud Rasmussen Glacier, and he quickly agreed. He was having as much fun as we were. Though the passage appeared to be blocked by a massive floe of bergs, Robart navigated his craft deftly through at twenty-five knots, and as we passed close to one growler we peered over the side at a ghostly blue tongue of submerged ice directly beneath the boat.

Beyond the floe we soon met the glassy expanse of Sermiligaq. The fjord was fully three and a half miles across at its junction with Ikateq Sound, and in the still air the snowcapped ridge lines

Fig. 31-7.   The east wall of Sermiligaq Fjord.

on its far shore were reflected in its mirrorlike surface. Eight
miles straight ahead was the frontal ice cliff of Knud Rasmussen
Glacier, and behind it were the horns and minarets of Schweizerland. Robart apologized that we could get no closer, but he was
running low on fuel, he said, and preferred not to risk being
stranded. We concurred. Robart cut the motor and we drifted
silently on the still water under a clear blue sky. The chill of the
air was balanced by the radiant heat of the Arctic sun. We rocked
easily to and fro, sipping in utmost contentment a cup of hot
coffee from Robart's thermos bottle.

Knud Rasmussen Glacier and its many branches have a surface area of perhaps two hundred square miles—a sizable mass
of ice by anyone's reckoning, but just a fair to middling part of
the great glacier complex north of Ikateq. All this ice in turn is
but a blip on the margin of the Greenland Ice Cap. As stunningly
beautiful and imposing as it is, Knud Rasmussen Glacier would
remain unnamed in most parts of Greenland, relegated to obscu-
rity in a realm of far larger bodies of ice. But here at Sermiligaq
it is readily accessible to view by boat or aircraft and is an apt
namesake for a great explorer who loved the icy land of his birth.

It was now time to leave Sermiligaq, and Robart jerked hard

245

on the recoil starter. Nothing happened. Three more jerks and it still didn't fire. Both Ellen and Lisbeth drew deep breaths. I thought about the distance to shore—a rocky cliff—and the fact that Robart had no oars for emergency use, no extra clothing or blankets, and no food. Not even life preservers. But Robart, unperturbed, loosened the cowling with a screwdriver, made a minor adjustment somewhere on the motor, and fired away. All this could have been a put on, but it wasn't. Robart had full knowledge of the operation of his boat and took it seriously—he had to; his life depended on it. We headed south and turned again into Ikateq Sound toward Angmagssalik, with the wind at our backs and the sun in our faces. The water had grown choppy. All too soon we would be back at the hotel sipping table wine, recounting the experiences of the day, and chatting with the Danes who gathered there to socialize. Some of them were astonished that anyone would travel to Greenland for a vacation, and all were astonished that anyone would ride fifty miles up Angmagssalik Fjord in Robart Christiansen's outboard motorboat.

The setting of Angmagssalik village is out of an Arctic story book. With about nine hundred people, the town sprawls across the rolling foothills hard above the shore of Tasiussaq. Sharp mountain peaks rise in all quadrants, flecked with snow and ice. Mountain tarns dot the landscape—lakes by some people's standards, the largest being Qordlortoq So, "waterfall lake," about three and a half miles long and more than two miles wide. Its outlet into Tasiussaq spills over a pretty waterfall, and its backdrop is a range of snowcapped horns. Rocky islands rise along its southern shore.

Kelly Nicolaisen arranged a walking tour for us around the village, led by a pair of young Greenlanders, a girl and boy, both of whom spoke Danish. The girl planned to attend college that fall in Copenhagen. The moonstruck boy mostly just watched the girl. They guided us along a path beside a splashy trout stream flowing through the tundra to a place called Blomsterdalen, "valley of flowers." There the stream pours from a tarn over a series of low waterfalls.

Blomsterdalen was well named. The ground was carpeted with flowers, mostly in rosettes or pincushion arrangements packed close to the ground in a mosaic of moss and sedges. Though short-stemmed, many of the flowers were large and

Fig. 31–8.   Iceberg in Angmagssalik Fjord.

showy, and many of them looked familiar. Among the eyecatch-
ers were fireweed, hairbell, gentian, ranunculus, various yellow
compositae, and cotton grass. A botanist could identify a lot
more. All except the cotton grass would be at home in the high-
mountain tundras of the western United States. Similar gardens
decorate Mount Washington in New Hampshire. We tarried a little while at the lake to watch some local fishermen, then turned
back, but instead of retracing our steps along the path to the
village we veered north from the lake and headed across country
toward Tasiussaq. A broad ridge intervened—rocky but abraded
smooth by the action of glaciers that once covered all of East
Greenland. Even on the side slopes of this broad ridge, rocky as
it was, we had to detour around many small crystal pools lined
with mosses, and we had to make our way through bogs of muskeg white with cotton grass. This was the habitat of the infamous
Angmagssalik mosquito, partial to visiting tourists, but we soon
were at the top of the ridge where a fresh breeze kept the mosquitoes in check and where the ridge line provided a great panorama of Tasiussaq and the crags above the far shore.

Tasiussaq was sprinkled with hundreds of small icebergs, all
drifting slowly with the ebb and flow of the tide. Strange that this

Fig 31-9. Wild flowers (moss campion) at Blomsterdalen.

bay should be so filled with ice, because it had no feeding glaciers. All the bergs drifted in from the North Atlantic, carried in
by the strong tidal currents that poured through the narrow strait
between Tasiussaq and the mouth of Angmagssalik Fjord.
Though a quirk, therefore, of marine hydrology, the bergs nevertheless were the delight of visitors from Europe, and they added
a picturesque touch that heightened the stark splendor of the
scene. Indeed, icebergs set apart the seascapes of Greenland
from the more familiar strands of the temperate world to the
south; Greenland and icebergs are synonymous.

I kept one eye on the changing panorama and another on the
rocks underfoot. Angmagssalik sits on a metamorphic complex
of ancient gneiss crumpled and contorted by millions of years of
movements deep within the earth and exposed at the surface by
erosion. Between the town and Blomsterdalen we crossed from
the gneiss onto a different terrane of dark-colored rock called
anorthosite or norite, a rock that does little for the average tourist
but raises the pulse rate and blood pressure of igneous petrolo-
gists. These eccentric scholars are engrossed in the composition
and origin of once-molten rocks. I say anorthosite *or* norite because even a petrologist can't flatly identify these rocks without
a microscope. Besides, they vary enough in character and ap-

pearance from place to place to demand different names—names that make the petrologist very happy. Learned symposia have been convened to discuss and name such rocks. A sort of black granite, our rock was best seen at the town quarry, where large rough boulders were hewn in 1964 to build up the footings for the then new town wharf.

Angmagssalik needed the wharf not only to provide unloading facilities at the rocky shore of Tasiussaq but also to protect vessels moored there from drifting icebergs. The wharf served another purpose: it was a social gathering place where grandmothers and small children could watch the bustling commerce of the short shipping season, and pipe-smoking elders could supervise the busy activity from a convenient perching place on the rocks. Here a fisherman proudly displayed his fresh catch of salmon as the onlookers nodded approval, and there a hunting party flensed a freshly killed seal. About half a dozen small ships and many motorboats may be in port at any given time. We watched as the ship *Einar Mikkelson* unloaded its cargo nearby.

Next to the wharf was the general store, carrying all manner of domestic and imported goods, ranging from canned European delicacies to adults' and children's clothing, magazines and books, trail gear, nautical charts, and native carvings in ivory and stone. Just to browse through this cosmopolitan marketplace was to enjoy this remote corner of Greenland. Young women in bright blouses and flaring skirts, wearing tightly curled permanent waves and flaunting outrageously high-heeled boots, pored through the clothing racks. In thirty-three years the glaciers of East Greenland had retreated noticeably, but the Greenlanders had advanced considerably in terms of Western staples and luxuries. The head clerk and cashier of the store was a solemn-eyed but helpful Greenlander, easily fluent in Danish, thoroughly European in her self-assured manner, and strikingly attractive as she neared middle age. We were dismayed, though, to learn that she would accept no American travelers' checks or credit cards for payment of goods. We had only a few Icelandic kroner, so we didn't buy the store.

Outside the store entrance was Angmagssalik's lone taxicab, a Toyota Land Cruiser that stood by to haul passengers up the steep hills of town to their destinations. Two hills stood between the waterfront and Kelly's hotel, but we declined help, choosing instead to sightsee our way back on foot, despite the mosquitoes.

Steep-roofed framed houses along the way had drying racks for seal meat and fish. Many houses had seal skins tacked tightly to their walls, curing in the sun. Flat-roofed porches were handy places to store dogsleds until winter or kayaks until summer, though I never saw a kayak, in or out of the water. They had been abundant in 1944 but all seemed to have disappeared by 1977.

The Arctic never had a tradition of fastidious sanitation, and Angmagssalik was no exception. From an open window close to the road a gnawed bone sailed out as we passed near. We weren't intended targets; we just happened to be there at that moment. Waste disposal is a problem everywhere in the Arctic. In the perennially frozen ground, the permafrost, underground sewer pipes would freeze solid even in summer. Kelly's hotel featured honey barrels, which had to be emptied daily during high season and hauled away for dumping behind a hill, just as ours had at Comanche Bay so many years before.

Litter is almost everywhere–especially tin cans, bottles, and plastic bags–sure signs of "civilization." Cans and bottles stay where they land, but plastic bags are carried far and wide by the wind. One otherwise pristine, serenely pretty lake downwind from town was littered with ugly plastic, both on shore and in the water. Of course, the litter is unnoticeable for nine to ten months of the year, when repeated snowstorms keep it discreetly covered. But who should throw stones? We in the army littered Greenland a whole generation before the Greenlanders did. Before our arrival, locally produced waste was biodegradable. My observation has been that developing countries around the world begin to wallow in litter as soon as they gain the accoutrements of industrial society. Hansen's law states that the Siamese twins of solid waste production and energy consumption increase exponentially with technological advancement and in direct proportion to the gross national product.

Our all-too-brief return to East Greenland was almost over. After a luminous, all-night twilight, when the shouting school kids on summer vacation played soccer until 2:30 A.M., we arose to a gray morning, enjoyed a last breakfast, packed our bags, boarded Kelly's cutter *Timmik*, and headed through the icebergs across the fjord to Kulusuk. The drizzly showers–even occasional snowflakes–were fitting mementos of the East Greenland summer, and I still remember the fog-shrouded peaks along the shore with a poignant touch of nostalgia. We tarried an hour or

Fig. 31–10.   Ikateq Sermia.

two at Kulusuk airport, stopping off to pay a call to the Americans
at the DEW line station while a new contingent of one-day travelers just off the airplane visited the village of Kap Dan.

Then a nervous flight attendant for Loftleider hustled everyone aboard. "We *must* get going!" Ellen tarried briefly in the terminal as a young airport employee asked if she could buy him a
low-cost, American-made parka. When she replied affirmatively
in Swedish he was astounded: "You speak Swedish, but you are
an American!" The flight attendant's pleadings intensified. The
gray shroud was thickening on the mountain tops. "*Please* get
aboard. We *must* be gone." Then we were in the air, Kulusuk
fell away, and we caught a last glimpse of the brooding coastal
mountains stretching endlessly to the north before they too disappeared in the mists. An old Danish expatriot, headed home to
Denmark for the last time, I judged, after years in East Greenland, asked if I would return again. "Of course," I replied, "and
will you?"

"Yes, of course," he nodded, and he lapsed into thoughtful
quiet.

Excerpts from Don Galbreath's Diary

June 9, 1943

Six of us were told we leave for Camp Myles Standish tomorrow. Wally Hansen left for Presque Isle.

June 11, 1943

From Camp Myles Standish we went by truck to Camp Edwards Rifle Range and shot 40 rounds each. At 1800 we boarded a train for Boston. There, we boarded the *Yarmouth* at 2100 as the band played "The Beer Barrel Polka" and "Over There."

June 12, 1943

We lifted anchor at 1200 and steamed out of Boston Harbor. None of us were allowed out on deck until we were out of sight of land.

June 14, 1943

The gun crews had gunnery practice today. In the P.M. destroyers and British corvettes started showing up from both sides.

After stops at Halifax, Nova Scotia and Argentia, Newfoundland, we arrived in BW-1, South Greenland, on July 2. We had a submarine scare after leaving Halifax. Poor "Doc" Johnson was seasick all the way over.

Maj. John T. Crowell is our C.O. at BW-1. We are no longer attached to 8th Weather Squadron but belong to the Greenland Base Command, 416 Air Base Squadron, Ice Cap Detachment. Capt. Franklin A. Wade arrived July 10 from the States. Wallace R. Hansen arrived from the States on July 14 (possibly July 13) from Presque Isle.

August 10, 1943

The advance crew went on board ship today bound for Comanche Bay – Major Crowell, Captian Wade, Bisson, Fincher, Force, and Johnson. [Ship was the *Izarah*, out of Newfoundland.]

August 22, 1943

At 2000 we went aboard the *Nevada* for the trip to Comanche Bay. Lifted anchor during the night.

August 26, 1943

At 1300 we started through the ice and after a while an A-20 [A-26?] flew over and routed us in through the ice field to Comanche Bay. We anchored at 1800.

October 2, 1943

We moved up the hill to the Base for winter.

October 3, 1943

The *Nevada* lifted anchor and steamed out of the bay at 0730 with all civilians aboard [plus Major Crowell].

October 6, 1943

At 1900 someone yelled "fire" and the radio shack burned to the ground with nothing saved.

October 17, 1943

The Navy patrol boat *Bluebird* came in today on its last patrol of the East Coast [of Greenland] this winter. It left as the fog lifted on Oct. 20.

October 24, 1943

"Scratch" [Phillips] and I sent out the first weather report as taken at Atterbury Dome. Grahl coded at Base.

October 27, 1943

Major Crowell and Major Sykes (BW-1 chief weather officer) arrived today. Crowell is no longer our C.O. but is in charge of all shipping to and from Greenland.

October 29, 1943

Major Crowell is captain of the ship that's in here. Just as they were leaving Major Crowell said, "If there is anyone who wants to go back, speak up." Bisson said he would like to go to BE-2. It seems he has lost weight and fears he could have T.B. Just 19 of us left here now.

November 11, 1943

Joe got a little stinko on something.

November 15, 1943

Wally Hansen and Joe left for a 17 mile trip [on the Ice Cap] to rescue a sled dog left there recently. They returned next day with the dog.

November 19, 1943

Wind reached a speed of 115 miles per hour as recorded on instruments and at times hit at least 125 mph.

Cadigan nearly froze to death at night in an attempt to go from the mess hall to the barracks, a distance of 75 feet [when] the guide rope came loose from the barracks.

November 23, 1943

Found out that the meat in the ice hole had apparently partly thawed in moving it from the ship, and it is all spoiled.

December 6, 1943

The guys made hydrogen today and intended to take pibals tomorrow, but due to wind and snow it was delayed until December 14 when they took one to 20,000 feet.

December 18, 1943

Captain Wade says we now belong to the Operations and Plans Division of the General Staff, Washington, D.C.

December 20, 1943

The sun rose at 0945 and set at 1300. [East and West Greenland shared same time zone; true solar time for East Greenland should have been about three-quarters of an hour later.]

December 23, 1943

For exactly 24 hours now (1600) the wind has been 50 mph or more. The highest this spell was 68 mph. Blowing snow has for hours held visibility and ceiling at zero.

December 24, 1943

Radiogram from BE-2 said to watch for a plane over in a last attempt to get Christmas mail. C-47 came over the dropped 30 mail bags in 4 trips over the Base. From Atterbury Dome it was like watching a bomb run. Bisson was on the plane.

December 25, 1943

Wind again with us and at 70 mph. Blackout called at 1915 local time.

December 28, 1943

Wind came up hard at 0400 and by 1300 was registered at 100 mph. By 1800 it had reached between 114 and 124 mph. Gusts checked at 144 mph and for 20 seconds averaged 135 mph.

January 5, 1944

Wind 115 mph at 1200. Gusts 156 mph with average 86.

May 10, 1944

Wind averaged 41 mph for 5 straight days.
Wind averaged 34 mph for 8 straight days.
Wind averaged 29 mph for 10 straight days.

May 16, 1944

Wind, snow, and rain. Snow even with peak of barracks roof.

May 20, 1944

Convoy [of snowmobiles] left for Ice Cap. Reached old [Demorest] station. Lost 2 differentials in bad surface conditions. May 21 returned to Base.

June 6, 1944

D-Day in Europe.

June 10, 1944

Bay ice breakup.

June 12, 1944

Convoy left base at roughly 0100. At 0200, and our first stop, it was found that Lt. Borden had forgotten his sleeping bag. Bob Johnson started back for it in his T-15. Radioed Base for "Scratch" [Phillips] to start out on his motor toboggan with the bag. After Johnson returned with the bag, we again pushed on. Stopped by snow and zero visibility. Found that lead machine (Captain Wade's) was within 40 feet of a ten-foot-wide crevasse. Set up tents in blizzard. Started out again when storm abated. Johnson's machine tore out its differential. All returned to Base. This was the 5th attempt to reach Ice Cap since March 21.

June 18, 1944

Snowmobile convoy of six machines left for Ice Cap at 0030. Made camp at 28 miles in snowstorm. Trouble freezing accelerators.

June 19, 1944

Drifting snow, poor surface. Camped at 54 miles. Low temperature reading of 8° F. Wind at Base Camp reached 63 mph.

June 20, 1944

Returned to Base Camp.

July 5, 1944

Snowmobiles set out for Ice Cap. Borden's differential broke down seven miles out; abandoned machine. Made camp 20 miles out. Steady wind during night, about 45 mph. Left cache of dog food at old Ice Cap Station [for Joe and Wally's team.]

July 6, 1944

Lost second differential (Cadigan's machine) as we left camp. Put Cadigan's gear in my [Galbreath's] machine. At 22 miles lost differential in Fincher's machine; laid over and installed new one dropped from airplane.

July 7, 1944

Low last night was 11.8° F. Plane dropped three differentials to returning party, but no mail. Dropped fresh meat at Base Camp. Joe Johansen and Wally Hansen are camped at 20 miles with dog team.

July 9, 1944

Lieutenant Dorsey decided to load up camp and move farther out. This without telling Captain Wade, but 55-mph wind delayed departure. Our tents are pounding and banging and we hope they don't blow down.

July 10, 1944

Wind this morning at 35 mph. Left camp site at noon. At 1400 we radioed in a FILNO ["not filed"] for the 1800 Z weather report, and on being questioned we said "moving." That remark by Lieutenant Dorsey. After travelling 22 miles we ran low on oil in T-15 and were forced to stop. At 2100 as we made weather radio contact we received message from Captain Wade saying in part, "Move unauthorized, TARFU now. Better start drilling for oil."

July 11, 1944

Snow fell all night. Today's temperature between 20° and 25° F. Talked to Wally Hansen by radio. He and Joe are camped at about 35–40 miles out. Are bringing oil for the T-15. Tex [Fincher] and I bypassed the oil filter, which was leaking badly.

July 12, 1944

Clear and sunny. Temperature reached 28° F. Today we ate pemmican, dried-eggs omelet, and hot chocolate. Radiation fog at 2200 hours; visibility about 1/8 mile; temperature 21.4° F; wind calm.

July 14, 1944

Convoy left Base Camp at 0530. Had a 4-way radio contact at 1500 (us, Wally, convoy, Base Camp). Convoy stalled at old Ice Cap Station replacing differential. Snow and fog all day.

July 15, 1944

Light snow most of day.

July 17, 1944

Moderate ground fog at 0300. Lieutenant Dorsey took off with full pack at 1155 intending to ski to crest of Ice Cap. Dog team arrived at 1220, tired out and needing rest. We unloaded them and set up their tent. Joe and Wally ordered by Wade to Bring back Dorsey. They took off around midnight, after surface hardened.

July 18, 1944

Dog team returned with Dorsey.

July 19, 1944

With loaded T-15 we pulled out of camp at 0330. The oil in the differential boiled several times. It took us a little over four hours to make the 23 miles back [to site of Ice Cap Station]. Arriving back at 54-mile site [station], the house was up and everything in running order. [The Ice Cap station was erected on site by Wade and another convoy while the Dorsey party and dog team were at 78-mile camp.] Three hours after our arrival Captain Wade and the rest of the convoy took off for home base. Joe and Wally arrived around 0100 and set up their tent.

July 22, 1944

Convoy left Base but had to turn back as they lost another differential.

July 26, 1944

Minimum temperature tonight: 7.8° F.

July 28, 1944

Low of 8° F; high of 25.

July 30, 1944

Joe and Wally left for Base Camp this morning. They rigged a sail on the sledge to take advantage of the 18 mph wind from the NW.

August 1, 1944

Evacuated Ice Cap Station at 1230.

August 19, 1944

Ship. [The *Polarbjorn* dropped anchor in Comanche Bay.]

August 22, 1944

Joe left on ship [for BW-1].

August 30, 1944

Bay has thin ice entire.

September 5, 1944
   Wind at 68 mph plus gusts.

September 9, 1944
   Aboard ship!

September 27, 1944
   Arrived BW-1.

Glossary

Weather Terms

Anorassuaq–"big wind"
Anore–wind
Anoritok–"the windy place"
Apuseq–snowy place, glacier
Apusiajik–the small snowfield; small glacier
Apuserajik–the big snowfield; big glacier
Aput–snow (on the ground)
Avangarsarneq–south or southwest wind
Iluliaq–iceberg (singular)
Iluliartukaje–extremely big iceberg
Ilulissat–icebergs; place of the icebergs
Kanangnaq–east wind
Navdordlugo–winter ice on the fjord
Ningeq–wet northeast wind
Perserpoq–drifting wind
Persoq–snowstorm
Piteraq–north wind
Pitoralikaseqaoq–"it is storming"
Qanik–snow (falling)
Qerneraq–"wind blowing across the water, making ripples"
Qineq–ice foot
Sastrugi–washboard-like ridges in a snowfield
Sermeq–glacier
Sermetaq–mountain icefield
Sermerssuak–the great glacier, the ice cap

Sikeq–dirty sea ice
Sikorssuit–field ice brought in by the wind
Siko sujornarnisaq–perennial ice
Sikuaq–thin ice
Suportoq–"a place that has many winds"

Place Names

Ajagitaq–the pillars (mountain)
Angmagssalik–where the caplin are
Iglutalik–house island
Igpik–slope, bluff
Ikardluk–skerry
Ikateq–shallow water
Ikeq–bay
Ikerasak–sound
Ikerssuak, or *ikertivaq*–big bay
Imeq–sea
Imavigssuak–ocean
Ivnertalik–place of the slope
Ivnarssuaq–big slope
Kalatdlit Nunat–land of the people
Kangeq–headland
Kujatdleq–south point of land
Kulusuk–shaped like a bird's back
Kungmiut–river people (or place of the river people)
Narsaq–plain
Narsarssak–unusual plain
Narsarssuak–large plain
Nunataq–belongs to the land
Pingo–gulls' hummock
Putulik–has a hole in it (place)

Qardlit Ikerat–bay shaped like trousers
Qasigissat–bay of the spotted seals
Qeqertaq–island
Qeqertarssuak–large island
Qeqertarssuatsiaq–rather large island
Qeqertaussag–peninsula
Qingo–head of the fjord
Qordlortoq–waterfall place
Sermiligaq–fjord with glaciers
Sermiligarssuk–small or unusual fjord with glaciers
Taseq–lake
Taseraq–small lake
Tasermiut–villagers who live on the shore
Tasiussaq–bay that resembles a lake
Tasiussarsik–small bay
Tunugdliarfik–turnaround place
Umanak–heart
Umanarssuak–big heart

Animals

Agtarajik–sea perch
Angmagssat–caplin
Angneq, or *ukssuk*–bearded seal
Aqaluk–salmon
Aqaluviaq–shark
Avataussaq–starfish
Erqernianagssaq–ptarmigan
Imerqutailaq–arctic tern
Kigssaviarssuk–Greenland falcon
Kilijitaq–mussel
Nagssugtoq–sculpin
Nalinginaq–saddleback
Nanoq–polar bear
Neriniarteq–bladdernose
Piseq–snow bunting
Pussugutilikasit–crab
Quparneq–black guillemot
Quseq–gull
Saggaq, or *tordluluatsiaq*–fjord seal
Sarugdlik–cod
Sikutoq–puffin
Sunaunaq–anemone
Tateraq–kittiwake
Tingmiavarssuk–ivory gull

Ugpaterqorteq–eider duck
Uvavfaq–snail

Miscellaneous

Akitseq–soapstone
Amigsaq–umiak skin
Angakoq–shaman
Angit–steering oar
Anorak–pullover windbreaker
Atertagaq–boot (West Greenland=*kamik*)
Autdarit–woman's boat (West Greenland=*umiak*)
Heire–right (Norwegian dog-sled command)
Imartit–ladle
Inuit–people, or Greenlanders (sing. *inuk*)
Iput–oar
Kalatdlit–Greenlanders' name for themselves
Kalatdlit Nunat–land of the people (Greenland)
Ligge ned–lie down (Norwegian dog-sled command)
Mamartoq–crowberry
Mataleq–mitten
Mortut–drill
Nunarssuk–rosewart
Nasaq–hood or hat
Niusivik–wooden bowl
Nukerutsiaq–thread
Nuliakeq–women
Pautit–kayak paddle
Pilautaq–knife
Qajarsit–kayak coat
Qarmaussaq–kayak-man's cap
Qavak–term denoting stupidity
Qavdlunaq–European or southerner
Quarlik–angelica
Sakoq–woman's knife West Greenland=*ulo*)
Sarqit–harpoon shaft
Savikataq–harpoon
Sijumiaq–bird dart
Stop–stop (Norwegian dog-sled command)

Timersit–mythical cannibal giants
Tingmiarmiut–bird people
Tungujortoq–bilberry
Tupilak–part-human, part-animal
carved figurines

Usikatak–harpoon bladder
Venstre–left (Norwegian dog-sled
command)

Further Reading

Akasofu, S. I. 1979. *Aurora Borealis: The Amazing Northern Lights*. Anchorage, Alaska: Alaska Geographic Society. 96 pp.

Balchen, B., C. Ford, and O. LaFarge. 1944. *War below Zero*. Boston: Houghton Mifflin. 127 pp.

Bates, Charles C., and John F. Fuller. 1985. *America's Weather Warriors*. College Station: Texas A&M University Press.

Brekke, Asgeir, and Alv Egeland. 1983. *The Northern Lights*. New York: Springer-Verlag. 170 pp.

Carlson, W. S. 1962. *Lifelines through the Arctic*. New York: Duell, Sloan and Pearce. 271 pp.

Churchill, Winston S. 1951. *Closing the Ring*. Vol. 5 of *The Second World War*. Boston: Houghton Mifflin. 749 pp.

Dunbar, Moira. 1969. "A glossary of ice terms." In *Ice Seminar*, a conference sponsored by the Petroleum Society of the Canadian Institute of Mining and Metallurgy (CIMM), Calgary, Alberta, Canada, May 6–7, 1968. Special vol. 10, pp. 105–110.

Escher, Arthur, and W. S. Watt. 1976. *Geology of Greenland*. Copenhagen: Grønlands Geologiske Undersogelse, 603 pp.

Fistrup, Borge. 1966. *The Greenland Ice Cap*. Copenhagen: Rhodes International Science Publishers, 312 pp.

Holm, G., and V. Garde. 1889. *Beretning om Konebaads-Expeditionen til Grønlands Ostkyst* [Report on Konebaads Expedition to Greenland's East Coast], 1883–85. Vols. 1 and 2. Copenhagen: Meddelelser om Grønland [Report about Greenland], 420 pp. and 400 pp. [in Danish.]

John, Brian S., ed. 1979. *The Winters of the World: Earth under the Ice Ages*. New York: Halsted Press, John Wiley & Sons. 255 pp.

Jones, A. V. 1974. *Aurora*. Dordrecht, Holland and Boston: Reidel, 296 pp.

Langway, C. C. 1970. *Stratigraphic Analysis of a Deep Ice Core from Greenland*. Geological Society of America special paper 125, 186 pp.

Larsen, Thor. 1978. *The World of the Polar Bear.* London and New York: Hamlyn, 96 pp.

Mathiassen, Therkel. 1933. *Prehistory of the Angmagsalik Eskimos*. Copenhagen: Meddelelser on Grønland [Report about Greenland], vol. 92, no. 4. 158 pp.

Miles, Hugh, and Mike Salisbury. 1986. *Kingdom of the Ice Bear.* Austin: University of Texas Press, 123 pp.

Murray, John E. 1969. "The drift, deterioration, and distribution of icebergs in the North Atlantic Ocean." In *Ice Seminar,* a conference sponsored by the Petroleum Society of the Canadian Institute of Mining and Metallurgy (CIMM), Calgary, Alberta, Canada, May 6–7, 1968. Special vol. 10, pp. 3–18.

Nansen, Fridtjof. 1969. *In Northern Mists: Arctic Exploration in Early Times* (Trans. by A. G. Chater). New York: AMS Press, 2 vols., 767 pp.

Ostermann, H., ed. 1938. *Kund Rasmussen's Posthumous Notes on the Life and Doings of the East Greenlanders in Olden Times.* Copenhagen: C. A. Rutzels Forlag, Meddelelser om Grønland [Report about Greenland], vol. 109, no. 1. 215 pp.

Rasmussen, Knud. 1933. "Explorations in Southeastern Greenland, Preliminary Report on the Sixth and Seventh Thule Expeditions." *Geographical Review,* vol. 23, pp. 385–93.

Rink, H. 1887. *The East Greenland Dialect* (Revised by W. Thalbitzer, 1911). Copenhagen: Meddelelser om Grønland [Report about Greenland], vol. 39. pp. 205–23.

Schultz-Lorentzen. 1927. *Dictionary of the West Greenland Eskimo Language.* Copenhagen: Meddelelser om Grønland [Report about Greenland] vol. 59. 303 pp.

Sharp, Robert P. 1988. *Living Ice; Understanding Glaciers and Glaciation.* Cambridge: Cambridge University Press, 223 pp.

Siscoe, G. L. 1978. An Historical Footnote on the Origin of "Aurora Borealis": *American Geophysical Union Transactions,* Vol. 59, No. 12, p. 994–998.

Thalbitzer, William, 1914. *Contributions to the Ethnology of the East Greenland Natives.* Copenhagen: Meddelelser om Grønland [Report about Greenland], vol. 39. 755 pp.

Thalbitzer, William, 1923. *The Ammassalik Eskimos.* Copenhagen: Meddelelser om Grønland [Report about Greenland], vol. 40. 564 pp.

U.S. Army (Arctic, Desert, and Tropic Information Center). 1945. "Comprehensive Report on Operations of Task Force 4998-A and the Ice Cap Detachment in Greenland, 1942–44," typescript. 182 pp.

Wade, F. A. 1946. Wartime Investigations of the Greenland Ice Cap and Its Possibilities: American Geographical Society of New York, *Geographical Review,* vol. 36, no. 3. pp. 452–73.

Index

(**Boldface** page numbers indicate illustrations or graphics.)